RIHANNA
Barbados World-Gurl in Global Popular Culture

EDITED BY Hilary McD. Beckles
and
Heather D. Russell

THE UNIVERSITY OF THE WEST INDIES PRESS
Jamaica • Barbados • Trinidad and Tobago

The University of the West Indies Press
7A Gibraltar Hall Road, Mona
Kingston 7, Jamaica
www.uwipress.com

© 2015 by Hilary McD. Beckles and Heather D. Russell
All rights reserved. Published 2015

A catalogue record of this book is available from
the National Library of Jamaica.

ISBN: 978-976-640-502-1
978-976-640-513-7 (Kindle)
978-976-640-524-3 (ePub)

Cover illustration: Jonna Twigg, Twigg's Bindery
Cover and book design by Robert Harris
Set in Scala 10.25/15 x 27
Printed in the United States of America

RIHANNA

CONTENTS

Selected Discography and Awards for Rihanna *vii*

INTRODUCTION "Baadest-Bajan, Wickedest World-Gurl" *1*
HILARY McD. BECKLES AND HEATHER D. RUSSELL

CHAPTER 1 Westbury Writes Back: Rihanna Reclaimed *14*
HILARY McD. BECKLES

CHAPTER 2 Rihanna as Global Icon and Caribbean Threshold Figure *38*
DON D. MARSHALL

CHAPTER 3 International Identity: Rihanna and the Barbados Music Industry *74*
MIKE ALLEYNE

CHAPTER 4 "What's My Name?" Reading Rihanna's Autobiographical Acts *96*
ESTHER L. JONES

CHAPTER 5 She Dances on the Holodeck *119*
CURWEN BEST

CHAPTER 6 From "F Love" to "He Is the One"? Rihanna, Chris Brown and the Danger of Traumatic Bonding *138*
DONNA AZA WEIR-SOLEY

CHAPTER 7   Rihanna and Bajan Respectability   159
               AARON KAMUGISHA

CHAPTER 8   Rihanna: Diaspora Citizen, Bajan Daughter,
               Global Superstar   181
               HEATHER D. RUSSELL

               Contributors   209
               Acknowledgements   211

SELECTED DISCOGRAPHY AND AWARDS FOR RIHANNA

DISCOGRAPHY

Music of the Sun. Produced by Carl Sturken, Evan Rogers et al. Def Jam Recordings. 2005.

A Girl Like Me. Produced by the Carter Administration et al. Def Jam Recordings. 2006.

Good Girl Gone Bad. Produced by the Carter Administration et al. Def Jam Recordings. 2007.

Rated R. Produced by L.A. Reid et al. Def Jam Recordings. 2009.

Loud. Produced by L.A. Reid et al. Label. Def Jam Recordings. 2010.

Talk That Talk. Produced by Carl Sturken, Evan Rogers et al. Def Jam Recordings, Roc Nation and Syndicated Rhythm Productions. 2011.

Unapologetic. Produced by Robyn Fenty, Roc Nation, Carl Sturken and Evan Rogers. Def Jam Recordings and Syndicated Rhythm Productions. 2012.

AWARDS

American Music Awards
2007 Favorite Female Artist – Soul/R&B
2008 Favorite Female Artist – Pop/Rock
2008 Favorite Female Artist – Soul/R&B
2010 Favorite Soul/R&B Female Artist
2011 Favorite Soul/R&B Album
2012 Favorite Soul/R&B Album
2013 Favorite Soul/R&B Female Artist
2013 Icon Award

BET Awards
2009 Viewer's Choice Award
2010 Viewer's Choice Award
2011 Best Female R&B Artist
2013 Best Female R&B/Pop Artist

BET Hip-Hop Awards
2009 Best Hip-Hop Collaboration
2009 Best Hip-Hop Video

Billboard Music Awards
2006 Female Artist of the Year
2006 Pop 100 Artist of the Year
2006 Female Hot 100 Artist of the Year
2006 Hot Dance Airplay Song of the Year
2007 Hot Dance Airplay Song of the Year
2007 European Hot 100 Song of the Year
2008 Female Artist of the Year
2008 Pop 100 Artist of the Year
2008 Female Hot 100 Artist of the Year
2008 Mainstream Top 40 Artist of the Year
2008 Top Digital Song Artist of the Year
2008 Top Dance Airplay Artist of the Year
2008 Top Canadian Artist of the Year
2009 Top Digital Song Artist of the Decade
2010 Top Dance Club Artist
2011 Top Female Artist
2011 Top Radio Songs Artist
2011 Top Rap Song
2012 Top Streaming Artist
2013 Top R&B Artist
2013 Top Radio Songs Artist
2013 Top R&B Album
2013 Top R&B Song

Billboard Latin Music Awards
2013 Crossover Artist of the Year

BRIT Awards
2011 Best International Female Artist
2012 Best International Female Artist

Grammy Awards
2008 Best Rap/Sung Collaboration
2010 Best Rap/Sung Collaboration
2010 Best Rap Song
2011 Best Dance Recording
2012 Best Rap/Sung Collaboration
2012 Best Rap Song
2013 Best Short Form Music Video
2014 Best Urban Contemporary Album

MTV Europe Music Awards
2006 Best R&B Artist
2007 Ultimate Urban
2012 Worldwide Act North American

MTV Video Music Awards
2007 Monster Single of the Year
2007 Video of the Year
2012 Video of the Year

MTV Video Music Awards (Japan)
2006 Best New Artist in a Video
2011 Best R&B Video
2011 Best Collaboration Video

MuchMusic Video Awards
2006 Best International Artist Video
2008 Best International Artist Video
2008 Most Watched Video

People's Choice Awards
2007 Favorite R&B Song
2010 Favorite Music Collaboration
2011 Favorite Pop Artist
2011 Favortie Music Video
2011 Favorite Song

2012 Favorite R&B Artist
2013 Favorite R&B Artist

Teen Choice Awards
2006 Female Breakout Artist
2006 Choice R&B Artist
2007 Choice Music: R&B Artist
2010 Choice Music: Rap/Hip-Hop Track
2012 Choice Movie Breakout

VIBE Awards
2007 Video of the Year

Introduction

"BAADEST-BAJAN, WICKEDEST WORLD-GURL"

HILARY McD. BECKLES AND HEATHER D. RUSSELL

THE WUK-UP

The revolution will be recorded. It has commenced. The Caribbean war for artistic and cultural space is resonating with recording studios everywhere.[1] *It is Rihanna's revolution. She is rupturing the old and redefining the new; and all we knew about Caribbean artists "out there" is dead. New attitudes have taken centre stage, and altitudes hitherto unimagined have been reached. Being pushed to the limits are metropolitan musical structures that once enticed and entrapped Caribbean art. Making space to make music is the new mantra. There is an age-rage on Rihanna's stage that has demanded the forging of a new age. It began with a head-on war of words. Then it moved up from the "cussing out" to the "cashing in". There is a new (she)riff in town. RiRi's war is now a revolution. The "revo" is a departure without a return ticket. You walk through a door of no return. You burn and bury the past and plot an irreversible break with the present. She has erased the past. Now she occupies another country. The Caribbean girl knows why she wants to be the only girl in the world; she lives on an island, all by herself.*

EASY NUH, GURL

Writing about an artist as dynamic, challenging, controversial and exciting as Robyn "Rihanna" Fenty is exhilarating and daunting.[2] The adage that an artist is not usually recognized in his or her own time remains an apt assertion. This is particularly true for Caribbean musicians, whose lyrical and rhythmic soundings are often grounded in highly specialized genres like reggae, calypso/soca, zouk and salsa, which do have global appeal but enjoy relatively modest success in comparison to artists working with US-global genres like hip-hop, R&B, pop and dance music. As a transnational cultural icon, however, Rihanna uses artistic stylings that criss-cross dance, pop, reggae, R&B and rock, even as her edgy, earthy voice unmistakably (re)sounds her Caribbean rootings. While Rihanna, affectionately nicknamed "RiRi", fully embraces her mainstream, popular appeal, she is openly and unequivocally Barbadian. Her uncompromising articulations of national belonging coupled with her unprecedented transnational success create a compelling case for putting together this volume. Focusing on Rihanna from multidisciplinary perspectives (history; literature; political science; cultural, feminist and gender studies) which are ideologically positioned in the global South, *Rihanna: Barbados World-Gurl in Global Popular Culture* is an attempt to intervene early in the discourse surrounding the Barbadian artist, with full cognizance of the ways in which black diaspora subjects and their art have historically been (mis)appropriated and (mis)represented by others.

In less than a decade, Rihanna has proven to be an undeniable, iconic cultural tour de force. She has sold more than 30 million albums and 120 million singles worldwide, making her one of the best-selling artists of all time.[3] Having achieved thirteen number-one singles on the *Billboard* Hot 100 chart, Rihanna is the youngest solo artist to achieve the feat and the artist who did so the fastest. In fact, *Billboard* named her the top digital songs artist of the 2000s and the top Hot 100 artist of the 2010s. In 2014, *Forbes* ranked her eighth on its Celebrity 100 list, naming her one of the world's most powerful celebrities, with earnings of $46 million, at the top of *Forbes*'s list of "Social Networking Superstars".[4] In fact, Rihanna's cutting-edge social networking is given brilliant Bajan context in this volume (see Curwen Best's essay, "She Dances on the Holodeck").

Unprecedented in terms of achievement, Rihanna has won multiple Guinness World Records, including being the first woman in the United Kingdom to have five number-one singles in five consecutive years, the singer with the most number-one singles in a year and the artist with the most digital number-one singles in the United States. In fact, Rihanna has been named the best-selling digital artist of all time in the United States, having sold 47,571,000 singles and albums. In January 2014, at the fifty-sixth Grammy Awards, Rihanna won her seventh Grammy Award, in the category Best Urban Contemporary Album, for *Unapologetic* (2013). In addition, it was announced that Rihanna had sold 3,868,000 records in the past year in the United Kingdom alone, making her the best-selling artist in the list of 2013 BRIT Awards artist nominees.

At the 2013 American Music Awards, after a moving tribute made by her mother, Monica Braithwaite, Rihanna was given the Icon Award. The show's producer, Larry Klein, said the following: "The first-ever Icon Award was created to honour an artist whose body of work has made a profound influence over pop music on a global level. . . . Rihanna's iconic and innovative sound has enabled her to become one of the most influential and best-selling artists of all time." The irreverent, politically astute and hugely popular television host Bill Maher, who introduced the award, referred to Rihanna as "the voice of our generation".[5]

The year 2013 was particularly Ri-markable. Not just content to make her mark in music, Rihanna launched a series of increasingly successful fashion ventures. For instance, in February 2013, she presented her first women's spring fashion collection at London Fashion Week.[6] She was also executive producer of the US version of "Styled to Rock", a fashion-design competition show that premiered in October 2013 on the Bravo network. In 2013, the singer collaborated with MAC Cosmetics and released her own summer, fall and holiday lines of makeup called RiRi Hearts MAC. In July 2013, Budweiser announced that Rihanna had become a part of their global "Made for Music" advertising campaign, co-starring Jay-Z.[7] Rihanna's fourth women's fragrance, Rogue, was released in September 2013. In June 2014, Rihanna received the Fashion Icon Award from the Council of Fashion Designers of America.[8] She has also ventured into acting, having been featured in four films, including a significant role in the 2012 film *Battleship*. In light of these dizzying achievements, in 2012 *Time* magazine named her one of the hundred most influential people in the world. (The essays by Don Marshall and Mike Alleyne which follow, in chapters 2 and 3 respectively, astutely examine these global achievements in relation to Barbados, and particularly Barbados youth culture, placing them in deeper context.)

Rihanna is arguably the most commercially successful Caribbean artist of all time. That she is from Barbados and has been unwavering in terms of publicly articulating her national pride is noteworthy. At the same time, there have been wide-ranging and oftentimes highly controversial responses to Rihanna's ascendancy in sectors of the Barbadian public and the Caribbean community at large – responses that in great measure reveal as much about the Caribbean's own national and regional anxieties and imaginings as they do about the artist herself. As Faith Smith asserts in her critically important, recently published collection, *Sex and the Citizen: Interrogating the Caribbean*, "Notions of sexuality are deeply inflected by colonial and imperial inheritances that have framed nationalism's discourses and silences and continue to inform, more or less, the structures of feeling of the region's people."[9]

While we recognize that the cutting-edge, boundary-transgressing cultural icon Rihanna is subject to anxieties about her body language and latitudes from her global audiences as well, the essays in this collection purposely seek to decentre and destabilize the primacy, and thus potency, of the Euro-American gaze, positing instead considerations of the Caribbean artist and her oeuvre from a Caribbean postcolonial critical/theoretical corpus of academic enquiry.

This is not to say that these essays constitute a facile endorsement of her celebrity. On the contrary, readers will undoubtedly recognize wide-ranging, and in some cases quite divergent views on issues such as the extent to which Rihanna's sexual expressivity can be said to be sociopolitically transgressive; the degree of artistic freedom that she in fact wields in her songs, music videos and public persona; and the extent to which her celebrity has significantly impacted the Caribbean in general and Barbados in particular.

Thus, in *Rihanna: Barbados World-Gurl in Global Popular Culture*, we work to read Rihanna in international, US, Caribbean and Barbadian contexts simultaneously and dialectically, at the same time as we foreground her Bajan roots, in terms of both her rootedness and her uprootings. Through situating Rihanna as both artist and symbol in historical, social, political, economic and cultural contexts, our hope is to engender an illuminating and critically relevant exchange which foregrounds what Ifeona Fulani describes as "the embattled terrain" impacting Caribbean women artists' performance of "transnational Caribbeanity".[10]

Underlying Fulani's thesis is a recognition of the performativity of gender and sexuality, which dynamically cross multiple sites of national and transnational commercial and ideological vectors. To this end, we have titled this introduction "Baadest-Bajan, Wickedest World-Gurl", first as an extension of Rihanna's earlier paradigmatic shift, signalled by her self-proclaimed status as a "good girl gone bad", but more centrally as an intentional act of signifying on the enduring patriarchal imposition of the madonna/whore binary, which, although devastating for all women, has particular resonance for women of colour, especially those emerging from the discursive economies of plantation slavery. Thus, we reject such violating formulations and claim "baadness" as a sign of transgression, of subversion of and resistance to Euro-American discursive and epistemological hegemony.[11]

Such baadness resounds, for example, in the following excerpt from a 2012 article in *Gentlemen's Quarterly* (*GQ*) magazine. Highlighting what he perceives as Rihanna's radical contradictory impulses, the *GQ* interviewer writes:

> Onstage, [Rihanna will] tap out the beat on her p—— and croon lyrics like *Suck my cockiness, lick my persuasion*. Online, she'll tweet a chicken-soup Bible passage to her 26 million followers and then an Instagram shot of a stripper's head between her thighs. . . . "That comes from my culture", she says with her Bajan steel-drum accent. "That's just the way it's always been, and I think that for people, especially in America, they make it like the forbidden fruit, but that only makes kids more curious."[12]

Here, Rihanna subverts the historical divide between raw sexuality and real spirituality, implicitly situating her culture as quintessentially informed by the traditional West African belief that the sacred and the secular are synergistically united. To this end, the essays in this collection trouble the long-standing mythology surrounding Barbados which simplistically reads Bajan culture as socially conservative, the "Little England", as it were, of the Caribbean. In other words, as Hilary Beckles points out in this volume, RiRi is not a Barbadian anomaly (see also Aaron Kamugisha's stellar contribution on Barbadian middle-classness in chapter 7); her unequivocal affirmation of black women's right to unfettered sexual mobility and expressivity, her highly publicized challenges to global racism and her radical nonconformity all mark her as 100 per cent Bajan.[13]

In a similar vein, *wickedest*, in Caribbean parlance, operates like its African

American counterpart *bad* as a classic instance of black vernacular signifyin(g). Radically engaged in reappropriating the power to define meaning, to be *wicked* is to be stylistically brilliant and adroitly unparalleled, with a hint of transgression against bourgeois respectability thrown in to make things interesting. As Henry Louis Gates Jr reminds us, "To rename is to revise, and to revise is to Signify."[14]

Likewise, we purposely invoke and signify on the term *gurl* in *world-gurl* to call attention to Rihanna's global/local dimensionality and the familial/kinship quality imbued in the term *girl* (as in "hey girl"), while at the same time rejecting the tendency to infantilize her or diminish her womanliness, as has been the case in some Barbadian national imaginings of their famous daughter (see Heather Russell's essay on Rihanna's diaspora citizenship in chapter 8). To invoke the womanist warrior Alice Walker, *gurl* is to *girl* as "purple is to lavender".[15] Walker's definition of a womanist includes:

1. A black feminist or feminist of color. . . . Usually referring to outrageous, audacious, courageous or *willful* behaviour. . . .
2. A woman who loves other women, sexually and/or nonsexually. . . . Sometimes loves individual men, sexually and/or nonsexually. . . . Traditionally universalist. . . . Traditionally capable. . . .
3. Loves music. Loves dance. . . . *Loves* the Spirit. Loves love and food and roundness. Loves struggle. *Loves* the Folk. Loves herself. *Regardless.*
4. Womanist is to feminist as purple is to lavender.[16]

Quintessentially *womanist*, the baadest-Bajan, wickedest world-gurl Rihanna continues to provoke and unsettle. According to cultural critic Muna Mire, the criticism of Rihanna is "too often anti-Black, anti-woman, anti-Caribbean, and in this case [speaking of Rihanna's video for "Pour It Up" (2013), which features strippers and Rihanna in the position of both sex worker and consumer, dancing in an all-female space marked by the absent male gaze], anti-sex work". Pointing to the fact that there are no men in the video and to the "athletic, synchronized, artful" aerial performances in the piece, Mire continues, "RiRi has no interest in being 'one of the boys', because she's down with the hoes. That is subversive. It's also pro-queer and deeply feminist."[17] (In chapters 4 and 6, Esther Jones and Donna Aza Weir-Soley take up these issues in illuminating ways, situating Rihanna's socio-sexual self-presentation in the context of her domestic violence survival.) According to David Halperin, "Queer is by definition whatever is at odds with the normal, the legitimate, the dominant. There is nothing in particular to which it necessarily refers. It is an identity without an essence. 'Queer', then, demarcates not a positivity but a positionality vis-à-vis the normative."[18]

If, as queer theory posits, we must arduously interrogate constructions of normativity (in all of its incarnations) that continue to perpetuate violating practices against those whom society constructs as other (whether it be sexually, racially, culturally or economically), then we fully agree with Omise'eke Natasha Tinsley that a queer black approach to reading must conceive itself historically, materially *and* metaphorically.[19] We have attempted as much in the following pages, which move unevenly and yet tellingly across the historical, figurative and material incumbencies which impact how, why and from where we "read RiRi".

VERSE

The chapters in this collection are organized to be interlocutors. Although not intending to be chronological, in chapter 1, "Westbury Writes Back", Hilary Beckles transports readers, through historical and cultural anthropological analyses, into the world of Rihanna's origins. Pointing to the entertainment careers of two cultural icons – Everton Weekes, ranked the best cricketer in the world during the dying days of colonialism in Barbados, and Robyn Rihanna Fenty, the global superstar of contemporary popular music, both of whose childhoods were spent in close proximity to the same ghetto street, Westbury Avenue, on the outskirts of Bridgetown – Beckles offers an illuminating comparative analysis about the ways in which their concomitant narratives speak to the nature of the Caribbean as a historically integrated space within modernity. By historicizing the context and content of their careers, Beckles argues for a necessary conflation of the global and the local into a continuum that diminishes the grip of geography and foregrounds the conception of the Caribbean as a cultural space at the core of what is loosely called "the West". The critical issue on stage, then, in Beckles's analysis, is that while the Caribbean might be situated in the economic South of "the West", culturally it belongs to its centre.

In chapter 2, "Rihanna as Global Icon and Caribbean Threshold Figure", Don Marshall situates Rihanna as a proxy for intervention in debates about Caribbean youth culture, nationalist sentiment and identity. Marshall discusses how Rihanna is both perceived and received by her many publics – particularly with respect to the charged dialogues of identity, self-definition and national obligation. In addition, Marshall reflects on what Rihanna's (post-)national attachments and world music tell us about the cultural effect of globalization on national boundaries. Interrogating claims of narcissism and apolitical historical abandonment among Caribbean youth, Marshall convincingly argues that the politico-ethical contestations they pose, albeit affectively distinct from the earlier decolonization period, do exist, but take on a different aspect because of the cultural effects of globalization and transnationalism. As a consequence, Marshall argues, artists like Rihanna are both propelled and repelled by vague obligations to history, state and ethno-oriented modes of national attachment.

Investigating the operationalization of Barbadian cultural production in the age of globalization, in chapter 3, "International Identity: Rihanna and the Barbados Music Industry", Mike Alleyne examines Rihanna's commercial impact, not only in the context of her own career but also in view of its implications for other internationally positioned Bajan recording artists. Asserting that Rihanna's global commercial success has dramatically raised the profile of Barbados in popular music, moving it from obscurity to a prime source of performing talent for the mainstream music business, Alleyne argues that Rihanna's ascent to pop superstardom has raised issues about the musical and cultural identity of Barbados within and beyond popular music. Highlighting "the spate of major record-label signings of Bajan artists in the R&B/hip-hop mould in the wake of Rihanna's breakthrough", Alleyne suggests that such hyper-commodification has fomented concerns about the distinctiveness (in comparison to the Caribbean genres of reggae/dancehall and calypso/soca) of the island's musical image being projected through these artists and their major-label outlets in the recording industry. The collective circumstances of Rihanna's marketplace arrival, Alleyne asserts, have on the one hand obliquely highlighted the raw economic realities of survival for musical artists in Barbados, and on the other given way to Rihanna's process of construction of an international identity for herself and her nation, both of which are projected through a music-business prism which is inextricably connected to the global identity of her homeland and the stylistic character of her music.

Shifting from the entailments of Rihanna's cultural production and its impact on Barbados, towards theorization of an aesthetics of Rihanna's domestic violence survivorship, Esther Jones's chapter, "'What's My Name?' Reading Rihanna's Autobiographical Acts", theorizes Rihanna's construction of her artistic self through readings of "post-incident" songs that collectively constitute the "artist's coming of age" (*Künstlerroman*) narrative – a narrative which, Jones argues, is distinctly shaped by Rihanna as an Afro-Caribbean woman artist navigating the international stage. As Jones points out, the *Künstlerroman* (from the literary tradition of the novel depicting the personal development of a lead character into an artist) maps an interrogation of identity and action: Who am I, how did I come to be here, and has the struggle been worth it? Chapter 4 explores the ways in which Rihanna continues to negotiate the complex discourse surrounding who she is, not only as a woman and artist but also as a survivor of domestic violence. Ultimately, Jones convincingly crafts a portrait of the artist in light of her own controversial responses to domestic violence, by suggesting that Rihanna is engaged in an ongoing conversation through her art form – song and music video – that experiments with and appropriates a politicized poetics of defiance in constructing her artistic self.

In chapter 5, in a compelling cyber-futuristic reading of Rihanna, "She Dances on the Holodeck", Curwen Best pushes further the themes of aesthetics, (re)presentation and postmodernity. Extending the notion of the holodeck, a virtual-reality facility found on starships and starbases in the fantastic world of *Star Trek*, Best analyses Rihanna's superstardom as an Internet and cyber sensation while simultaneously proposing that many Barbadians of her generation are no less embedded in the world of cyberspace. Positing Rihanna's contact with the arena of cyberspace as highly symbolic, Best argues that the Barbadian society that spawned her development was, in the late 1980s, a society in flux, caught somewhere between the analogue era and the digital wave in tech culture. This transition, Best suggests, had substantial impact on the way citizens lived their lives and how they thought about themselves and others. Given Rihanna's rise to stardom via new, robust technologies, Best affirms the necessity of interrogating new mediums and technologies, such as YouTube and computer-generated video, by way of opening up an understanding of *how* Caribbean citizens of the digital age are being reconstituted and reimagined. Such an investigation, Best points out, also reveals how some Caribbean citizens are taking these same tools to fashion new versions of identity and subjectivity.

Through feminist readings of media and new media, in chapter 6, "From 'F Love' to 'He Is the One'? Rihanna, Chris Brown and the Danger of Traumatic Bonding", Donna Aza Weir-Soley cogently discusses Rihanna's dual position as both megastar and battered woman. Analysing Rihanna and Chris Brown's turbulent on-again, off-again relationship, Weir-Soley argues that despite Rihanna's (possibly) misguided responses to media portrayals of her as a hapless victim and Brown as an irredeemable bad boy, something deeper is afoot. Beneath the purported motivating factors for reunion – reckless abandon on the one hand and the allure of "true love" on the other – is, according to Weir-Soley, a deeper psychological response to abuse, common to victims of domestic violence, called "traumatic bonding". Setting her subject within a broader socio-historical context within which black entertainers, particularly women, have always been problematically positioned vis-à-vis mainstream popular-cultural discourse, Weir-Soley suggests that this syndrome of traumatic bonding is exacerbated in Rihanna's case by virtue of the flippant and reductionist media hype surrounding the continued dramatization of the problematic relationship between two megastars whose personal problems are treated as little more than fodder for the consumption of a merciless, and sometimes mercenary, public.

In chapter 7, "Rihanna and Bajan Respectability", Aaron Kamugisha importantly sets Rihanna in the context of a larger and long-historical discourse interpellating Barbados and global middle-class identity. Problematizing the claim that Rihanna "put Barbados on the map", Kamugisha argues that Barbados has always been visible in and integral to North Atlantic modernity since that project's inception. In this chapter, Kamugisha considers Barbados's role in the production and reproduction of a global black middle class – and the place of Rihanna within it. Often lauded as the most "successful" independent majority-black country in the world, Barbados, Kamugisha reminds readers, has one of the lowest rates of abject poverty and largest middle classes in the region, and a high rate of class ascendancy, which, he argues, cannot be delinked from Rihanna's "success" story. Thus, Kamugisha claims, the conflictual embracing and disavowal of Rihanna in Barbados cannot be reduced to, respectively, the Barbadian state's interest in using her image as a marketing tool or a reaction from the conservative religious right to her behaviour, but is a product of a deeper anxiety about youth culture, tolerance to diversity and middle-class respectability in which the state is constantly engulfed. Such national imbrications occur, Kamugisha argues, precisely because middle-classness in Europe has always been linked to ideas of respectability, and given the high price paid for black psycho-existential freedom in the Americas, this has been doubly so in the Caribbean. Such recognition demands, Kamugisha implies, that we read Rihanna, and reactions to her in Barbados, in more nuanced, socio-historical, culturally inflected ways.

In the final chapter, "Rihanna: Diaspora Citizen, Bajan Daughter, Global Superstar", Heather Russell examines Rihanna's "diasporic citizenship" as a way to tease out the politics of her location(s). Simultaneously identified as Barbadian "daughter" and global "superstar", Rihanna, Russell argues, must navigate inevitably conflicting, contesting and reinforcing sites of transnational belongings. As Russell points out, Rihanna is a hugely commercially successful artist operating in a popular-cultural market dictated by US-global musical tastes, and at the same time, she is youth ambassador of Barbados and has signed a multi-year deal to promote her country for the Barbados Tourism Authority. And, too, local discussions surrounding Barbadian national pride, Victorian notions of female propriety and Christian ideas about decency that Rihanna's emergence and ascendancy have provoked, continue to capture the Barbadian public's imagination and dominate the opinions expressed in their newspaper columns. Through readings of popular responses to Rihanna, her (re)presentations and respective entailments, primarily in Barbados, chapter 8 proposes theorizing Rihanna and her aesthetic corpus under the alembic of diaspora citizenship. Such an approach attempts to explore how ideas around nation, diaspora, gender, identity, sexuality and global economy converge in illuminating ways. These ideas are, as Russell asserts, necessary for reading Caribbean cultural production in the age of postmodernity.

While undoubtedly, because of the common subject matter of these essays, there is inevitably some repetition regarding certain incidents, cultural production and analysis, for the most part the authors whose work is compiled here approach the subjects of Rihanna, globalization, gender and sexuality, commerce, transnationalism, Caribbean regionalism, and Barbadian national identity and development from radically different disciplinary and ideological perspectives. We hope you will read both the moments of convergence and those of divergence as equally meaningful and instructive. Whether you are a Rihanna aficionado, an unrepentant Caribbean paternalist, a sceptical consumer or some intriguing admixture of all of the above, we offer the following pages as generative material.

NOTES

1. *Wuk-up* is a Caribbean term used to describe a sensual dance based on skilful gyrating that is central to calypso/soca music and culture. It is mostly female-identified and celebrates women's free expression of and with their bodies.
2. In Caribbean parlance, *easy nuh* refers to the idea that someone has done well – and can be a way to say you are in awe of those achievements, depending on the context of the utterance. We use the word *gurl* as opposed to *girl* to signal Rihanna's womanliness, while still using the commonplace term of reference as a sign of close kinship, as in "hey girl".
3. "The Evolution of Rihanna", BET.com, http://www.bet.com/music/photos/2011/03/the-evolution-of-rihanna.html.
4. Dorothy Pomerantz, "Rihanna Tops Our List of Social Networking Superstars", *Forbes* online, 9 August 2012, http://www.forbes.com/sites/dorothypomerantz/2012/08/09/rihanna-tops-our-list-of-social-networking-superstars/.
5. "Biography", RihannaDaily.com, http://rihannadaily.com/rihanna/biography/.
6. Her clothing-line launch was for British street-fashion brand River Island, in collaboration with her personal stylist, Adam Selman. Together, they published two more collections for the brand: a summer edition released in May 2013 and an autumn edition released in September 2013. The fourth and last collection for River Island, the winter edition, was released in November 2013.
7. "Rihanna and Jay-Z Partner with Budweiser for Global 'Made For Music' Campaign", *Vibe* online, 10 July 2013, http://www.vibe.com/article/rihanna-and-jay-z-partner-budweiser-global-made-music-campaign.
8. "Introducing the 2014 CFDA Fashion Icon of the Year", CFDA.com, 24 March 2014, http://cfda.com/the-latest/introducing-the-2014-cfda-fashion-icon-of-the-year.

9. Faith Smith, ed., *Sex and the Citizen: Interrogating the Caribbean* (Charlottesville: University of Virginia Press, 2011), 2.
10. Ifeona Fulani, ed., *Archipelagos of Sound: Transnational Caribbeanities, Women and Music* (Kingston: University of West Indies Press, 2012), 6–7.
11. Édouard Glissant writes about the brutality of "ethnocultural hierarchy" in *Caribbean Discourse: Selected Essays* (Charlottesville: University of Virginia Press, 1989).
12. Jay Bulger, "Rihanna: Obsession of the Year", *GQ* online, December 2012, http://www.gq.com/moty/2012/rihanna-cover-story-gq-men-of-the-year-2012?current Page=1 (emphasis added).
13. Dorkys Ramos, "Rihanna Tweets Angry Response over Dutch Magazine's Racist Comment", BET.com, 20 December 2011, http://www.bet.com/news/fashion-and-beauty/2011/12/20/rihanna-tweets-angry-response-over-dutch-magazines-racist-comment.html.
14. Henry Louis Gates Jr, *The Signifying Monkey* (Oxford: Oxford University Press, 1988), xxiii.
15. *Womanism* is a feminist term coined by Alice Walker in her germinal collection of essays, *In Search of Our Mothers' Gardens* (New York: Harcourt Brace, 1983). See also "Womanism", in *A Feminist Theory Dictionary*, 17 July 2007, http://afeministtheorydictionary.wordpress.com/2007/07/17/womanism/.
16. Walker, *Our Mothers' Gardens*.
17. See Muna Mire, "Talkback: In Defense of Rihanna", *Feminist Wire* (blog), 16 October 2013, http://thefeministwire.com/2013/10/rihanna/.
18. See David Halperin, *Saint Foucault: Towards a Gay Hagiography* (Oxford: Oxford University Press, 1995), 62.
19. Omise'eke Natasha Tinsley, "Black Atlantic, Queer Atlantic: Queer Imaginings of the Middle Passage", *GLQ: A Journal of Lesbian and Gay Studies* 14, nos. 2–3 (2008): 191–215.

1

WESTBURY WRITES BACK
Rihanna Reclaimed

HILARY McD. BECKLES

Rihanna's Barbados, a rising star as a global entertainment site, has not sufficiently intrigued any formal "school" of social scientists or community of literary critics engaged in postcolonial discourse and cultural theory. In the streets of towns and villages, however, in bars and food joints, pundits and raconteurs, scholars of orality, drink rum and ruminate on the issues in the media and beyond. They are busy at work defining and claiming their space and important developments within it.

The effervescence of the informal stands in stark contrast with the inertia of the formal. The lapse in the latter is due in large measure to the diminished influence of historical perspectives in social investigation. This is particularly evident in the case of some recent Caribbean cultural studies. Barbados, for instance, is branded from the outside as a decent rather than decadent destination (read: country) whose natives (read: citizens) are simply too orderly in their postcolonial conformity to contribute to the "body badness" performance expressions of Caribbean dancehall discography. On the inside, citizens do not recognize this construction and see it as describing another country, an unrecognized foreign place.

Heather Russell, for example, in an insightful inquisition of Caribbean/Barbadian official ambivalence about its superstar's reputation for what might be called by some "Jamaican-style" stage and social boldness, has drawn attention to the presence of disbelief (denial?) in many places with respect to Rihanna's identity as an artistic creation of the allegedly conservative country.[1] Magazines and monographs alike have taken their readers on a hike up and down the mythical mountain of interpretation and narration. Unable to imagine the Barbadian social origins of the diva's "sensual slackness" reputation, writers have fallen into an ahistorical pit from which is heard an echoing chatter that the island is "too small to matter". From this crumbling depth, there is a disturbing Caribbean consensus of either silence or empty noise on the social energy and fuel of her flight.

In the deep, it is difficult to see if anything of significance can emerge. Instead of reason and research, the literary lacuna is filled and refilled with political stereotypes about size and culture that reproduce their own arcane geo-cultural hype. While it is undoubtedly true that on websites (*Feminist Wire*, for example) and in magazines, there have been some quality discussions on Rihanna, North American consumers are still swamped with media manuals such as *The Rihanna Handbook: Everything You Need to Know about Rihanna*. Such texts are honed to conceal rather than reveal what is of substance and therefore importance about the icon to her community and the islands around it. In them, Robyn Fenty does not sing.[2]

On the ground, in her hometown, there is a "calling out" of cultural critics, academics and media moguls. Rihanna's rise to the top of global pop, and the solidification of her reputation as an irreverent icon without comparison, her "homies" say, should serve to reaffirm what they always knew: that analytic focus should seek to engage the histories and integrities of all communities and place them on a level field for equality in enquiry.

The suggestion from folks in the street is that academic observers should not dwell on the obvious and should not be oblivious to the hegemony of geography. Instead, they should embrace the collective intellect of marginalized communities and frame the eruptive universal success of local citizens in such contexts. The categorical call, then, is for critical field research into social consciousness and cultural identity beyond the simplicity of land surveyors' eyes.

A better understanding of Barbados, and by extension of its golden girl, RiRi, can promote this path of enquiry into the postcolonial Caribbean. But trapped conceptually in the big island/small island and island/continent dichotomies that inhibit effective postmodern readings of the archipelago, only something akin to a seismic shakeup, a hurricane-like howling or a Reaganite instruction can tear down these walls. The primacy of the historical perspective is the point where the demolition should begin. There is much rubble to be "rubbished" before important insights can be revealed.

At the outset, it is to be noted that tiny Barbados, in the post-Columbus colonial feeding frenzy of Europe, was huge in the seventeenth century. It was here that England's earliest expressions of imperial hunger and inhumanity led to the crime of mass enslavement of Africans. It was also here that English entrepreneurs and their state supporters built modernity's first black-majority Atlantic society. Everyone who was paying attention to the colonial project as a strategy of morally unfettered capital accumulation had heard of the place as the "richest little spot of earth in the world".[3]

These imperial practices had colonial consequences, which in turn have morphed into the oppressive legacies of nationalism. In this way, Barbados and Britain are minted as two sides of a cultural coin that symbolize modernity's descent into the indecency of chattel slavery, dichotomized today into a culture that promotes blackness as badness, whiteness as goodness and, critically, the creole as lesser than the metropole. The commercialization of the black body as commodity is built into the global cultural DNA. The plantation is no more; the hotel is the new lure. Sugar and slavery have given way to sea and servitude.

With the turn to tourism, the tide has turned. The imagery of white planter on horseback whipping black bodies to productivity lies submerged beneath the new fantasy of white eyes desiring black bodies on golden sand and blue sea. Colonial oppression gave birth to nationalist dislocation. Vexation simmers beneath the concept of total relaxation that signifies the perfect vacation. Rihanna is a "pickaninnie" of the periphery, the urban ruin of the abandoned sugar plantation.

"Get out the ghetto", however, is not a unifying theme in every community. There is always "home" within decay, destruction and death. The cultural entertainment of "the plenty" by the poor is more than a pantomime of mendicancy and the fantasy of flight. It is also about the fight for possession, ownership and legitimization of the creative imagination.[4] The street is filled with the voices of the counter-discourse. There is no silence; there is no noise;

just the sharp, focused sound of a society in defiance and determination to stand its ground.

Here at Beck's Bar, in Rihanna's backyard in Bridgetown, there is discursive intensity on the conceptual issues relevant to the function of the community as career curator. The community rejects as a project external interpretations of the origins of RiRi's commercial career, and sees this posture as a politic rooted in a legacy of resistance to cultural erasure. These sage imbibers might not be speaking to the specificity of literary and cultural criticism, nor indeed revisionist social theory, but they do believe that big slices of scholarship have gone astray in the way they improperly portray their progeny.[5]

Top of the menu, for instance, are the assumptions and projections of analytic argument found within Stuart Hall's interchange with Immanuel Wallerstein on relations between the local and the global in social theory. Hall asks, "Is globalization nothing but the triumph and closure of history by the West? Is this the final moment of a global post-modern where it now gets hold of everybody, of everything, where there is no difference which it cannot contain . . . ?" Wallerstein answers: "What is striking about the political history of the modern world-system, as it has historically developed, is the ever more frequent and ever more efficacious utilization by oppressed elements of what might generically be called cultural resistance. Of course, cultural resistance is an eternal theme."[6]

Westbury is a keen informal participant in this polemic. It sees itself as part of and not apart from "the West", and as an agent and site of resistance in the appropriating politics and policies of the economic North of this "West". The community, therefore, has its own epistemic understanding and posture in the disputed borderland. Its understandings are fluid and informed by a keen grasp of the history and sociology of community formation within the long trajectory of colonialism.

This sense of self-awareness and self-interest is found in no formal text. But it is real; it exists. It requires no literary intervention to trigger an articulation. Like Rihanna before her recording phase, it is ready to burst forth. A tourist can unleash a tirade merely by entering Beck's and asking whether it is true that Rihanna is really from around here. The response is always swift and rendered with veracity in the vernacular. Thereafter, invariably, the stratosphere is suddenly thickened. There is respect for the impostor. But the raw nerve is exposed. There is acute sensitivity, born of a perceived injustice that under no circumstances will be accepted.

Answers are comprehensive, reflective and projective. There is generational solidarity in the cosmology of this community. "Rihanna is not from here! She is here! Here is [in] her". The question is understood to mean that implicit in the answer, "yes she is from here", is a kind of touristic condescending incredulity. Offence is taken by the implication. The asker is understood to be in control of truth and seeking an arrogant affirmation. The answerer rejects the polarity as a vulgarity. The collective face of the place is turned against the cultural force that seeks to define and defame, desecrate and appropriate that which they have created. The bar is ready for battle. It is more than a war of words; it is a military operation for primary rights over ownership of Rihanna's space and authorship of her persona. The community is writing back in the ways it knows best: offerings in orality that speak to cultural confidence in identity; vocal domestication of internationalism as local.[7]

Beck's Bar – owned and built by Omar Beckles (no known blood relation, but small places are filled with big secrets, and one has to be open and big-minded) – is situated at the centre of the community that curves around the perimeter of a public cemetery. It is in voice reach of RiRi's birth base, a discursive place filled with street scholars and popular pundits. It is still a young enterprise, and no night is without its intellectual surprise. Conversations with commuters and in-house regulars provided the evidentiary basis of the community's critique presented here. It is a source that might not satisfy standards of scientific scrutiny as scholarly interventions, but it shows the passions of people determined to have their voices and visions included and institutionalized.

"She from just down the road", says an elderly man (he is ninety-something). "This place is way up there [he points to the sky] with the best. Oprah come in here and she drink a rum with the people. Nobody ain't push pen and paper in she face for she signature. She sent down she rum and coke in peace and quiet. Simple so! We in Westbury accustomed to the best; we like bigness and we love badness. So God bless David, if Miss Ri wants to mix in we own local *c*-word with all the bad foreign *c*-words like *CNN*, we tell she to go right ahead 'cause that is how we raise she in Westbury: to grow fast and spread free and flowery like a frangipani tree [he laughs]. She does curse too sweet when people mess with she; a true child of Westbury!"[8]

Here, in the belly of the community, every imaginable mixture of the global and the local is known and sewn into the fabric of street fellowship. The story of neighbourhood stars is told with pride. Metropolitan myth of "big" producers discovering "raw" girls for refining and recasting as divas from the diaspora holds no power here. The community is concrete in the assertion that one person's "local" is another person's "global". It is simply, they say here, a matter of deciding and defending what and where is the centre – the place from which you see and speak. They are secure in the truth that their centre is here; right here around and within Beck's Bar. It is from here that a thousand ships have been launched. Those that return laden have licence to go respected and unmolested as royalty.

In Westbury, RiRi was bred to bacchanal – badness, slackness and boldness, sassiness and sexiness forged in the beat and heat of the night. Westbury is a community like no other on the poor periphery of Bridgetown, England's first sin city in the formative days of its imperial glory. How fascinating: it still seems to many visitors that this straight and narrow little street is home to a day/night culture that says, *Everything your body or heart desires can be secured in exchange for the dollar.* Kids play games outdoors in the sunlight; adults convert street games into business in the moonlight. Cash rules! This is how pleasures are measured. Priests ignore the sin within; police have bigger fish to fry.

Backing onto Westbury is New Orleans, an extension of the community that competes with and loses nothing to its larger partner in Louisiana. These streets are the springs that irrigate RiRi's irrepressible desire. She is the "baddest" diva that recent decades have adored. Knowing Westbury is reading Rihanna. It is the key to her cadence. There is no mystery in her history. While the global gloats about the "bad" girl going gold, the local mocks their hubris with laughter as its pop princess takes the top spot. The old man in Beck's says that the hype of the celebrity media is hollowed. It lacks substance and seriousness. "There is no strange fruit on the tree", he insists. "Talent is a blossom. It blooms in its own season. It was just a matter of time." The cultural certitude that sweeps these streets enables the "inevitability thesis" to hold its ground. There is resolve in their communal reasonings; it is seen in the eyes of the elderly and in the attitudes of adolescents. It is as unmistakable as it is remarkable.[9]

Westbury is a metaphor for diverse worlds mangled together by the cultural power of colonialism. The creolity created in the crucible has spawned its own cultural mores that bubble like hot tar upon the surface. This creolity runs in the veins of the vernacular and finds expression in all that is said and done. It holds the community together. It is an outward-looking space that knows its inner values and worth. It is tolerant yet tenacious. There is, therefore, no counterclaim to RiRi's domestic raising and professional rise. Her Guyanese father and Barbadian mother represent the rhythm of a Caribbean space shaped by migratory movement. Westbury is simultaneously a crossroad and a hub where cultural inflows coalesce into a community that knows modernity as an insider.

Inside the community, each street connects to the town's major public symbols of life and death. To the east is the city's cemetery, where the curtains come down for the final time on the rich and rapacious and the poor and polite. The "big-ups" who own the government and the "barefooted" who possess the street find common ground in "West-bury". To the west is Spring Garden, the liveliest street, which is home to the annual Crop Over carnival, the biggest and "baddest" live show the society has conceived. Here rum and the drum run riot in celebration of liberation from slavery and in anticipation of freedom and redemption.

From the centre of these worlds of life and death, sounds and silence, energy and eternity, RiRi stepped out, riddled with teenage turbulence and the preparation of a community confident that it empowers its citizens from cradle to casket. Fenty's girl, my confidant commented, knew "big-people business from she was little bit". She was bred, for sure, to know the vitality and mortality of an avenue that connects the badness of bacchanal to the introspection of internment. The community serves as an incubator that accelerates the growth of talent with tenacity. In this crucible she was "forced ripe", matured beyond the normal trajectory of common nurture.[10]

Westbury seeks to liberate rather than incarcerate its citizens; it empowers the energetic and enterprising. Flight from the cultural scaffold of slavery is an imperative still driving the imaginative. The ruins of what was Westbury's slave sugar plantation are still evident in the minds and manners of inhabitants. Emancipation has come and gone, leaving the slave village to evolve into an urban ghetto, a Caribbean tale often told. "Up from poverty" is a powerful philosophy that calls for an escape from the mindscape of the enslaving estate. The community deifies the door to global destinies that is the sea at the end of the street – the bluest backdrop to the brown of internal decay.

In the recesses of the Caribbean mind, Miami to the west has replaced London to the east as the yeast that enables the cake to rise. Forces fashioned in England directed much of the history, but the present repositioning of imaginings favours Uncle Sam. The sea is seen as the seamless survival escape to "the States". Any movement along this trajectory is read as domestic rather than foreign travel. Citizens traverse this terrain daily – New York, Miami, and Washington, DC. For them, London was a long time ago and a long way to go.

Barbados, then, conceived in the "wickedness and sin" of sugar and slavery, was born to Africa and England, with cousins on the continent and siblings in each island in the sun. It is a cultural world that embraces inputs from far and wide. RiRi, the community says, is as Bajan as sugar, as Caribbean as slavery, as American as emigration, and as English as imperialism. Westbury holds the centre in this history and insists upon the right to write what is new within the news. Historical perspectives lead to a place from which it can be said that Barbados occupied a more central location in the rise of capitalist modernity than any other Caribbean colonial construct. As the first fully formed slave economy in the New World, it was also home to the first black-majority society. The slave-based wealth generated in the seventeenth century by the English, and circulated by the pirates of the Caribbean, was unprecedented. While it was deemed "a place worse than hell" for Africans, the English branded it "the richest little spot on earth". By 1680, when its first population census was taken, it was classified as the financial capital of England's America. The trade value of the little place was more than all the American colonies combined.[11]

The legacy remains, buried in the abandoned plantations but bubbling in the consciousness of every child in Westbury and beyond. Rihanna's revolution is an eruption in the erudition. The elderly man in Beck's knows this, though the young within the town might experience it at a more subliminal level, as a feeling. But none is disconnected from the historical narrative in which they expect their global success to be expressed as domestic common sense. They know the connections between their impoverished past and empowered futures; and they are not afraid to party.

The proof of the pudding is in the eating. From the back of Beck's Bar, less than five minutes' foot time away is the mecca of national popular-sport culture: Kensington Cricket Oval. This towering stadium has seen decades of black achievement on a global scale. It is a monument to the poor in its vicinity, as it is to the rich wherever cricket is played. Community stars before Rihanna was imagined took the world by "hurricane" in this stadium, democratized and transformed it with their indigenous strokes. For many disciples of the sport, the Oval is the greatest cricket stadium in the (New) World. It is the home of community legends – black heroes who rose from neighbourhood poverty to parade their genius upon a global stage.

Outside the Oval, in a garden facing Westbury, is an impressive statue that captures the performance art and style of Sir Garry Sobers, the greatest global living legend of cricket. He stands there, fifteen feet high, cast in bronze, glittering in the sunlight that illuminated his career. Like his friends and contemporaries Muhammad Ali and Pelé, Sobers was the greatest performer of his discipline in his time (the 1960s and 1970s). He was a supreme artiste whose fan base in Bridgetown and beyond was fanatical about his stagecraft. For many, he possessed the performance magic. His movements were bold, beautiful and awe-inspiring.[12]

The pundits poured into Bridgetown from the corners of the cricket earth to witness the king. His kingdom stretched from the island to England; from India to Australia; from New Zealand to Pakistan; and from South Africa to the black diaspora. Children ran behind him in the streets; their fathers made way as he walked about the city. He was the most world-famous Barbadian of his time, a household global name captured in verse and calypso.

Like King Sobers, Queen RiRi raises eyebrows and pulses everywhere she journeys. Sobers's lane on the other side of town mirrors Westbury in many ways, without the cemetery and "sin city" imagery. Both are part of post-plantation poverty, with dense concentrations of inner-city children. Cut loose to fend for themselves, many discover their gifts, with which they apply intense discipline and determination to succeed. The concept of the child genius is old to this town. The king and queen came to their thrones with an inheritance of community brilliance, which was the sole source of their sovereignty. At twenty-two years of age, Sobers had broken the prized global cricket record and Rihanna was selling more records than any other artiste from the region, and more than most others throughout the world. They were rated and ranked at the top of their tables. Pundits and experts have rushed to print and Internet in recognition of the need to interrogate the alleged phenomenon. None has yet unearthed what every child knows in Westbury: that Columbus did not discover their island and neither did Jay-Z discover RiRi.

Truth has its own compelling logic and unrelenting legacy. There is much to be understood about the power of past achievements within the popular imagination. How historic knowledge is recorded as community memory and expressed for global consumption is in many ways about the politics of organized power. A generation before Sobers ruled the town, there was another. His name was Everton Weekes. He came from Pickwick Gap, the space adjoining RiRi's. Twice in the 1950s, Sir Everton was rated by spectators and statisticians worldwide as the number-one cricket batsman.[13]

"Not bad," Sir Everton wrote in his cricket memoirs, for a Westbury boy to take the number-one spot in the world. He was "the one", and the street did not need the world to tell them. He was born, he wrote, "in Pickwick Gap [a stone's throw from Rihanna's home], in a typical chattel house in the inner city of Bridgetown. Maybe I was born to be a cricketer as I grew up on a street a ball's throw from the historical Kensington Oval which loomed large in my mind as a child. It was the only place within the community that captured my imagination. There was no museum, no library; just Kensington Oval, a place of legend. I was determined to find my way out in that middle, one way or another. All of the boys in the community had the same ambition." He found the way to the "centre" of the Oval, and took centre stage in the universe.[14]

Weekes dazzled crowds with his genius. He explains the key to his case – the rationale for his rise:

> The poverty we experienced had to do more with . . . history than with our ability as a people. I grew up surrounded by some very gifted and bright people whose ability was well known and who in a different, more humane circumstance, would have been outstanding citizens in terms of their contribution to human advancement. I was blessed, endowed, I suppose, like many of my fellow villagers, with a little gift; a mind that enabled me to concentrate for long periods, and to apply it in ways that supported my desire to be a disciplined person.[15]

Weekes prepared the way for the day when kings and queens from Westbury would rise within the world of arts performance. In this way, the village would vigorously ventilate its cultural capability, recognizing no limits within itself.

The only walls within Westbury are those erected around the cemetery. They have no significance for spirits possessed of creative imaginations and destined for greatness. The sound of music and the rounds of cricket are not contained. The high performance standards set by Weekes and Sobers would apply to all art. Rihanna did not expect that she could escape the cultural hegemony of cricket. The Bridgetown brand banished the thought of an exception. Like Weekes and Sobers, she grew to maturity in awe of the Oval.

Rihanna was socially made, therefore, to crave the big stage. Madison Square Garden or the London Palladium held no advantage in the imagination over the Oval. She knew intuitively that she had to win her stars and stripes in the streets of her creation. This meant the Oval. Like Weekes and Sobers, she had to find the way to the "centre" and show the locals what they were craving.

"Pure pandemonium rocked Kensington Oval last night", screamed one article on 6 August 2011. A crowd of twenty-nine thousand, in a stadium of eighteen thousand seats, had pushed its way into the Oval starting at six p.m., when the gates opened. No cricket crowd that large had ever graced the Oval. The recorded attendance for the Cricket World Cup Final in 2007 between Australia and Sri Lanka was twenty thousand.[16]

The event was billed as Rihanna's "first ever hometown concert". It was the last leg of her Loud tour. Conceptually, it was the first forward movement back to the beginning – a return to source. It was also, symbolically, a confrontation of the outer world with the imagination of an inner-city soul intent on bending reality into a shape to call its own. This was simultaneously the end and the beginning of the tour. Saving the best for last would be a test. Singing in the Oval is as global as it gets. The magnificence of the metaphor resonated.

Rihanna's innings at Kensington rolled back the time mnemonically to the first moment in which the inner city had taken over the world. It was 1967. It was Bridgetown, and the world was assembled to pay homage. Barbados had achieved political independence the previous year, after 339 years of British colonial rule. The 240,000 islanders were breaking with the Brits and "going alone". Prime Minister Errol Barrow, an attorney just forty-six years old, had announced to the world that the time had come for him, and them, to "cease loitering on colonial premises". It was time to go home. The political performance was superb.[17]

The celebration of political freedom took the form of a cricket match. It was art propelled to the centre of political (re)creation! But it could not be a local match; historical reasoning and political engineering required the largest possible canvas on which to paint the tale whose telling would be universal. Barbados would take on everyone from everywhere. The match – to be held at Kensington Oval, from 8 to 11 March 1967 – would be between two teams: the national team and the best team assembled from the "Rest of the World". The Barbados team was led by "King" Sobers, and the rest of the world's best were led by William Lawry, the Australian national captain.[18] The global cricket event, staged to signal the enormity of the political moment, was more than a celebration of Barbadian excellence in popular culture. Critically, it was the world coming to the community to pay homage to the greatest performer it had ever seen.[19]

The world team was keen to contest the best in the Oval. There was nothing unusual about the event. Barbados had within its team some of the finest cricketers in the world. International teams had been defeated before by the island's best. Nations of millions knew how readily they could be bundled by the Barbadians. A confidence bred by its global depth had seeped into the sap of the determined little nation. The Oval is situated at the heart of this national ethos. Rihanna's strategy to win and hold the centre meant storming Kensington. This was also the community's expectation.

RiRi's words echoed those of Weekes a half-century earlier. Before taking to the stage, she told the media, "I remember when I was growing up, just two streets across from the Oval, in Westbury Road, and singing and annoying our neighbours. I always wanted to perform in there."[20]

In the culture of art performance, there is no hierarchical structure that ranks small places below big places. Beyond the crassness of race and class consciousness, art pushes away the discriminatory debris and insists upon a level playing field. When, for example, King George V of England sought to kick-start international cricket after the recess of the Second World War, he invited Learie Constantine of Trinidad and Tobago to lead a world team to compete against England at Lord's Cricket Ground, the home of English cricket. Constantine was the cricket king in the king's commonwealth. He stepped forth and took control of the centre, marginalizing the mountain of racial and colonial prejudice.

RiRi's arrival at the Oval, like Constantine's entry at Lord's, fulfilled a dream drenched in childhood cultural preparation. It was not simply that she desired to enter the physical space as a performer, to sing and dance in the den of cricket crusaders. It was that the Oval is the only global performance space on the island with a pedigree recognized over several generations. It is the only institution in Barbados that is celebrated in song, expressed in multiple vernacular versions. She climbed a steep childhood curve on a diet of such praise-songs detailing Sobers's many ovations in the Oval.

RiRi's Oval debut and departure, then, were filled with fables, a history of glory sustained by generations in the gap. The cricket fraternity heard that RiRi had expressed the desire to wind up her world tour in the Oval. There was anxiety that cricket pundits and purists would object to the sacrilege of it all and engage in a desecration discourse. There was silence. There was consent. RiRi's time had come. She had conquered the outer space. It was time to prove herself before a jury of the vicinity – the folks from Westbury, Pickwick Gap and the environs of the Oval.[21]

The timing was impeccable! RiRi was on the ball. "The girl has game", a security guard said. At 10:20 p.m., after the longest wait in the Oval's history, four hours, the queen strutted across a stage chandeliered in blue and yellow lights – national colours – and shouted, "Barbados, I love you." Then it came: the moment of compelling – the performance of "Only Girl (in the World)". There was no space on this stage for a critic! The "only girl in the world", dressed in national colours, expressing universal love, mobilizing BET's live broadcast to entertain millions of global viewers from the heat of the Bridgetown night. When the skies opened and rain descended upon the show for ten minutes, it was christened by a shower of blessing and welcomed by all from Westbury. The walls around the Oval came down for the "only girl". It was RiRi's triumph.[22]

It was an innings filled with master strokes. Not even Sobers at his best, some suggested, could have played it so perfectly. Two exquisite political comments on masculine violence gave her "family" the opportunity to choose: "Man Down" was followed by a declaration of her rise and triumph in "Run This Town". The Oval undulating, she unleashed the "Rude Boy", urging him to "get it up". "What's My Name?" seemed a redundant refrain; she was the only girl in the Oval. She had been groomed for the moment long before she knew.

All in the Oval were under her "Umbrella" for the 110-minute coronation.[23]

Those who did not witness the sight that night resorted to reading what the world wrote. This has been a vexation to their spirit. A brother in Beck's "pooed" the report in *Esquire* magazine of October 2011 in which RiRi was dubbed "the sexiest woman alive". "The white people in the world", he said, "have this harassing habit of discovering things the rest of the world already knows. Who give them this right to write about things they just see? They have no right to claim copyright for something that we made and belong to us. I was there, in 2004, when she ran away with her school's beauty pageant [at Combermere Secondary]. God bless David, she was the most beautiful thing on the earth since Sheba stun Solomon. Beauty not in the eye of the beholder; it does behold the eye, and if you have a good eye you can see it coming. I saw it when she was fourteen. The world can twist it or put the fix on it, but we know the truth; we know the difference."[24]

The will to turn the world the right way up arises from the judgements of plaintiffs at Beck's. Pouring out of this place is a passion to have wrongs made right; there is a politic that assaults any pretence to authority by outsiders. Jay-Z, for them, did not "make" RiRi. This perspective, coined and minted by an Internet intellect, causes the rum to run while the outrage is denounced. RiRi was world-ready, produced in Westbury and sent out to find a sponsor. "He opened doors for sure," my elderly friend says, "but she brought him into her interior. . . . She travelled on his vehicle for sure, but the man who has his private jet still has to land it on somebody's strip! You don't make your own road, just because you rolling in a Rolls!" The world, for him, comes to Westbury. "We are at the centre of things," he says, "we run things from here."[25]

The rejection in Westbury of the notion that the community exists on the periphery calls for a review of the tendency to dichotomize in social science. This is consistent with pseudo-historical perspectives which seek answers to questions like "What is Barbados?" and "Who is Rihanna?" Caribbean historians, from C.L.R. James and Eric Williams to Walter Rodney and beyond, have refused from the outset to accept the concept of the Caribbean as anything other than centre.

Economists, on the other hand, have too often upheld the dichotomy, resulting in leftist political scientists asserting that Caribbean development requires a critical delinking, or more effective re-linking, to "the West". RiRi's

Westbury, and Barbados at large, have for four centuries been at the centre of what is known as "the West".

Indeed, an argument can be sustained that "the West" began, at least in a financial way, in Barbados, because it was here that Africa, Europe and the Americas met in unholy slavery. It was here that free-roaming European capital, enchained labour from Africa and stolen material resources from native America, combined in mines and managed on plantations, mass-produced commodities for world trade and accumulated wealth at an unprecedented global level. Globalized greed also produced songs of freedom. This ancestry continues to shape voices in Westbury.[26]

While Barbados might reside in the economic South of "the West", it originated and was sustained because RiRi's enslaved ancestors resided at its cultural centre. Her reason for occupying the Oval, the primary globalized institution in her domestic space, was precisely to insert herself into the discourse with a powerful political statement. Her journey home to the centre had little to do with *home* in a literal, pedantic sense. *Home*, here, is a metaphor for simultaneous recognition of beginning and end, the conflation of deep historical roots and probing routes through the contemporary into new worlds.

At the crossroads of Westbury and the Oval is President Kennedy Drive, which leads to Princess Alice Way, and so on and on. It is a community punctuated with political symbols of global power and ownership. Rihanna's arrival at JFK Airport in New York to begin her Jay-Z journey can hardly be understood as "foreign" travel. Momentous in many ways, it was essentially a movement along pathways known to Westbury and familiar to its world travellers. The challenge for folks in Beck's, then, was not posed by the globalization of RiRi, or of Barbados, for that matter, as they know and live it daily, but by interpreters of the interaction who see only from *their* centre. This quarrel with these scribes of the crossroads is in part a plea for a partnership approach to scholarship.

Acrimony in the divergence of testimony, however, is reserved for elements in the domestic rather than global discourse. The rage in discursive representation is directed at the citizenry in local evangelical suburbia rather than global academia. This is also where a brutal battle is being waged to claim RiRi. Westbury has no fear of media missiles launched from New York, London, Paris or Rome. But passionate sermons of parish priests engender an enmity that constitutes the battleground for a progressive Barbadian cultural and artistic sensibility that respects the "body" and its poetics as naked truths to be revealed.

The notion of a "good girl gone bad" invokes a humorous response in Beck's. "But God knows, she bad badbad from the start", says my conversationalist. "We mek she bad! She bad like all ah we." There is humour in this reading of the narrative. Jay-Z, the story is told, found a cute island sweetie, innocent in every way, incorporated and corrupted her core in order to make the music in his mind. Unpacking and dispatching this allegory requires the juxta-position of Westbury's real body politics, which drip in brown sugar–molasses sassiness, with the artificial studio makeover of the American video. The reaction to this literary recreation of RiRi's evolution is that Jay-Z better watch his ——— because the "Westbury devil" will turn his world upside down with her Bajan badness.[27]

RiRi's unleashing of Westbury's Western ways upon the wider local society has invoked an evangelical, moralist mantra. Incantations of indignation resonate in many places, while they violate spirits in her community. Flesh exposed is as Westbury as apple pie is New York; it is common and carries no censorship. But the outcry against RiRi in the outskirts that her skirts are too skimpy and her tops too topless sends tongues wagging aplenty. Too much of the icon's inner body is bare, they pray; she portrays a virtue that is not consistent with the national core value. For Westbury, what matters is that its "sin" is lawful. It finds short shrift with the perception that it is awful. Divided by brown skin, society's official love of the queen is conditional; the cover girl must cover more, or be chastised.

Westbury ignores this ignominy. It reads these critics as advocates of an anthropology of antiquity, and replies with its own hype that speaks of hypocrisy in high places. "Bare and beat your chest, child," my elder advises her, "and show the world the legs on which your achievements rest." He adds, "Be brazen without a bra, pretty girl; raise your rear wherever you feel reason." Writing back from Westbury involves the hurling of such missiles at reactionary elements in the "heights and terraces" who continue to prefer the rule of the obsolete orthodoxy of puritan Christianity: the same lips that launched a thousand slave ships.[28]

RiRi's legs-apart, butt-pride, finger-licking choreography is the brand of gap culture that creates and certifies her familiar dance movements. As an effective cultural messenger, she takes pride in precision of performance and knows all too well the importance of community cultural ownership. The street rejects criticisms of its art as vulgar and takes umbrage to accusations of its cultural icon as being responsible for moral arson. The "legs apart and astride a prostrated sister" stunt is a common woman-on-woman street simulation designed to stimulate diversity in the sin city market. It is wicked Westbury playing the game of tease without release. Every girl on the go knows the first rule of the game: see the crotch but don't move to touch!

It is not that RiRi has blown the lid on libido liberation. Neither is it that she represents a public parody of imported immorality. Rather, it is that official society has made a failed attempt to submerge its cultural extremities under a porous cloak of respectability, which has been rejected. Beneath a widespread commitment to form a mythical English conformity resides an insurgent African cosmology. RiRi is the latest liberator to be dragged before the local laity. Her sentence has been a kind of stoning. There will be others.

This theology is well known to those concerned with drafting the text of the "Westbury write-back". To suppress the message is to support the oppressor. To empower the messenger is to spread the ideology of the uprising. "One day coming soon", says the refrain of a popular calypso, the people will excavate their sound, long buried beneath the rubble in each imprisoned soul. They will chant down the walls of Bridgetown and sing to Westbury's Enlightenment. Then, and only then, will the queen sit on her throne with no fear of a single stone.

Then there is the persistence of the Jamaica/Barbados comparison. For example, a headline in the Barbados *Nation* on 29 November 2012 asked a strangely constructed question which, more than anything, identified RiRi as peculiar within the spectacular: "Where are the Jamaican Rihannas?" The clipping is pasted upon a wall at the Oval. Its intention is to delegitimize as much as to rationalize. On the one hand, the phrase invokes the rebel sound of "Jamdown", the "get up, stand up" lyrics of the Kingston garrison in contrast to the seemingly apolitical vocals of the North Atlantic "bad girl" world of Westbury. On the other hand, ideas about the unruly, unprofessional parochialism of the Jamaican artiste resound in calls to, in the words of one industry insider, "look at an artiste like Rihanna as a template. It was working directly with international producers which allowed her to break out. I don't see any of the [Jamaican] female artistes doing any active collaborations with international acts."[29]

Discourses of cultural interaction between the local and the global too often serve to generate notions of servility in the former, with their attendant sterile stereotypes, and systems of superiority in the latter. But in this instance, the article does more, even without intending to. Although the author's query is seemingly steeped in a discourse which attempts to highlight the internationalization of the Barbados "sophisticate", it inevitably dichotomizes Caribbean music into two broad categories: the minstrel entertainment sound of the "small islanders", who are shrewdly apolitical and thus able to capitalize by prioritizing mainstream desires, and the "rebel music" of Jamaica, which is stuck in a time warp. Such simplification furthers the idea of Rihanna as both anomaly and mystery, and misses important opportunities to read her radical Bajan badness within a broader sociopolitical context. Still, it is true that Jamaica has an undeniably strong national performance arts culture, informed by and branded in its grassroots liberationist ideology of centuries' vintage. Deeply rooted in an African sensibility, and nurtured by a philosophy of redemption, Jamaican musical thirst is quenched at a deep well sunk in the African aesthetic. Barbados, in many ways, is a Caribbean disapora within the African diaspora. The shape of its music reflects this demographic. Barbados has evolved further along the Caribbean creolization trajectory.

Of the blacks emancipated from physical slavery in 1838, just 1 per cent in Barbados were African born, compared with 25 per cent in Jamaica.[30] These are significant demographics that impact the cultural rubrics of these countries. Jamaica has retained a strong African heartbeat that drives its magnificent musical heritage. Barbados, at the other end of the scale, has a stronger "New World" identity that is informed by but not anchored in an African epistemology.

The emergence of "brand Barbados", an attempt to globalize national identity around images of corporate integrity, diplomatic sophistication, financial flexibility and other such assets befitting a centre of Western capitalism, is therefore significant in reading the subtext of RiRi's choices and charm. The North Atlantic catalogue of sound, from thirties blues to sixties jazz and soul, through to seventies rock and funk and post-nineties pop, constitutes the textual images of musical internationalism that propelled Rihanna into the spaces she occupies with the medley that is her brand. She is an ocean into which many rivers flow. None begins in her hometown. All have arrived, passed through, left their legacy and moved on.

Jamaica's artistic assets are manufactured differently. "Made in Jamaica" has an altogether different postcolonial meaning. The global world has found no primary traction in Jamaican musical trenches. *Homegrown* means, above all else, made with local materials with an indigenous integrity. The global reggae explosion of the seventies did not reach Barbados with any intensity until the nineties, and Marley was resisted by the popular consciousness that embraced Elvis, the Beatles, Jim Reeves, Johnny Cash, and Simon and Garfunkel. Calypso got a look in, but local stars struggled to make a living. Music was not a part of the corporate rubric. This island remained under the global recording radar.[31]

The initial attempt to tie RiRi's tongue to the "island in the sun" legacy of Harry Belafonte, jerked with a faint flavour of Jamaican reggae and spiced and fried in a "Trini" calypso pan, was inevitable, given the absence of a dynamic indigenous sound in Barbados. It was also doomed to failure on account of its false assumptions and fragile foundation. The prime program had to be inserted if RiRi was going to be real. She was not reinvented. She returned to self: the sounds of the Atlantic. This is where her spirit is located.

Mr Fenty, father to the prodigy, has been the singer's harbinger. A "session" musician of quality in the vicinity, he is recognized as a talent bred within the creative diversity of the community. He plays everything; he knows it all; he is known for his range. This Bajan musical approach, long in place, harnessed RiRi's gift in the home. She was Jay-Z's afterthought. The call had gone out to another. RiRi was asked to audition after her friend, whom she had accompanied, did not impress the investor. The afterthought blew away the forethought. The talent sang for itself. It was ripe and ready. She exploded because her clock was already ticking towards the big bang.

The combination of domestic nurture and Westbury's nature prepared the path for RiRi's journey to her audition in New York City where the first tale of the long story ends. The dazzling young beauty from Westbury sealed the deal. There is nothing of the fairy in the tale. Rather, it is the same old allegory about hard work, mental preparation and toughness, and desire for development. Outside of the personal is the structural. The counter-narrative is well scripted by academics: foreign capital is invested in Caribbean raw materials; these are extracted, processed, packaged and marketed in the metropole as First World products. It is the story of Caribbean sugar, bauxite, cocoa and oil, and it mirrors the mythology that surrounds its sounds from RiRi back to Marley.

By returning and claiming the Oval, RiRi knew, intuitively and intellectually, the need to proclaim a national strategy to bring home a larger ration of the bacon. There is the beginning of an anti-systemic political ideology at work. Though it has not yet matured in the way that led to Marley's Tuff Gong kingdom in Kingston, the lights along the future are lit. Honed at Combermere, one of the most prestigious academies on the island, Rihanna's sharp intellect allowed for sight beyond the glitz of the global into the roadways of revenue flows. She has effectively reaffirmed the island as a global centre/home for her political sovereignty. This, then, is how the "Westbury Reclaim RiRi Project" enters the polemic – as a declaration of personal and community independence. The rest, they say at Beck's, is poo!

Rihanna's persona is unmistakably political and postcolonial. When Prime Minister Errol Barrow, during a fiery electoral speech in Bridgetown in 1986, asked citizens the question "What is your mirror image?", it created for the youth an opportunity to unleash "baaaad" body politics in expressions of freedom from fear and to unfetter their minds from mental slavery. The folks in Westbury rejoiced; they were happy to hear that their political leader had finally caught up with them. And so, when a Dutch magazine referred to Rihanna as a "nigga bitch", Citizen R's response came from deep within the Westbury vernacular. She went for the jugular: "You put two words together, with the intent of abasement, that made no sense. . . . Well with all respect, on behalf of my race, here are my two words for you . . . F—— YOU!!!" Likewise, when she was racially abused in similar fashion in a Lisbon hotel, her tweet was sweet for her Westbury base: "Needless to say, the #NIGGA in me came out! Bajan accent and all."[32]

The Barbadian government's decision to appoint the global star national cultural ambassador opened a Pandora's box. "Sometimes a person looks at me and sees dollars", she says. "They see numbers and they see a product. I look at me and I see art. . . . But I am a [Westbury] woman", she says, "and I have to be in control."[33] Personal proprietorship and national representation constitute a mulled-over cocktail that remains explosive. "I am no role model", the ambassador insists. "I cannot raise your kids; that is your job. I do the art, not the aunt." Her refusal to participate in a polemic in which she is framed as the "good girl" in need of redemption and salvation is consistent with the discursive disconnect artists generally experience between constructs of personal freedom and the controlling impulse of their nation(-states).

As cultural ambassador, RiRi paints an abstract picture that centres her personal creative dynamic above the reactionary piety retained in the postcolonial cultural realm. The "bad girl" is entirely Bajan and a far shout from bohemian. Westbury loves her just the way she is; they are not prepared to have her modified and mentored away in any discourse that alienates and appropriates. The community is leading the charge to reclaim their baby from the co-opting/adopting parents. It is writing back. And here at Beck's Bar, a narrative has matured. War words – including the common c-type – have been made and are sharpened. "Talk That Talk", RiRi's response, is the silent signal that tells her community not to let up but to step up the battle for Barbados.

NOTES

1. Heather D. Russell, "Whose Rihanna? Diasporic Citizenship and the Economics of Crossing Over", in Ifeona Fulani, ed., *Archipelagos of Sound: Transnational Caribbeanities, Women and Music* (Kingston: University of the West Indies Press, 2012), 299. See also Carolyn Cooper, *Sound Clash: Jamaican Dancehall Culture at Large* (New York: Palgrave Macmillan, 2004); *Noises in the Blood: Orality, Gender and the "Vulgar" Body of Jamaican Popular Culture* (Durham, NC: Duke University Press, 1993); Esther Tyson, "Slackness and More Slackness", *Jamaica Gleaner*, 6 April 2008, http://jamaica-gleaner.com/gleaner/20080406/cleisure/cleisure5.html.

2. Tanisha Murilo, *The Rihanna Handbook: Everything You Need to Know about Rihanna* (n.p., 2010). See also Antonio Benítez-Rojo, *The Repeating Island: The Caribbean and the Postmodern Perspective*, trans. James E. Maraniss (Durham, NC: Duke University Press, 1996), 1–6; Timothy J. Reiss, "Introduction: Music, Writing, and Ocean Circuits", in *Music, Writing and Cultural Unity in the Caribbean*, ed. Timothy J. Reiss (Trenton, NJ: Africa World Press, 2005), 1–34.

3. See Hilary McD. Beckles, "The 'Hub of Empire': The Caribbean and Britain in the Seventeenth Century", in *The Oxford History of the British Empire*, vol. 1, *The Origins of Empire: British Overseas Enterprise to the Close of the Seventeenth*

Century, ed. Nicholas Canny (Oxford: Oxford University Press, 1998), 218–40; Paul Gilroy, *The Black Atlantic: Modernity and Double Consciousness* (Cambridge, MA: Harvard University Press, 1993); Anthony Bogues, "Politics, Nation, and PostColony: Caribbean Inflections", *Small Axe* 6, no. 1 (2002): 1–30.

4. See Édouard Glissant, *Caribbean Discourse: Selected Essays*, trans. Michael Dash (Charlottesville: University of Virginia Press, 1992); Guillermina De Ferrari, *Vulnerable States: Bodies of Memory in Contemporary Caribbean Fiction* (Charlottesville: University of Virginia Press, 2007); Charles W. Mills, *Radical Theory, Caribbean Reality: Race, Class and Social Domination* (Kingston: University of the West Indies Press, 2010); Diane Austin, "Culture and Ideology in the English-Speaking Caribbean: A View from Jamaica", *American Ethnologist* 10, no. 2 (1983): 223–40; Brian Meeks and Norman Girvan, eds., *The Thought of New World: The Quest for Decolonisation* (Kingston: Ian Randle, 2010).

5. Informal conversations were recorded with a group of patrons in Beck's Bar on Saturday, 30 March 2013. Permission was granted to quote statements, but not to reveal identities. For more on Beck's Bar, see "Slice of Life: Bringing Life to Westbury", *Daily Nation* (Barbados), 7 February 2012, 16.

6. Stuart Hall, "The Local and the Global: Globalization and Ethnicity", in Anthony D. King, ed., *Culture, Globalization and the World-System* (New York: Macmillan, 1991), 33; Immanuel Wallerstein, "The National and the Universal: Can There Be Such a Thing as World Culture?" in King, *Culture, Globalization and the World-System*, 99.

7. This is consistent with the ideas and themes expressed in the conversations found in Bill Ashcroft, Gareth Griffiths and Helen Tiffin, *The Empire Writes Back: Theory and Practice in Post-Colonial Literatures* (New York: Routledge, 1989). See also the following by Curwen Best: *The Popular Music and Entertainment Culture in Barbados: Pathways to Digital Culture* (Lanham, MD: Scarecrow Press, 2012); *Culture @ The Cutting Edge: Tracking Caribbean Popular Music* (Kingston: University of the West Indies Press, 2005); "Barbadian Music: An Overview of Barbadian Calypso", *Clockwatch Review: A Journal of the Arts* 10, nos. 1–2 (1996): 24–37.

8. Conversations, Beck's Bar.

9. Ibid. See Margeaux Watson, "Caribbean Queen: Rihanna", *Entertainment Weekly* online, 2 June 2007, http://www.ew.com/ew/article/0,,20043393,00.html; "Our World of Entertainment: The Rihanna Debate", *Barbados Advocate*, 24 February 2008, 33.

10. Conversations, Beck's Bar.

11. See Hilary McD. Beckles, *A History of Barbados: From Amerindian Settlement to Nation-State*, 2nd ed. (Cambridge: Cambridge University Press, 2006), 22–47;

Ulf Hannerz, "Cosmopolitans and Locals in World Culture", in *Global Culture: Nationalism, Globalization and Modernity*, ed. Mike Featherstone (London: Sage, 1990), 237.

12. See Hilary McD. Beckles, "Tribute to Sir Gary Sobers", in *The Development of West Indies Cricket*, vol. 1, *The Age of Nationalism* (Kingston: University of the West Indies Press, 1998), 173–80. See also Garry Sobers, *My Autobiography* (London: Headline Books, 2002).
13. Sir Everton Weekes, with Hilary McD. Beckles, *Mastering the Craft: Ten Years of Weekes, 1948–1958* (Kingston: Ian Randle, 2007), 124–70.
14. Ibid., 1–2.
15. Ibid., 17.
16. Jay Blessed, "Rihanna Rocks Barbados in Her First Ever Hometown Concert", JayBlessed.com, 6 August 2011, http://www.jayblessed.com/2011/08/06/rihanna-rocks-barbados-for-her-first-ever-hometown-concert-Loud.
17. Hilary McD. Beckles, "Radicalism and Errol Barrow in the Political Tradition of Barbados", in *The Empowering Impulse: The Nationalist Tradition of Barbados*, ed. Glenford D. Howe and Don D. Marshall (Kingston: Canoe Press, 2001), 221–32.
18. See "Barbados v. Rest of the World XI, Barbados, 8–11 March 1967", ESPNcricinfo.com, http://static.espncricinfo.com/db/ARCHIVE/1960S/1966-67/R-O-W_IN_WI/R-O-W_BDOS_08-11MAR1967.html.
19. Sobers also captained the "Best of the World XI" that played against England in 1970 and Australia in 1971. See Sobers, *My Autobiography*, 140–49.
20. http://www.nationnews.com/nationnews/news/39102/ri-markable.
21. See Ricky Jordan, "Rihanna Does It All in 2011", *Sunday Sun* (Barbados), 1 January 2012, 23A.
22. Ibid.
23. See Allison Ramsay, "Rihanna LOUD Tour Rocks Kensington Oval", *Barbados Advocate*, 7 August 2011.
24. Conversations, Beck's Bar.
25. Ibid.
26. See Kenneth Morgan, *Slavery, Atlantic Trade and the British Economy, 1660–1800* (Cambridge: Cambridge University Press, 2000); Matthew Parker, *The Sugar Barons: Family, Corruption, Empire and War in the West Indies* (London: Windmill Books, 2012).
27. Conversations, Beck's Bar.
28. Ibid.
29. Maxine Stowe, quoted in Richard Johnson, "Out of Tune: Can Female Artistes Make a Comeback?", *Jamaica Observer*, 23 November 2012. Reprinted as "Where

Are the Jamaican Rihannas?", *Weekend Nation* (Barbados), 29 November 2012, extra, 12.
30. Slave Compensation Files: for Barbados, Department of Archives, Black Rock: for Jamaica, Jamaica Archives, Spanish Town.
31. See Curwen Best, "Popular/Folk/Creative Arts and the Nation", in Howe and Marshall, *Empowering Impulse*, 232–56.
32. See "Racial Slur 'Bad Joke'", *Daily Nation* (Barbados), 21 December 2011, 6A; Jordan, "Rihanna Does It All".
33. Jay Bulger, "Rihanna: Obsession of the Year", *GQ* online, December 2012, http://www.gq.com/moty/2012/rihanna-cover-story-gq-men-of-the-year-2012?currentPage=1; "Ri Ri Bares It All", *Daily Nation* (Barbados), 27 November 2012, 5; "Flayed Going and Coming", *Sunday Sun* (Barbados), 1 January 2012, 24A.

2

RIHANNA AS GLOBAL ICON AND CARIBBEAN THRESHOLD FIGURE

DON D. MARSHALL

Youth culture in the contemporary anglophone Caribbean features a world of interactive media, brands, brevity in linguistic expression, eclectic musical styles and dance. It is countercultural primarily because it shapes as it mocks the mainstream, but there are many voices under the rubble: exuberant, subversive, contemplative and others of this or that coolness paean. The voices, inherited and discovering, emanate from both subaltern and bourgeois class factions. Some are driven to the American manner of society, unappealingly atomized, as they celebrate a sovereign *I* in the acquisition of brand and "bling". Others, upon closer observation, are pursuant of a quantum leap in aesthetic perception – that is, to definitively escalate, with explosive innovation, the expressionism of their twentieth-century forebears.

If these early twenty-first-century Caribbean moderns are to celebrate their humanity and culture, it will be interactive and commercially hyped, relying less on the immediate surroundings and structures of the nation than on the surreal world of digital media and popular discursive manners of being. This is captured, for example, in musical styles not yet categorizable but decidedly crossover; the artful manipulation of appearances, such as the so-called colour blocking that flouts the rules of conventional fashion; the mockingly licentious use of YouTube; and the reach for iconic self-representation, as with Usain Bolt's thunderbolt pose.

Such is the flamboyancy and release of youth culture. But whatever its posture, this culture runs up hard against a twentieth-century Caribbean middle-class paradigm of a lost inheritance of struggle following the attainment of self-government and political independence (circa 1970). The oft-repeated lament is that the commensurate capacity to discern, to question – indeed, that latent radical strain implicit in anti-colonial discourse rooted in self-reliance, cultural self-making and economic nationalism – has been cashiered. Twenty-first-century information technologies, we are told, encourage self-absorption, with the task of art and expression being its own self-realization, outside and beyond historical memory and local context.[1] There is no Bob Marleyesque counter to this counter, it seems. Or, put differently, no popular artist has emerged beckoning a "re-enchantment of the world" – an incorporation of spirituality into our lives to balance the consumerism, individualism and scientism of late modernity.

This essay pursues a discussion about Rihanna as proxy for intervention in debates about Caribbean youth culture, nationalist sentiment and identity. In the fifty years since "youth culture" was created as a consumer category and deployed for sociological application, young people's attachment to music and musical artists has constituted a rich vein of enquiry about youth styles.[2] In terms of the level of attention and meaning that young people invest in it, music remains unmatched by any other organized activity in society. By focusing on a young, black, female, Caribbean music artist who is also an officially designated youth ambassador for Barbados, I want to call attention to how Rihanna is perceived and received by her many publics – particularly with respect to the charged dialogues of identity, self-definition and national obligation – and, in the same manoeuvre, reflect on what her (post-)national attachments and world music tell us about the cultural effect of globalization on national boundaries.

Methodologically, this is accomplished through the verbal optic of her narratives, interviews and social media responses to her supporters and detractors in the period between 2005, when her first album was launched, and 2013. The selected scripts correspond to the conceptual under-clearance generally pursued in discussions about Caribbean nationalism and identity, youth culture and the political predicates of twenty-first-century Caribbean personhood. The hope is to puncture grandiosity – that is, to make inroads into discussions about Caribbean youth culture and nationalism, showing that a different world than that imagined and confined within a state exists. This endeavour goes beyond arguments that Caribbean youth suffer from a classic case of "me before anyone else" or cultural assertions about their abandonment of historical sense. I argue that everyday contestations against the operations of power are constitutive of a different ethical and emotional valence from those of the decolonization period because the cultural effect of globalization is the disregard of territorial sovereignty. Here, the agent – in this case, the artist – is both propelled and repelled by vague obligations to history, state and ethno-oriented modes of national attachment.

WHY RIHANNA?

The Achievements

Rihanna, a Barbadian born of an Afro-Guyanese mother and a Barbadian father of mixed African and Irish descent, is as global a celebrity pop star as any in the music industry. While she currently resides in the United States, she frequently returns to the familiarity of home, indulging family and close friends, the mas (a street carnival with theatrical display), local cuisine and the beaches. Still, we need a broader understanding of *home*, for in a sense, Rihanna exists in a Caribbean American diasporic community constituted as a series of musical events rather than in terms of territorial extension. It is not singularly Los Angeles, Barbados, New York or Jamaica, for example, but between these spaces exist a language, a culture and a history of fused sounds that go by the names jazz, bebop, reggae, hip-hop, pop, soca, salsa, and rhythm and blues. It is an imagined community, and this nation exists where African Caribbean and African American music is being played or associated dance attitudes are being exuded.

Situating and Claiming Her Stardom

Grounded and bounded by the problematics of territory, identity and communal morality, Robyn Rihanna Fenty, an official youth ambassador for Barbados and a US-based international pop star, allegorically stands as a threshold figure re-situating globalization not as modernity's final form, but as a process of connection that regularly intercalates one time and one space with others, historical and creolized, contemporary and Anglo-American, black diasporic and fragmented. Her career and iconic trajectories encourage contemplation about nation-centredness, (multiple) territoriality, struggles for race and gender equity, identity, corporate ownership and influence in the music industry, and music itself as a site of enunciation. Graced with charisma, unique vocal talent and the good fortune of being signed by Def Jam Recordings – a successful subsidiary label of Universal Music Group – she has had to confront a mainstream media at "home" and "abroad" that insists on conformity and containment.

Confirmed by *Forbes* as the top social networking superstar in 2012 and affirmed by Music-News.com as the most viewed artist on YouTube in the following year, Rihanna is not protected from the delimiting public sphere for women, cross-hatched by race, class and sexuality.[3] Born and raised in Westbury Road, an urban, inner-city, working-class district in Bridgetown, Barbados, she went on to such achievements and earnings that American magazine *Time*, in 2012, named her among the one hundred most influential people in the world. Rihanna's publicity grew in 2013 in the wake of her seven-date 777 tour, during which she performed seven concerts in seven different cities in seven different countries (within North America and Europe) accompanied by a group of fans and over 150 journalists drawn from eighty-two countries. By the end of the 777 tour, the single "Diamonds" had reached number one on the *Billboard* Hot 100 chart, and her album *Unapologetic* had topped the *Billboard* 200. But even before 2013, based on income from record sales, touring, endorsements, merchandise sales and other ventures for the period May 2011 to May 2012, Rihanna had joined Britney Spears, Taylor Swift, Lady Gaga and Katy Perry among the top-earning women in the music industry.[4] The terms of these women's participation as "superstars" notwithstanding, executive male power pervades the music industry through the dominance of the "Big Four" record labels and their subsidiaries, from the financing of local, regional and international distribution systems to the naming of genres themselves, including the fusions (that is, deciding what constitutes hip-hop, gangsta rap, Latin music, pop and so on).[5]

Rihanna's personal life continues to fuel mass-media discussion, particularly the on/off romantic reunions with Chris Brown, who assaulted her in

February 2009. What has emerged is a rich conversation about domestic violence and its impact on the women who are most likely to be victimized; attitudes of cultural complicity supporting male abusers; ubiquitous support of masculinity as *naturally* violent; and the scapegoating of those who experience abuse, particularly working-class, black women.[6] In keeping with the social regulation of women's lives, this fillip of discussion simultaneously ventures into commentary about Rihanna's sexuality, particularly with regard to her appropriateness as a role model and a youth ambassador for Barbados – a point to which I shall return.

Nationalism's Aura, Post-Plantation Societies and Caribbean Personhood

Beyond the din of tabloid reporting about Rihanna's popular-culture rituals and behaviours in the public sphere, the more relevant question might be, is there any other discourse through which to see Rihanna other than as a product of exhibitionistic pop culture, and as a participant in "divadom" who enjoys alcohol, fame and the material comforts money can buy? By levering discussion back to an understanding of her Caribbean heritage and home, beyond the exoticization of her Barbadian accent and the erotica summoned in her performances, this discussion aims to recast questions about politics, national identity and power onto issues of subjectivity and personhood. Rihanna emerges, like many of her migrant Caribbean forebears and today's Caribbean youth, as a navigator of the complex interplay between the boundaries and limits of race, class, gender, sexual difference and national/territorial allegiance – all encased within the unconscious psychodynamics of anti-colonial resistance. Intriguingly, of course, this navigation – featuring Rihanna's alterations in gendered identity, her insistence on being Barbadian and Caribbean, and her declaration of a right to be, as well as her errors, frailties and contradictions – occurs in the full glare of a world audience, in real time.

We engage in difficult dialogues when seeking to apply an analysis of nationalism to social formations like those in the Caribbean where the colonial encounter featured plantation slavery and a concomitant resistance to white, imperial, patriarchal power. Indeed, the concept of the national produces different political inflections and competing discourses.[7] From the vantage point of relative powerlessness, a constant struggle is generated by successive generations to create an elusive authenticity around what is considered "national".

In the context of the global South, the slippage between the original meaning of *nation* as an ethnic or racial group and its later meaning as a politically organized entity oscillates in different historical and geographical contexts. In Giddens's construal, *the state* refers to the political institution with centralized authority and monopoly of coercive agencies coeval with the rise of modern capitalism, while *nationalism* denotes the diverse configuration of peoples united by a commonality of symbols, beliefs, traditions and shared sentiments of belongingness.[8] Beyond this formalism, a reactive nationalism that resists colonization and subordination by a hegemonic power cannot be equated with a proactive nationalism with expansionist ambitions. Cooppan refers to the traces, haunting effects, ambivalences and other "oscillating temporalit[ies]" that animate nationalism in postcolonial spaces.[9]

Arising out of the lived experience of plantation slavery and society, freedom has served as the counterpoint to domination, demanding equality.[10] In the case of western Europe, freedom arising out of the Enlightenment has been equated with supreme rationality as a way of managing oneself and the world. This was McNeill's cue to point up a localizing motivation behind the emergence of a capitalist state, presenting it as an agency to rally the populace to serve the needs of the commercial and industrial elites and the goal of accumulation.[11] On the other hand, the multiple modes of resistance in the anglophone Caribbean in the seventeenth and eighteenth centuries – against conquest, slavery, indentureship and colonial rule, condescension and dispossession – expressed a negotiation of empowerment far more complex than can be captured in a materialist analysis of the contradictions that gave rise to a bourgeois state, or a quasi-Hegelian interpretation that hails the rise of Caribbean nation-state forms as part of the locomotive of world expansion.

Resistance in the anglophone Caribbean featured (and continues to feature) desires for political autonomy, socio-economic progress and social uplift. These power struggles were and are saturated with class, race, gender and sexuality dynamics that intersect and are always in motion. As a consequence, the nation ought to be conceived as an evolving, imaginary construct rather than an originary essence with its contingent emergence in the nation-state form in the global South linked to ending colonialism.

To be sure, the conversation about nationalism within postcolonial scholarship is animated by the discussion of modernity/coloniality matrices and the dialectics of resistance arising from various arenas of contention, whether within territorial states or across diasporas.[12] Without delving into the inventory of charges made against the nation-state – ranging from the indictment of its disciplinary apparatus to the "us versus them" binaries produced by claims of homogeneity – there is a richness to the postcolonial observation that we situate an understanding of *nation* and its corollary term *nation-state* within the trauma, melancholia and changing political aesthetic of progress and autonomy.

From the vantage point of how struggles for power among various groups and subjects play out, let us briefly consider a postcolonial reading of the anglophone Caribbean project of ending colonialism. This project was central to a black male nationalist agenda. Edmondson argues that black and brown professional men demonstrated their civility and capacity for self-rule by serving as leaders of public institutions and by "ruling" their women.[13] The latter took the form of policing the public images of women, often by scrutinizing their public behaviour. Deborah Thomas connects the values associated with the postcolonial state and those generated in and through popular culture.[14]

Here, Thomas points up tensions between a macroeconomic understanding of growth and development and a cultural understanding of progress, highlighting the transformation from the multiracial, creole nationalism of the first thirty years of Jamaican independence towards an urbanized black identity. This "modern blackness" to which Thomas refers is multifaceted and variably constructed through a youth culture influenced by African American culture. Indeed, in the Caribbean, modernity is associated with information technology connectivity, African American youth culture and a conflation of nationalist sentiment with global ambition.

If there is to be a discussion about Rihanna's public performances in the "lowbrow" arenas of carnivals and parties and the "middlebrow" venues of international stages, then it becomes necessary to acknowledge that she emerges from a social space where traditional attitudes pathologize these performances as social violations of women's femininity. If, at the same time, we seek to make sense of her paradoxical use of the public sphere to celebrate femaleness, to perform the transgressive Barbadian "wuk-up"[15] as a decorous alternative to Miley Cyrus's "twerk", it is appropriate to acknowledge that it is distinguishable within and synonymous with an evolving Caribbean nationalism. This nationalism accents while it troubles "authentic representation", and insists that Caribbean culture is part of the new cultural order. From the perspective of class and gender, this is a Caribbean that witnesses its women, particularly black Caribbean women, increasingly assuming positions of power and authority, as with former Dominican prime minister Dame Eugenia Charles.

Caribbean Nationalism and Anti-colonial "Subject Effects"

Not unlike the Euro-American experience, Caribbean nationalist sentiment over the past fifty years has waxed and waned on the degree of socio-cultural economic alienation or inclusion that the community is experiencing in a given moment. This has related in part to the limits of formal sovereignty and what such limits have meant, and still mean, for defending property rights and the right to private accumulation and for facing up to the cold winds of international competition. Nationalist sentiment in the English-speaking Caribbean remains fissured and fractured by growing inter-island rivalries for market share in tourist traffic, foreign direct investment and development pre-eminence. This continues to Balkanize regional identity and diminish imaginings of a West Indian nation. Indeed, island-national cultural propagation remains in full command, despite gains in anglophone Caribbean functionalist cooperation in education, meteorology, cricket administration and representation, and market access. Reggae, for example, is, along with its origins and influences, proclaimed for Jamaica, as calypso/soca is for Trinidad and Tobago. Such is the discursive power of nation-stories that they appropriate musical and other idioms from within and outside the domestic space to constitute communal attachment and origins. For Barbados, this is the case for spouge music, despite the sonic contributions from various Caribbean musicians who were part of the leading bands promoting and identifying with this short-lived style.[16]

While nationalisms are invented, performed and consumed in ways that do not follow a blueprint and are not experienced the same way by different groups (that is, classes, genders, ethnicities, generations and so on), Caribbean nationalisms, because of the plantation experience, distinctively entail what Fanon might describe as the psychodynamics of anti-colonial subversion.[17] Here, relations between the individual, unconscious, political life and belongingness are neither separable nor reducible to each other. Instead, they comprise criss-crossing and dynamic mediations, reciprocally and messily transforming each other. Caribbean societies are thus understood as emerging out of racist experiences entailing the internalization of inferiority among Caribbean black men and women and other people of colour and a companion belief that their lands, kept from them "before", are structurally delimited from achieving a meaningful "after".

In short, as part of the contiguous crises of identity and paradox, Caribbean people wrestle with the vestigial effects of white supremacist ideologies and the disparagement of their social space. The constant battle to avoid erasure, together with the overwrought effects of globalization on sovereignty and territoriality, constitutes key power relations of the everyday experience of Caribbeans at home and abroad. Second- and third-generation Caribbean Americans integrated in the American national imaginary, for example, still refer to both assimilative and disruptive moments in American collective nationhood.[18]

In the crucible, nation-state sovereignty operates at one level as a site of closure for peoples within the state and at another as a site of defence against global subordination.[19] The national power elite sets firm boundaries around who counts as worthwhile citizens and outlines descriptivist ideals of authentic behaviour, the traditions to maintain and the political contests to engage. The main problem with such prescription is that the "merely different" in society is turned into the "absolutely other". Rihanna's risqué performances, suggestive lyrics and "rude girl" posture challenge mainstream conventions of appropriate behaviour for women, which in turn has enlivened debate in Barbados about her suitability as a youth ambassador, mirroring the Victorian preoccupation with virtue and sexuality.

The net result, or the "subject effects",[20] have been an abiding ambivalence to questions of home, identity and self, all of which, Fanon suggests, require a "sociodiagnostic".[21] Certainly, the problem is wrongly understood as one about twenty-first-century Caribbean youth unmoored by a sense of national belonging or anti-colonial subversion. The contradictions and complexities then, as now, extend to the effects of changing technology on territoriality and the imagined community. Technologies compressing time and space are shattering how people enact agency and exhibit global forms of belonging.

Indeed, the idea of nationhood and belonging is becoming much more fluidly akin to thinking of diaspora and cosmopolitanism along a continuum. This dynamic complicates understandings of the nation-state as a central political site for change, action and allegiance. The idea of geographic belonging, as described by Croucher and Hartnell, should encompass citizenship, nationhood, gender, ethnicity and emotional dimensions of status or attachment.[22] With the rise of global civil society and that of social media, imaginary geographies extend beyond those that are yoked to territorial sovereignty, leading to what Campbell describes as a new "political prosaics".[23]

In this formulation, everyday life becomes a site of contestation, with individuals and organizations as loci in which a variety of relational determinations interact. Questions of self/other erupt in conflict. Globalized life is often represented as a series of struggles rather than as a complex of international, multinational or transnational relations, because these modes of representation have powerful investments in the very borders being questioned. Campbell thus treats the global as presenting a plurality of challenges.

If we accept Campbell's formulation that politics and agency are mutating in an outer-territorial manner, then we should consider how this bears upon Fanon's previously cited observation that postcolonial subjectivity is bound up with the psychodynamics of anti-colonial subversion. This is the prism through which I seek to locate Rihanna as a young Caribbean woman and global celebrity. What exactly have been her political effects? What is it that she perpetually destabilizes and disrupts that, for example, leads critics at home and elsewhere to question her suitability as a role model for youth? Is there an evident Fanonian Caribbean anti-colonial consciousness at work, or some meta-critical casting off of prevailing self-definitions? Is she an updated "natural rebel" *pace* Beckles?[24]

UNDERSTANDING RIHANNA'S AGENCY

Rihanna's life story after her debut hit single "Pon de Replay" (2005) reveals a young woman living dangerously between the social expectations of home and the wilderness of stardom, between love and autonomy, obedience and scandal. Now around a decade into celebrity status, Rihanna has consistently resisted socially produced scripts of oppression which expect black women to remain safely in lanes of servitude and invisibility. Indeed, two years into her fame, her album title *Good Girl Gone Bad* (2007) signalled that she was prepared, sexually, to be a renegade.

By getting out on tours, frequently returning to Barbados despite tight schedules, and assuming a sexually suggestive image, Rihanna affirmed women's right to mobility and sexual independence. With skin tone and long hair to fit the beige ethnic model of high-fashion marketing and pop-music artists, she could have conceivably settled into or become boxed in by corporate and mainstream expectations of women's looks, based on variations of white beauty standards.[25] But Rihanna's charismatic fashion appeal, her penchant for style, her playful exploration of androgyny, sexuality and sensuality, and her control of wardrobe smothered the possibility of stereotypical industry formatting. On the control of her image, Mel Ottenberg, her long-time personal wardrobe stylist, stated:

> We definitely have some back-and-forth moments, but she's in control of her image. I show her different ideas, and we talk about it. Sometimes, figuring out what it'll look like has already been done, and other times, it's more spontaneous and collaborative. . . . In this day and age, everyone thinks it's all the same watered-down looks, and Rihanna isn't like that. She's not looking at other people for competition; she's just doing her own thing, and that's fun to work with because she'll let you do something different.[26]

Rihanna's unconscious and conscious acts of nonconformity have made her a controversial figure. Take for instance the criticisms made in a 2013 article by Liz Jones, a columnist for Britain's *Daily Mail*. This opinion piece is important, as it appropriates oft-repeated themes in mainstream and tabloid reporting on the proper role of young female celebrities and recirculates framings of offstage deviations that are commonly applied to women of colour. In the article, entitled "Pop's Poisonous Princess: Glorying in Drugs, Guns and Sleaze, Rihanna's [a] Toxic Role Model for Her Army of Young Fans", Jones states that Rihanna's sexually suggestive performances on stage, her revealing fashions and her penchant for marijuana and alcohol use all combine to make her a bad role model for young girls and young women. As she puts it:

> I don't care if she has the voice of an angel and is self-made, feisty and confident. All these qualities pale to nothing when we know she went back to her abusive

boyfriend, Chris Brown, who pleaded guilty to assaulting her in 2009; that she promotes drug-taking, drinking and the sort of fashion-sense on stage that surely invites rape at worst, disrespect at least. . . .

I wish she'd stop infecting our High Streets with her gun tattoos, her false nails and fake hair, her bogus bad-ass shenanigans that try to portray her as "real", as "street", as her own person, as strong and single-minded.

While Rihanna knows when to tone it down in order to pull in advertising deals and keep her record label sweet . . . the message she's sending to her young fans, through her explicit lyrics, vile dance moves and pictures on Twitter, is utterly toxic.

This poisonous pop princess should come with a government health warning.[27]

This article prompted an angry response from Rihanna through her Instagram account:

LOL!!!! My money got a bad habit of pissing people off!! If you sincerely wanna help little girls more than their own parents do, here's a toxic tip: don't be amateur with your articles, you sound bitter! What's all this about hair and nails and costumes and tattoos?? . . . That shit ain't clever!!! That shit ain't journalism! That's a sad sloppy menopausal mess!!! Nobody over here acts like they're perfect! I don't pretend that I'm like you, I just live . . . My life!! And I don't know why y'all still act so surprised by any of it!! "Role Model" is not a position or title that I have ever campaigned for, so chill wit dat! I got my own f——ed up shit to work on, I'll never portray that as perfect, but for right now it's ME!! Call it what ya want!! Toxic was cute, Poisonous Pop Princess had a nice ring to it, just a lil wordy! And P.S. my first American Vogue cover was in 2011 . . . APRIL!!! #ElizabethAnnJones[28]

There were 519 comments on *Mail Online* responding to Jones's article twenty-four hours following its publication and Rihanna's Instagram response. Of this, a total of 117 entries are here discounted, as these were follow-up or repeat submissions. Among the rest, opinion on the tone and content of the exchange was divided, as were the levels of support for either Jones or Rihanna (see tables 2.1 and 2.2 and figure 2.1). While determining the sex of each contributor was not straightforward, based on the names that commenters provided, it does appear that more females were moved to comment than males. The four sample entries shown below also provide a snapshot of the dominant thrust of the commentaries, which touched on themes such as the social responsibility of public figures and gender roles, particularly what it means to be a woman for both a female celebrity and a female critic-as-journalist.

MAPPING THE INITIAL ONLINE REACTION TO LIZ JONES'S *MAIL ONLINE* ARTICLE AND RIHANNA'S RESPONSE (2013)

Table 2.1. Commenters by Country

Country	Number of Comments
United Kingdom	269
United States	73
Australia	15
Canada	13
Jamaica	6
France	3
Other countries*	23
Total**	402

*Countries with fewer than three entries were placed in this category. The *Daily Mail* is a British newspaper, which explains the overrepresentation of UK entries and English-language responses. Other countries represented include the United Arab Emirates, Brunei, Cambodia, China, Finland, Germany, Italy, Malta, the Netherlands, Russia, Singapore, Spain, Switzerland, and St Vincent and the Grenadines. (See "Rihanna Responds with Fury After She's Dubbed a 'Toxic Pop Princess' by Liz Jones", *Mail Online*, 25 June 2013, http://www.dailymail.co.uk/tvshowbiz/article-2348108/Rihannas-fury-shes-branded-toxic-pop-princess-Liz-Jones.html#ixzz2XzLI38oK.)

**This number does not include the 117 repeat and follow-up comments.

Table 2.2. Commenters by Sex*

Male Commenters	Female Commenters	Commenters Using Pseudonyms
45 (11%)	144 (36%)	213 (53%)

*The sex of each commenter was determined, to the extent possible, by his or her screen name. In cases of ambiguous names, entrants were grouped under the rubric "Pseudonym", along with those who used initials or nicknames.

Rihanna as Global Icon and Caribbean Threshold Figure

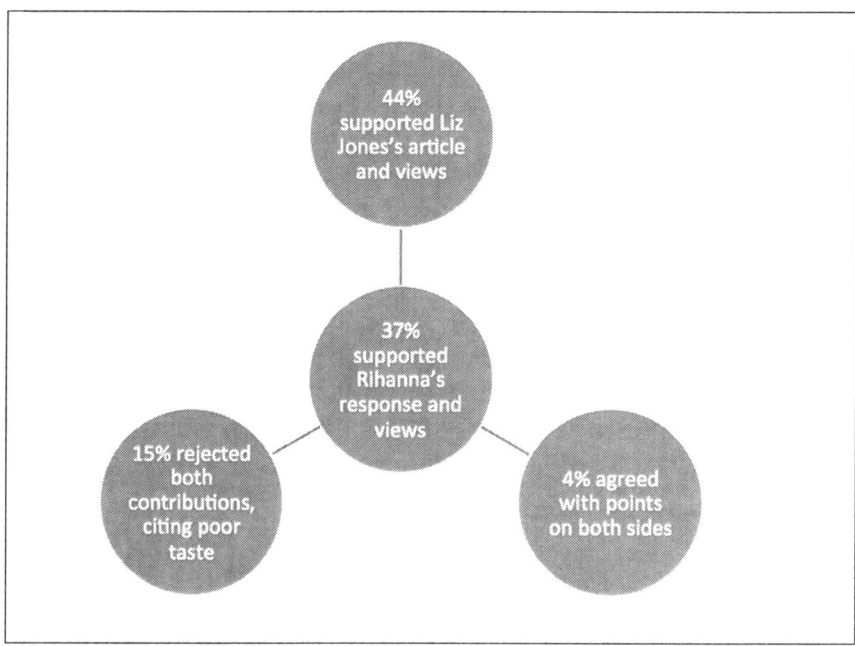

Figure 2.1. Levels of Support for Liz Jones and Rihanna among Online Commenters

Note: These statistics were drawn from 636 comments on the *Mail Online* website. If a name or pseudonym appeared more than once, only the initial entry was counted. Such repeat or follow-up comments accounted for 117 responses. Of course, dividing opinions by the sex of respondents was problematic, as over half the sample (53 per cent) submitted responses under pseudonyms. ("Rihanna Responds with Fury After She's Dubbed a 'Toxic Pop Princess' by Liz Jones", *Mail Online*, 25 June 2013, http://www.dailymail.co.uk/tvshowbiz/article-2348108/Rihannas-fury-shes-branded-toxic-pop-princess-Liz-Jones.html#ixzz2XzLI38oK.)

FOUR SAMPLE COMMENTS ON THE *MAIL ONLINE* ARTICLE AND RIHANNA'S RESPONSE

> Once she's given a mega platform like that where millions upon millions of young girls look up to her, she can use it to roll in and out of clubs, promoting strippers, drugs, etc., posting endless pictures with her a$$ out, dating volatile woman beaters . . . Or she could be this strong, sassy modern woman who holds herself with class and dignity and sets this amazing example to her fans and women across the world. But instead she criticizes everyone for "expecting" her to do it without really taking any responsibility for her position. Shame people bother to buy her music really.—issabellababy14, Toronto, Canada

I don't think you get to have a say in whether or not you're a role model . . . Once you're in the industry with your multi-million Twitter followers, you're setting an example whether you mean to or not.—Em, Sydney, Australia

The reason why so many young girls look up to Rihanna is that she is not afraid to be herself and doesn't hide her imperfections. That is the beauty of her. It doesn't matter how many times you call her trash or write nasty articles about her, her fans are still going to support her. I wish Rihanna wouldn't have responded because Liz Jones is just another nobody trying to gain publicity off of her. Anybody with a brain knows that just because a pop star does something doesn't mean you're going to do the same thing. Children are more influenced by their peers than anyone else. The reason they start smoking weed is because their friends do it, not because Rihanna is doing it. Who said smoking weed and drinking alcohol was bad anyway. Who are you to judge? People are constantly trying to knock Rihanna down because she's been number one for so long now. Find another way to do it because calling her trash and saying she is a bad role model hasn't worked and will never work.—Chris, everywhere, United States

Rihanna and all the rest of these hyper-sexualized female performers HARM women by globally portraying them as sex objects and re-enforcing some very ugly belief systems. The results of men viewing women as sex objects are unhealthy and even dangerous. Women KNOW what happens when men think this way, and Rihanna is one of the women that is actively cultivating the belief system that women are just sex objects. Women like Rihanna make a lot of money by doing this, and now she is all outraged that other women are NOTICING how incredibly toxic she is for ALL western women? She HARMS people and claims that's just how she is. Liz Jones was so right on the money – Rihanna, Madonna, Beyonce, and all the rest of these performers ARE toxic, and their behaviour has had and will have ugly physical, emotional, and even financial repercussions for other women.—MWeather, Riverside, UK

To be sure, the online reactions included condemnation both of Jones's rape apologism, captured in her comment that Rihanna's fashion sense "invites rape", and of Rihanna's ageist remark with respect to her characterization of the article as "a sad sloppy menopausal mess". Of some importance, references to Rihanna as an "Illuminati princess" went without challenge. Across the blogosphere, this charge, located in speculation and extraordinary attention paid to cultist symbols, has acquired the status of a fugitive truth, the scope of which cannot be addressed here, but which offers intriguing future possibilities for analysis.[29]

RIHANNA'S ETHICAL AND EROTIC DRIVE

Since blackness itself marks the Caribbean space in the international gaze, it is worth exploring the series of negotiations that Rihanna engages in as she works to avoid erasure. Rihanna consistently rejects the tag of "role model". This is but one of the regulatory mechanisms with which she refuses to comply. Another is to do with expectations that she serve activist intentions from the standpoint of being a woman. Put another way, some commentators expect Rihanna to speak up exclusively on gender by virtue of being herself a female subject. As a black Caribbean woman, she experiences complex, braided connections of race, class, gender and sexual orientation that tenuously map her sense of identity and community. These axes work in a fluid manner, and one dimension of existence cannot be subtracted from the others – a point underscored in black feminist thought.[30]

Many leading columnists and commentators, however, subscribe to the notion that by virtue of being a woman, Rihanna is imbued with a specific mode of reasoning, and a maternal nature or a specific erotic nature, and that as a global celebrity she could be a reliable voice for feminist liberation. Here, we ought to be reminded of the profusion of criticism and dissent against the idea of the coherent female subject that arose from the work of early radical and liberal feminists. Whether it is in the words of Sojourner Truth's 1851 speech "Ain't I a Woman?", the pages of Anna Julia Cooper's *A Voice from the South: By a Black Woman from the South* (1892), or the scholarship of, say, Jacqui Alexander, Eudine Barriteau, Patricia Hill Collins, bell hooks, Kamala Kempadoo, Ania Loomba, Chandra Mohanty or Gayatri Spivak, the (female) subject is presented as complex and indeterminate. As Moya Lloyd puts it, "[Feminism] needs to embrace an alternative version of the subject, understood as ambivalent, in-process, indeterminate, and terminally open to reinscription; a subject whose identity is always precarious, contingent and ambiguous."[31]

The point that all subjects are in-process, and that identity is precarious, ambiguous and contingent, is crucial. Nowhere is this made more explicit than in Rihanna's views about issues of gender as these affect her personal and professional life.

In the interviews and tweets presented below, Rihanna unconsciously allows insight into both her erotic and ethical drives. That the two drives bring about political stalemates is not surprising, for they have contradictory objects and aims. I begin with her response to a question posed by Ellen DeGeneres in an exclusive interview in November 2011, before taking up another example in which Rihanna responds to critics of her music video "Man Down".[32] In the DeGeneres interview, Rihanna speaks about the qualities that matter in her ideal type of man:

> I like men that are more aggressive, but mysterious, but I like a man to be very sure. I like them to be sure of themselves and know that [he's] the man. I'm the lady and the only way for us to make this work is for us to play our roles. You know, I really can't be the man for you. I don't want to be. I'm the man at work all the time.

Here, she articulates a point of view that corresponds to the traditional idea that social limits should be placed on gender roles, and that men and women should stay within these lines. She can also be said to be drawing from a socially prescribed sense of maleness and manliness that is a reaction to colonial discourses of degeneracy and superior white patriarchy. This should not be underestimated, since the Caribbean space throughout the nineteenth and twentieth centuries was figured in the imperial imagination as inherently degenerate in a symbolic triangle of deviant sexuality, deviant race and deviant gender.

Decolonization and Afro/Indo-Caribbean nationalism were also about patriarchal regeneration, involving an overturning of the degeneracy narrative. Caribbean women participated in the independence project partly in solidarity with their husbands, lovers, fathers and sons, and also to effect a transgression where, with the cult of domesticity, women faced multiple oppressions: black mothers under the imperial gaze suffered from the idea that their bodies incarnated the very nadir of human degeneracy. From this cultural vantage point, when Rihanna describes herself as being "the man at work" instead of referring to herself as being in control when at work, she may not be using gender to imply that women are weaker than men so much as she may be overturning her mother's and grandmother's burdens and heaviness of being.³³ Still, she is drawing heavily from the man-as-breadwinner notion, and this unwittingly perpetuates an underappreciation of Barriteau's point that throughout the region, Caribbean women have *always* worked, whether this was paid or unpaid labour.³⁴

Rihanna's ethical drive and her erotic drive may pull in contrary directions, but daring to point up an unbidden dimension in her psychic life as a Caribbean female subject allows for an upping of the "anti" in anti-colonialism, leading to a more complex level of analysis. Her point of perspective may be a reinscription of masculinist discourse, but it is born out of the socio-historical experience of Barbados and evidenced in her attempts to self-identify, if she is to avoid patriarchal erasure.

Rihanna's tweets following reactions to her music video for "Man Down", drawn from her album *Loud* (2010), provide another example of how her ethical and erotic drives slide discrepantly against each other. The music video debuted on BET's *106 & Park* on 24 May 2011. In the video, which is set in Jamaica, its distinctive Caribbean rhythm and staccato style apparent, her character struggles with the choice she has made to kill her rapist. This follows sensual scenes and erotica on the dance floor, which the video clearly indicates should not be interpreted as consent for future sexual activity. Her message in the video is straightforward. She declares rape as wrong and not at all linked to women's prior behaviour. By shooting her attacker in the full view of the public, she makes it clear that rape shall not go unpunished. Some commentators criticized the apparent callousness of gun use by her character. Indeed, the US-based advocacy group the Parents Television Council unsuccessfully tried to have the video banned, deeming the song "an inexcusable, shock-only, shoot-and-kill theme song".³⁵

Initially (on 24 May 2011), Rihanna tweeted:

> I'm a 23 year old rock star with NO KIDS! What's up with everybody wantin me to be a parent? I'm just a girl, I can only be your/our voice. Cuz we all know how difficult/embarrassing it is to communicate touchy subject matters to anyone especially our parents! And this is why! . . . Cuz we turn the other cheek! U can't hide your kids from society, or they'll never learn how to adapt! This is the REAL WORLD! . . . The music industry isn't exactly Parents R Us! We have the freedom to make art, LET US! It's your job to make sure they don't turn out like US.

As the controversy raged, she made a live call to *106 & Park* and stated:

> Rape is, unfortunately, happening all over the world and in our own homes, and we continue to cover it up and pretend it doesn't happen. Boys and girls feel compelled to be embarrassed about it and hide it from everyone, including their teachers, their parents and their friends. That only continues to empower the abusers. Making that into a mini-movie or video, we needed to go back to why it happened. Obviously, she's not a cold-blooded killer. It had to be something so offensive. And we decided to hone in on a very serious matter that people are afraid to address, especially if you've been victimized in this scenario. . . . I've been abused in the past, and you don't see me running around killing people in my spare time. I just really want girls to be careful. Have fun, be sassy, be innocent, be sweet, be everything that you are. But just try not to be naive. That's not coming from a parent but from a peer.

Following the show, Rihanna tweeted:

> Young girls/women all over the world . . . we are a lot of things! We're strong innocent fun flirtatious vulnerable, and sometimes our innocence can cause us to be naïve! We always think it could NEVER be us, but in reality, it can happen to ANY of us! So ladies be careful and #listentoyomama! I love you and I care!

In the foregoing, a feminist ethical drive is apparent. She abhors rape and is insistent that exhibitionism and erotica – figured in her words as "fun", "flirtatious" and "sassy" – do not provide excuses or justifications for such violence and violation. While it could be true that her follow-up comments were in keeping with advice from her image consultants, her position in this case is consistent with prior positions. In other words, Rihanna's ethical drive is bound up with respect for bodily autonomy. Given Rihanna's album successes, her command of her attire and her penchant for reinvention of image and style, it is difficult to conceive of her as powerless. The risqué poses and dance moves that she performs do produce an objectification, but it has a different charge. Hers might be termed "Caribbean feminist opposition to compulsory virtue".

RIHANNA, THE CHRIS BROWN AFFAIR AND CELEBRITY CULTURE

Ever since February 2009, when images of a battered Rihanna appeared in the media, she has had to respond to political reactions to her on/off relationship with Chris Brown. She has also had to respond to expectations that she play the role of celebrity survivor, or poster child against domestic violence, neither of which she embraced. Perhaps it was her interview with Diane Sawyer on 20/20 in November 2009 that encouraged such expectations. At that time, she stated, "When I realized that my selfish decision for love could result into some young girl getting killed, I could not be easy with that part. I couldn't be held responsible. . . . If Chris never hit me again, who is to say that their boyfriend won't? Who's to say that they won't kill these girls?"[36]

In January 2013, Rihanna confirmed her reunion with Chris Brown, in *Rolling Stone* magazine. Her simple statement was, "Even if it's a mistake, it's my mistake."[37]

At first glance, some paradoxes seem apparent. Rihanna's stance against rape corresponds to the common themes of intimate partner abuse: violence, possessiveness and isolation. This should make her an ally against intimate partner violence. But she is irritated by having to live up to the tag of "role model" and to bear the cause of fighting violence against women through abandonment of the risqué and of her hope of reconciling with Chris Brown, her professed first love. These expectations represent for her an intrusion into the sphere of her private life. But this ethical ambiguity is also due in part to the surveillance and double standards at the heart of celebrity culture.

Celebrity culture has become an important site where debates about the proper roles for men and women often take place. Particularly, the scope of attention falls on young female celebrities where the boundaries between public and private, ordinary and extraordinary, are blurred in the surveillance of their lives. Some scholars make the point that a gendered double standard exists in which mainstream press coverage of celebrity young men who fall from grace is marked by gravity and distance – "Boys will be boys" – while celebrity young women in similar circumstances become objects of derision and titillation. As Negra and Holmes argue, media coverage of female celebrities such as Britney Spears, Lauryn Hill, Amy Winehouse and Lindsay Lohan constructs them as either "out of control" or cautionary tales, while male celebrities' behaviour "is largely immune from public referendum".[38]

More crucially, these newly created spaces help to circulate a backlash rhetoric that sets back the efforts of the women's movement to break the silence on intimate partner violence by repositioning women in celebrity culture as attributed with capacity.[39] As "can-do girls", they are portrayed as capable of taking responsibility for their own abuse by monitoring their actions and refusing to be seen as a victim. This deflects attention away from the perpetrator and from how men and women treat each other, and heralds choice, individual freedom and responsibility as key to issues surrounding domestic violence. The extant social surveillance and regulation of women's actions thus remains intact.

So on the one hand, Rihanna can be praised for trampling underfoot any number of Western aesthetic expectations: how a "good girl" should behave; the notion that a Caribbean female subject ought to perform servility as sign of gratitude for Western acceptance; that she ought to acquiesce to erasure instead of authoring her own style, vernacular, and liminal being. But on the other hand, she is criticized for her attraction to rugged, aggressive manliness. This purportedly sets her up to be a *deserving* victim of male partner abuse. The problem, of course, is that the diva caricature is intended to both portray the female subject as devoid of complexity and position her as one of any of the voguish female mimetic depictions that circulate simplicity – femme fatale, Barbie, wonder woman, Jezebel, Sapphire, supermom, celebrity housewife and so on.

RIHANNA AS *"UNRULY"* POLITICAL SUBJECT

But there is more to this than the double standard of female celebrities' experience. The concerns about Rihanna's erotic style and her example to young women carry over across the perilous threshold of race, as witnessed in the storm of controversy arising from the launch of the music video to her song "Pour It Up". The video, which was largely directed by Rihanna,[40] features a scantily dressed Rihanna in a strip club, pole dancing amid strippers and other pole dancers. The signature lines "Pour it up, pour it up, that's how we ball out" and the money-grabbing persona she portrays in the refrain "I still got mo' money" combine to showcase a raw female sexual agency.

From the perspective of some commentators, the song's lyrics and visual display slip too easily into a treatment of women as sexual currency, exemplifying the common objectification of women in music videos. Hobza summarizes and affirms the range of critiques arguing that the music videos of top female pop artists such as Rihanna, Miley Cyrus and Britney Spears correspond to misogyny. These artists, Hobza writes, are being exploited for their sexually charged public personas while sharing the naïve belief that the music video provides a liminal opportunity for negotiating entrenched images of respectable femininity. These female performers often wish to be defined by how much money they earn, their everyday fashion and the sex appeal they exude. Hobza thereafter proceeds to reproduce Sinéad O'Connor's 2013 open letter to Miley Cyrus, one that received widespread circulation in online magazines. In the letter, O'Connor admonishes Cyrus for confusing sexualized public performance with empowerment. As O'Connor puts it, Cyrus is pimping herself or is being pimped by the music industry, and women like her ought to be "protected as a precious young lady" from a "dangerous world".[41]

Mire and Bradshaw enter the dialogue about Rihanna's "Pour It Up" video by rejecting these responses as overblown and anti-feminist. "It's paternalistic and anti-feminist to condemn what a woman chooses to with her body", declares Mire. Bradshaw explains that men are not featured in the music video, that it is women making the money, and notes that the music video shows women behaving sexually without any visible patriarchal figure. Both columnists acknowledge the importance of Rihanna's promotion of Nicole Williams's audition performance for lead pole dancer before the "Pour It Up" video was released. This gesture, from Bradshaw's perspective, represents a gesture of empathetic cooperation and empowerment on the part of Rihanna. Mire also notes Rihanna's positionality as sex worker (in which she dances on the pole) and consumer (in which she showers the strippers with money while rapping about her dollar bills). She highlights the singer's back-and-forth movement between these roles as well as her Caribbean dancehall rapping style. Mire concludes that the music video, instead of promoting falsely feminist ideology, presents an ironic, witty take on male fantasy, deviant sexuality and sanitized eroticism.[42]

As a woman in the rap game, Rihanna, in this music video, disrupts the trope of black-identified degeneracy by adopting an aggressive, in-your-face sexuality and a chanting style reminiscent of Caribbean dancehall queens such as Patra, Lady Saw and Carlene – only this time through her brown/beige hybridized appearance. The combination of lowbrow culture ("vulgar" black dancehall woman and pole dancer) and highbrow pretensions (erotic, beige, brand-advertising, genteel woman) could not be in starker contrast as she manipulates the viewer's gaze. The recognition of such artistry is, however, lost in oversimplified claims that the music video is in poor taste and that it remains mind-numbing and annoying.

For Bradshaw, the claim that "Pour It Up" is not art reflects an easy reversion to "the unfortunate trope of black people and black culture being aesthetically and ethically inferior".[43] Indeed, this discursively dovetails with popular representations of black teenage girls across the United States as being either "at risk" for teenage pregnancy, obesity and sexually transmitted diseases or helpless victims of inner-city morbidity. As Oneka LaBennett explains, such pervasive portrayals make for a reading of black adolescents' consumer and leisure culture as uncivilized and pathological.[44] Such tropes and discourses recirculate in popular music, where black music and styles are marked as innately degenerate, "sending white mainstream into a frenzy".[45]

Rihanna allegorically stands as a figure of intense ambivalence in terms of the threat her agency poses. She does not see being female, black, sexy and undomesticated as hazards to be overcome or concealed. She indulges in alcohol use and regular late-night parties but insists on professional readiness for the stage. Here, she intends for her body to be viewed as sensuous and as sexy in the female form, and as androgynous in her occasional power attire, command on stage and execution of the songs. There is no passive pose anywhere while she is on stage. Hers is a persona that is intentionally and simultaneously feminine and controlling. While these postures and acts affirm a black woman's right to be, or a twenty-first-century autonomous adventure of selfhood, they may also be read as an extension of the Caribbean's emergence as a legitimate cultural cipher and signifier.

NEGOTIATING "HOME"

As Rihanna challenges social scripts of behaviour and authority in the global public space, she is sensitive to surveillance at home in Barbados. The mantle of ambassadorship officially conferred upon her in February 2008 offers opportunities for critical comment about how Barbados should be represented. The official declaration read:

> Whereas the Government and the people of Barbados truly acknowledge and celebrate the remarkable achievements of Robyn Rihanna Fenty;
>
> And whereas such an accomplishment has brought significant honour and deserving recognition not only to Rihanna but also to her beloved country and has elevated Barbados to the forefront of the entertainment world;
>
> And whereas this phenomenal success has come at so tender an age evoking invaluable inspiration and motivation to youth everywhere;
>
> And whereas all Barbados stands proud in the face of this honour and gives full support to Rihanna on her continuing path;
>
> Be it now proclaimed in Bridgetown, Barbados . . . that the Government of Barbados designates Robyn Rihanna Fenty an honorary Youth and Cultural Ambassador of this country.[46]

This designation was mostly enthusiastically received by Barbadians. Three years later and after greater album success for Rihanna, the Freundel Stuart administration, through the Barbados Tourism Authority, sponsored a homecoming concert on 5 August 2011, coincident with Rihanna's international Loud tour. It also sought to formalize a closer relationship between Rihanna and the Barbados Tourism Authority with respect to marketing the island. The homecoming concert was sold out to the largest audience the country had known. It was during this concert that she thanked Barbadians for their support and hailed the community of Westbury Road, acknowledging her socio-historical location.

A few months later, Rihanna, in a moment of rhetorical excess, sought to defend her use of a profanity, the *c*-word, pointing to Barbadian lingo and everyday manners of speech. The furore on talk radio and in social media served as an entry point for criticism of Rihanna's risqué performances and her overall example since the conferment of the ambassadorship. Below are a few samples of the online comments that were made after the story broke in the *Barbados Free Press* (4 October 2011). These are representative of the dominant views expressed at that time in the various media.

> Will somebody, anybody – BTA [Barbados Tourism Authority], PM Stuart – please fire the girl? Barbados is an upscale tourism and offshore investment destination. Our potential tourists and investment clients will surely realize

that we're a classy place because – according to Barbados Tourism Authority spokesperson Rihanna – we normally address each other using the "c" word.

We at *Barbados Free Press* always thought that Rihanna was the wrong choice for a Barbados Tourism Authority representative because the demographic that appreciates her music and public persona is not the upscale demographic we hope to attract to Barbados. Our country . . . can't be competitive in mass-market tourism and Rihanna as our spokesperson doesn't resonate with the folks who have money . . . or class. Do we really need more proof?—Zing with Cliverton

I knew she was a bad choice from the beginning. Tell me, was she so ignorant and illiterate not to know that the "c" word was degrading and belittling. Ladies don't use those words. You representing Beautiful Barbados? You have done so much damage to this country. I pray and hope that those business folks will ignore your sayings, because girl you made yourself look like a complete jackass and you disgrace you folks from your neighbourhood.—Spinelli

She like she has lost touch with REALITY! Money and fame corrupts, this attitude is IGNORANT. While as a Bajan I understand what she is saying, it is not really that way. She is [exaggerating] this as she exaggerated herself image and look!! Ya CAN'T!!! While friends and close buddies say this in amongst themselves it should not be broadcast to the world as they cannot understand Bajan culture!—barbadian

I'll tell you exactly where we went wrong. It is the way that we speak to our children. It shocks me to hear how rough people, mothers and fathers alike, carry on with their kids. I see it on the street, in the supermarket and even among some parts of my family.

The coarse manner in which many of us speak to our children lays a base on which crassness turns to crudeness and eventually leads to people calling one another cu˜ts.—X

Rihanna generalizing her behaviour to that of all "Bajans" is like the rapper Lil Kim generalizing her image as that of all "Americans" to everyone outside America, except that if Lil Kim tried that she would very easily be exposed as either a liar or ignorant because American culture and diversity is visible enough to speak for itself. Her ego is such that she has inflated her self-image to being synonymous with that of "Bajans" because it makes her seem exotic to her international market who don't know better, rather than the individual from a particular community within Barbados that she is. I'm black, I'm Bajan and I don't use words like that in my everyday vernacular and I'm offended that she would tell lies on me and my country like that. She has a tendency of explaining her behaviour as "We in Barbados don't . . ." this or "We Bajans always . . ." that. In a recent interview she was asked if she ever played Battleship growing up and her answer was "We don't play that in Barbados" and I know for a fact that I did as a child.—Unabashed

Reb'l Fleur

"I love the way you lie"
Be careful if you do "S&M" in a "California King Bed"
You might have to use an "Umbrella" to protect yourself
"SOS" and don't be "Unfaithful" to Barbados and Bajans
"Te Amo" and I don't "Hate [That] I Love You"
We sometimes wonder if you need to check into "Rehab"
"Live Your Life" and don't play "Russian Roulette"
"If It's Lovin' That You Want" leave out the "Rude Boy"
"Cheers I'll Drink to That!"
We don't need "Disturbia" or a "Man Down"
Then the police will ask you "What's Ya Name"
I hope you find someone who thinks you are the "Only Girl in the World"
So "Please Don't Stop the Music"
We want to hear all your songs "Pon de Replay"
Especially the "Music of the Sun"
—Pearl

I think Rihanna plays well to the "Rude Boy" crowd. They are her fans. To the more mature audience, she is seen as "trash". Alluding to the fact that she has put Barbados on the map – certainly. However, as a person who has lived overseas, I can see where and how the generalizations come in. When strangers ask a person of what they consider an "exotic" country about life there, they expect the person they are asking to speak for "all" the country and its natives. Rihanna is yet young and may not be able to fend off the pressure that the fans, press, paparazzi . . . may constantly place on her for ready responses to their questions. So, the first thing on her mind falls out of her mouth. She has to learn how to "pause" before she speaks and come to grips with the fact that everything she says, and even some she does not say, will get aired or published. It is a tough job. Maybe that is why she says that she does not want to be a role model. I don't know.

How many of you can do what she is doing? She may act like she is having fun – and maybe she is some of the time, but what she is doing is a lot of hard work under pressure. Maybe the *c*-word expressed helps her to relax under the pressure. At the same time she should be careful to tell the world that Barbadians use this word as part of their everyday vernacular. Not all of us speak in those terms every day, but if we were to be placed in the same pressure cooker that she finds herself, it may be amazing what some of us will embarrassingly utter.— Lending Support[47]

Here, Rihanna functions under a high-surveillance gaze as a young black woman in the public sphere. From the perspective of those who regard maleness as a normative humanity, Rihanna represents the unruly feminine that has to be disciplined and contained. From the perspective of those who believe that ambassadorial rank ought to be preserved for experienced citizens who serve the nation with distinction, Rihanna is deemed far too young and her success in the entertainment industry too unfamiliar for a country with a trained eye for the professions and public service.

Pearl, in a poem of song titles, feels compelled to advise Rihanna on her right to be, beginning first with a plea for conformity; Spinelli cautions "ladies" against the use of the *c*-word, berates Rihanna for "embarrassing" Barbados and reduces her to a condition of infancy – "a girl" who needs to "grow up"; and Zing calls for the removal of her ambassadorial role, allegorizing the rescue of the presumed weaker sex from such an obligation.

Apart from the surveillance and condescension, some of the accounts also reveal an identity preoccupation with how Barbados is perceived by "outsiders", meaning North Americans and Europeans. While Lending Support goes on to suggest that Rihanna should be praised for "put[ting] the Barbados brand on the world map", Spinelli and Zing state that she ought to be aware that she is representing "beautiful Barbados". For the latter, this is "classy Barbados", a country that has forgone competing in the mass tourism market as it seeks to attract the "upscale demographic", meaning "folks who have money . . . or class". Indeed, while Spinelli simply states that Rihanna is a "bad choice" for ambassadorship since her manner "disgrace[s] . . . folks from [her] neighbourhood", Unabashed goes further, noting that the scope of the ambassadorial role is broader than what fits "the individual from a particular community within Barbados that she is". These comments are classist and sexist, in effect if not in explicit intention.

There is a kind of mainstream loyalty expected of Barbadians, who have been long socialized into accepting that catering to a non-resident clientele is the most efficient way to build society and economy. The development model of all-out services, having reached its limits in accumulation with the financial crisis in 2008, did serve to sustain levels of growth, welfare spending and social reproduction for the wealthy elite and middle class. Questions of allegiance and patriotism easily slide into issues of how to safeguard Barbados's image to further augment tourism and financial services promotion.

While Rihanna's iconic status can assist with the marketing of the island, moralistic and puritanical comments by some in Barbados about Rihanna's state of undress on, say, the cover of her latest album, *Unapologetic*, and about her penchant for body art suggest a great sense of unease. The puritanical Barbados imaginary is a project that Rihanna cannot easily subscribe to while navigating imperial social space. Barbadian youth do not feel like they belong to that construction or the quaint cultural norms, given their diverse interest in music and ways of being both within and outside the Caribbean diaspora.[48]

The burden of representation for a Caribbean, black female celebrity is onerous within the hermeneutics of domination. The financial scandals of Wall Street and London in 2008 were not seen as a negative reflection on white power. Yet for Rihanna, each utterance, each concert and music video performance, and each act of everyday life is overcharged with allegorical meaning for black women, Caribbean people and what Barbados stands for.[49] As an artist, hers is an eruptive power and a distinctive style. Her music and lyrics do not correspond to or encourage national affiliation and contemplation in the same way as, say, those of Red Plastic Bag or Mighty Gabby, both celebrated local exponents of calypso music. The intricate coding of Rihanna's anti-colonial subversion is a decidedly black, feminist predicate. Whatever the intentions of Island Def Jam, Rihanna's style, the musico-aesthetics of her work, represent a resistant singularity not unlike that which emerged from the bowels of the plantation in the black diaspora throughout the Atlantic.

Three songs, each of which she negotiated to be included in her albums, are of relevance here.[50] There is, in their linguistic play and musical form, and in their wilful abuse, a defiance and evasion of prevailing structures of meaning and dispersed structures of feeling that transcends nation-state space. "Disturbia" (2008, *Good Girl Gone Bad: Reloaded*) is a song reflecting mental anguish, anxiety and confusion. "Hard" (2009, *Rated R*) is a song about emulating power and strength. The protagonist dares to be the best at what she does. "S&M" (2010, *Loud*) presents the sexual fetishes of the protagonist, encoding an ironic mocking of her critics. As Rihanna put it, "S&M" is about strength: "People can talk . . . people are going to talk about you, you can't stop that. You just have to be that strong person and know who you are so that stuff just bounces off."[51] The protagonist is a young woman throwing off the social surveillance, the puritanical, the displacement, and the cult of domesticity of the black woman, and proclaiming her autonomy. She cannot be expected to reflect back the ideals projected onto her, given the music-business world she inhabits.

YOUTH CULTURE, NATIONAL SPACE AND RIHANNA'S SUBJECTIVITY

What might be gained or lost by Rihanna's continued navigation at the intersection of race, class and gender is a political question. It is rooted in how we understand resistance to domination. In the nation-state discourse, socio-ecological and economic security will entail efforts to secure investment, manage rising debt and ensure citizenship security. Access to global capital, technology and markets will prove crucial, but care must be taken on the part of state managers to avoid the denationalizing of the local economy by foreign capital. From the vantage point of Caribbean youth culture, the global is a moment in the national as the acquisition of "bling", transnational goods and handheld telecommunications constitutes what it means to be a twenty-first-century modern.[52] However, young Caribbeans refuse to be objects of global culture and have used instant technology to "represent" or to "big-up" who they are in an ironic reconstitution of individualism. This is the mimetic surface through which elite powerholders can seek to enliven cultural authenticity and entrepreneurial expression as a pathway to economic renewal.

Navigating identity and scotching cultural erasure represent part of the constellation of forces re-embedding the national imaginary and its silhouette, personhood. Rihanna exemplifies as much as she pre-empts battles against a singularity of being. Destabilization is transformative when limited to questions of subjectivity, representation and recognition. It is less so when applied to examining structural and institutional forms of domination. The transformation, in fact, might entail new forms of dependency and subordination. Still, it is necessary to understand how sundry relations of power converge to produce a hegemonic effect. It is for this reason that I suggest we track Caribbean anti-colonial resistance in its various modes, including the resistance vernaculars of the youth, none of which is more complex and fascinating to trawl than that of Robyn Rihanna Fenty.

NOTES

1. Curwen Best, *The Politics of Caribbean Cyberculture* (New York: Palgrave, 2008).
2. Angela McRobbie, "Shut Up and Dance: Youth Culture and Changing Modes of Femininity", *Cultural Studies* 7, no. 3 (October 1993): 406–26.
3. With 59.6 million fans on Facebook and 23.8 million followers on Twitter as of August 2012, Rihanna was in that month declared *Forbes*'s number-one social networking superstar. See Dorothy Pomerantz, "Rihanna Tops Our List of Social Networking Superstars", *Forbes* online, 9 August 2012, http://www.forbes.com/sites/dorothypomerantz/2012/08/09/rihanna-tops-our-list-of-social-networking-superstars/; "Rihanna Snatches Justin Bieber's YouTube Crown", Music-News .com, 1 March 2013, http://www.music-news.com/shownews.asp?H=Rihanna-snatches-Justin-Biebers-YouTube-crown&nItemID=63389.
4. See Zack O'Malley Greenburg, "The Top-Earning Women in Music 2012", *Forbes* online, 12 December 2012, http://www.forbes.com/sites/zackomalleygreenburg/2012/12/12/the-top-earning-women-in-music-2012/. "Music industry" here refers to the *Billboard* charts of chiefly mainstream American popular music.
5. Letrez Myer and Christine Kleck, "From Independent to Corporate: A Political Economic Analysis of Rap *Billboard* Toppers", *Popular Music and Society* 30, no. 2 (May 2007): 137–48.
6. Lisa M. Cuklanz and Sujata Moorti, "Television's 'New' Feminism: Prime-Time Representations of Women and Victimization", *Critical Studies in Media Communication* 23, no. 4 (October 2006): 302–21. Here, the working-class woman is stereotyped as "Sapphire" – meaning annoying, antagonistic and in opposition to a black man. She is then depicted as "asking for abuse", and her willingness to reconcile is presented as tacit admission that she was not a true victim of domestic violence. For more on this, see Autumn Sandeen, "Chris

Brown, Rihanna, and Domestic Abuse in the News Cycle", *Pam's House Blend* (blog), 7 November 2009, http://pamshouseblend.firedoglake.com/2009/11/07/chris-brown-rihanna-and-domestic-abuse-in-the-news-cycle/; DeNeen L. Brown and Ashley Surdin, "Chris Brown Averts Prison, but Not the Debate Over Justice", *Washington Post*, 23 June 2009.

7. Benedict Anderson, *Imagined Communities* (London: Verso, 1991); Jürgen Habermas, "The European Nation-State: On the Past and Future of Sovereignty and Citizenship", *Public Culture* 10, no. 2 (1998): 397–416.

8. Anthony Giddens, *Social Theory and Modern Sociology* (Cambridge: Polity Press, 1987), 172.

9. Vilashini Cooppan, *Worlds Within: National Narratives and Global Connections in Postcolonial Writing* (Stanford: Stanford University Press, 2009).

10. Glenford D. Howe and Don D. Marshall, eds., *The Empowering Impulse: The Nationalist Tradition of Barbados* (Kingston: Canoe Press, 2001); Mimi Sheller, *Consuming the Caribbean: From Arawaks to Zombies* (New York: Routledge, 2003); Gordon K. Lewis, *The Growth of the Modern West Indies* (Kingston: Ian Randle, 2004).

11. William H. McNeill, *The Rise of the West: A History of the Human Community* (Chicago: University of Chicago Press, 1992).

12. See, for example, Linda Basch, Nina Glick Schiller and Cristina Szanton Blanc, eds., *Nations Unbound: Transnational Projects, Postcolonial Predicaments, and Deterritorialized Nation-States* (London: Gordon and Breach, 1994); Rosemary J. Coombe, "The Properties of Culture and the Politics of Possessing Identity: Native Claims in the Cultural Appropriation Controversy", *Canadian Journal of Law and Jurisprudence* 6, no. 2 (July 1993): 249–85; Anne McClintock, Aamir Mufti and Ella Shohat, eds., *Dangerous Liaisons: Gender, Nation and Postcolonial Perspectives* (Minneapolis: University of Minnesota Press, 1993); Julia Marie Praud, "Nationalism's Discontents: Postcolonial Contestations in the Writings of Mariama Ba, Assia Djebar, Henri Lopes and Ousmane Sembene" (PhD diss., Ohio State University, 2005); Cooppan, *Worlds Within*; Walter D. Mignolo, *The Darker Side of Western Modernity: Global Futures, Decolonial Options* (Durham, NC: Duke University Press, 2011); Maria Rovisco, "Towards a Cosmopolitan Cinema: Understanding the Connection Between Borders, Mobility and Cosmopolitanism in the Fiction Film", *Mobilities* 8, no. 1 (2012): 148–65.

13. See Belinda Edmondson, "Public Spectacles: Caribbean Women and the Politics of Public Performance", *Small Axe* 7, no. 1 (2003): 1–16.

14. Deborah A. Thomas, *Modern Blackness: Nationalism, Globalization and the Politics of Culture in Jamaica* (Durham, NC: Duke University Press, 2004).

15. This is a dance style featuring the gyration of the waist, hips and buttocks,

punctuated with thrusts to the staccato sounds of drums or the rhythm section. As a spectacle, it is the embodiment of the sonic, the spiritual and the erotic, capable of conveying a range of emotions.

16. Spouge is a style of Barbadian popular music from the 1960s which fuses ska, reggae and calypso, but is also influenced by a wide variety of musics from the British Isles and the United States. The sound relies heavily on the cowbell and percussion, with a choppy rhythm of the guitar reminiscent of a quickened reggae beat. Its popularity waned after nearly a decade of success.
17. Frantz Fanon, *Black Skin, White Masks* (London: Pluto, 1986).
18. See Charles Green, *Manufacturing Powerlessness in the Black Diaspora: Inner-City Youth and the New Global Frontier* (Walnut Creek, CA: Altamira, 2001), especially chapters 1 and 3; Sheila L. Croucher, *Globalization and Belonging: The Politics of Identity in a Changing World* (Lanham, MD: Rowman and Littlefield, 2004); Fazila Bhimji, "Cosmopolitan Belonging and Diaspora: Second-Generation British Muslim Women Travelling to South Asia", *Citizenship Studies* 12, no. 4 (2008): 413–27.
19. Ella Shohat, "Imaging Terra Incognita: The Disciplinary Gaze of Empire", *Public Culture* 3, no. 2 (Spring 1990): 41–70.
20. Anne Friedberg, *Window Shopping: Cinema and the Postmodern* (Berkeley: University of California Press, 1993).
21. Fanon, *Black Skin, White Masks*, 10.
22. Croucher, *Globalization and Belonging*; Helen E. Hartnell, "Belonging: Citizenship and Migration in the European Union and in Germany", *Berkeley Journal of International Law* 24, no. 1 (2006): 330–400.
23. David Campbell, "Political Prosaics, Transversal Politics, and the Anarchical World", in *Challenging Boundaries: Global Flows, Territorial Identities*, ed. Michael J. Shapiro and Hayward R. Alker (Minneapolis: University of Minnesota Press, 1996), 7–31. To elaborate, Campbell reverses the priority of sovereignty over anarchy in conditioning possibilities. Action and agency operate against a backdrop freed of metaphors like *territories* and *boundaries*. A political prosaics "subverts those terms by thinking of action and agency in terms of anarchy". For Campbell, *anarchy* does not refer to Hobbes's state of nature or the absence of central authority. Instead, the etymology of the Greek word *an-arche* is deployed, meaning "being without first principles, foundations or grounds" (22–23).
24. Hilary McD. Beckles, *Natural Rebels: A Social History of Enslaved Black Women in Barbados* (New Brunswick, NJ: Rutgers University Press, 1989).
25. Sheila Whiteley, *Women and Popular Music: Sexuality, Identity and Subjectivity* (London: Routledge, 2000); Susan Willis, "I Shop Therefore I Am: Is There a Place for Afro-American Culture in Commodity Culture?", in *Feminisms: An*

Anthology of Literary Theory and Criticism, ed. Robyn R. Warhol and Diane Price Herndl (New Brunswick, NJ: Rutgers University Press, 1997), 992–1008.

26. Theresa Dinh, "Five Things We Learned about Rihanna from the Man Behind Her Style", GlobalGrind.com, 24 April 2013, http://globalgrind.com/style/5-things-we-learned-about-rihanna-man-behind-her-style-photos.

27. Liz Jones, "Pop's Poisonous Princess: Glorying in Drugs, Guns and Sleaze, Rihanna's Toxic Role Model for her Army of Young Fans", *Mail Online*, 24 June 2013, http://www.dailymail.co.uk/femail/article-2347680/Rihannas-toxic-role-model-army-young-fans/html.

28. Kate Dries, "Rihanna Unleashes Her Wrath on Noted Troll Liz Jones", *Jezebel* (blog), 25 June 2013, http://jezebel.com/rihanna-unleashes-her-wrath-on-noted-troll-liz-jones-572105743.

29. I am deeply concerned about the complex racialized terrain of demonization that Rihanna will have to continue to navigate in the midst of vigorous celebration among communities in Barbados, the Caribbean and the related diaspora. For some, her achievements fit well with the exploits of Bob Marley, Harry Belafonte, Grace Jones and Jimmy Cliff. But for others, her success has come through a pact with the occult, a powerful trope that has its genesis in the mythology of the natural inferiority of "blacks". This trope is powerful because of the discursive appeal of the paranormal as entertainment and discovery. This is refracted through the lens of the camera and the cinematic lens. A nexus is drawn between the discovery of stolen artefacts and symbols of past cosmologies and teeming discussion about religious orders. However, its popular representation invokes narratives of degeneracy extending back to imperial slavery. Those blacks most visibly enjoying success are thus considered to be exceptional and attract such explanations by those eager to point up the power of otherworldly forces. This requires significant study that is outside the scope of this essay. For a freewheeling discussion of cult symbols and black musician success, see "Rihanna 'Where Have You Been' Illuminati Explained" and associated comments, *Memoirs from Morocco* (blog), 2 May 2012, http://memoirsfrommorocco.blogspot.co.uk/2012/05/rihanna-where-have-you-been-illuminati.html.

30. See, for example, Patricia Hill Collins, *Black Feminist Thought* (New York: Routledge, 2000); Eudine Barriteau, "The Relevance of Black Feminist Scholarship: A Caribbean Perspective", *Feminist Africa* 7 (December 2006): 9–31; Tracey Reynolds, "Rethinking a Black Feminist Standpoint", *Ethnic and Racial Studies* 4, vol. 25 (2002): 591–606. The idea of the simultaneity of oppressions as fundamental to the experience of marginality is also found in women's writing from the standpoint of the global South. See Chandra Talpade Mohanty, "Cartographies of Struggle: Third World Women and the Politics of Feminism",

in *Third World Women and the Politics of Feminism*, ed. Chandra Talpade Mohanty, Ann Russo and Lourdes Torres (Bloomington: Indiana University Press, 1991), 1–50.
31. Moya Lloyd, *Beyond Identity Politics: Feminism, Power and Politics* (London: Sage Publications, 2005), 27. To be clear, this is not a charge against essentialism; on the contrary. Feminism's passionate attachment to the idea of a coherent unified feminist subject has been critical in circumstances where the repression of women is exacting, absolute and normalized. It is because Lloyd is inclined to address this as historically contingent that I am drawn to accent the indeterminacy of the female subject.
32. Becky Bain, "Rihanna Tells Ellen DeGeneres She Likes 'Aggressive but Mysterious' Men", *Idolator*, 21 November 2011, http://idolator.com/6087091/rihanna-ellen-dating-interview.
33. Indeed, Rihanna openly shared her grief at losing her grandmother, "Dolly", with whom she was very close and who was special in her upbringing. For an Instagram message by Rihanna sent out in tribute to her grandmother on the first anniversary of her passing, see "Rihanna Pays Moving Tribute to Late Granny on Instagram", *Bolega India*, 2 July 2014, http://www.bolegaindia.com/gossips/Rihanna_pays_moving_tribute_to_late_granny_on_Instagram-gid-31911-gc-15.html.
34. Eudine Barriteau, *The Political Economy of Gender in the Twentieth-Century Caribbean* (London: Palgrave, 2001).
35. See Gil Kaufman, "Rihanna Defends 'Man Down' Video's Violent Scenes", MTVNews.com, 3 June 2011, http://www.mtv.com/news/articles/1665057/rihanna-defends-man-down-video.jhtml.
36. Rihanna, interview with Diane Sawyer, *20/20*, ABC, 6 November 2009.
37. "Rihanna on Chris Brown: 'We Know Exactly What We Have Now'", *Rolling Stone* online, 30 January 2013, http://www.rollingstone.com/music/news/rihanna-on-chris-brown-we-know-exactly-what-we-have-now-20130130#ixzz3A2Nzuzsb.
38. Diane Negra and Su Holmes, "Introduction: Going Cheap? Female Celebrity in Reality, Tabloid and Scandal Genres", *Genders* ;8 (2008): para. 12, http://www.genders.org/g48/g48_negraholmes.html.
39. Anita Harris, *Future Girl: Young Women in the Twenty-First Century* (London: Routledge, 2004).
40. The video was actually co-directed by Rihanna, but in the closing stages of its production, the other director withdrew his name from the project. See Muna Mire, "Talkback: In Defense of Rihanna", *Feminist Wire* (blog), 16 October 2013, http://thefeministwire.com/2013/10/rihanna.

41. Kat Hobza, " 'Pour It Up' Video: Will Sinead O'Connor Write Rihanna Next?", SheKnows.com, 3 October 2013, http://www.sheknows.com/entertainment/articles/1019383/rihanna-pour-it-up-video-sinead-oconnor-miley-cyrus-letter.
42. Mire, "In Defense of Rihanna"; Melissa Bradshaw, "All I See Is Controversy: Rihanna's 'Pour It Up' ", *Red Bull Music Academy* online, 12 October 2013, http://www.redbullmusicacademy.com/magazine/all-i-see-is-controversy.
43. Bradshaw, "All I See Is Controversy".
44. Oneka LaBennett, *She's Mad Real: Popular Culture and West Indian Girls in Brooklyn* (New York: New York University Press, 2011).
45. Bradshaw, "All I See Is Controversy".
46. For more on this, see "Rihanna Named Cultural Ambassador", Caribbean360.com, 22 February 2008, http://www.caribbean360.com/news/rihanna-named-cultural-ambassador.
47. Comments cited here were posted on the article "Rihanna Explains to *Vogue* Readers How Bajans Normally Call Each Other C_nt", *Barbados Free Press*, 4 October 2011, https://barbadosfreepress.wordpress.com/2011/10/04/rihanna-explains-to-vogue-readers-how-bajans-normally-call-each-other-c_nt/.
48. Curwen Best, *The Popular Music and Entertainment Culture of Barbados: Pathways to Digital Culture* (Plymouth: Scarecrow Press, 2012).
49. White power is dominant, and socially empowered groups need not be unduly concerned about stereotypes, tropes and distortions. But under-represented groups and historically marginalized races are and will be especially sensitive about representations.
50. On the song "Disturbia", L.A. Reid, then CEO of Def Jam, stated: "It was the first time Rihanna actually came to me and said, 'Here's the song I want to put out.' She played me the song. That was her taking control. . . . She understands what hits are, and she knows what she wants to say. She's at that place where she can do that." Rihanna co-wrote "Hard". The song features hip-hop, militant horns, and a rapper's style of phrasing. In Rihanna's words, the song "had such an arrogance to it, which is so far from who I am . . . which is part of why I wanted to do it". "S&M" was released in 2011 and noted for its sexual lyrics, which Rihanna insists are all metaphorical. Shaheem Reid, "L.A. Reid Says He's 'Loaded' with Music for Rihanna's Next Album", MTVNews.com, 11 February 2009, http://www.mtv.com/news/1604904/la-reid-says-hes-loaded-with-music-for-rihannas-next-album/; *Wikipedia*, s.v. "Hard (song)", accessed 9 July 2013, http://en.wikipedia.org/wiki/Hard_(Rihanna_song); *Wikipedia*, s.v. "S&M" (song), accessed 9 July 2013, http://en.wikipedia.org/wiki/S%26M_(song); Shaheem Reid, "Rihanna 'Loves, Loves, Loves' Young Jeezy's Verse On 'Hard'", MTVNews.

com, 10 November 2009, http://www.mtv.com/news/1625977/rihanna-loves-loves-loves-young-jeezys-verse-on-hard/.
51. "Rihanna Discusses 'Bad Ass' New Album", *Spin* online, 19 October 2010, http://www.spin.com/articles/preview-rihanna-discusses-bad-ass-new-album/.
52. Thomas, *Modern Blackness*; LaBennett, *She's Mad Real*.

3

INTERNATIONAL IDENTITY

Rihanna and the Barbados Music Industry

MIKE ALLEYNE

> Through the digital technological complex in popular music, a kind of cultural quantization has been activated, limiting the scope for diversion from commercially viable norms, and extending the continuity of Western influence.
> —Mike Alleyne, "The Digital Imprint on Caribbean Music"[1]

This chapter examines Rihanna's commercial impact, not only in the context of her own career, but also in view of its implications for other internationally positioned Bajan recording artists. Rihanna's global commercial success has dramatically raised the popular-music profile of Barbados, moving the country from obscurity to being a prime potential source of performing talent for the mainstream music business. However, Rihanna's ascent to pop superstardom has raised unresolved issues about the musical and cultural identity of Barbados within and beyond popular music. The spate of major record-label signings of Bajan artists in the R&B/hip-hop mould in the wake of Rihanna's breakthrough has also sparked concerns about the distinctiveness of the island's musical image being projected through these artists and their corporate outlets in the recording industry. Moreover, the collective circumstances of Rihanna's marketplace arrival have obliquely highlighted the raw economic realities of musical artist survival in Barbados, drawing into question whether a true industry exists there or whether Rihanna's rise creates or reveals illusory ideals.

The visual commodification of Rihanna also plays a crucial role in the international identity-construction process of the singer and her nation, both of which are consequently projected through a music-business prism. Her wide-ranging commercial product endorsements and her three-year promotional deal with the Barbados Tourism Authority (beginning in 2011) demonstrate the power of her image and the extent to which it is inextricably connected to the global identity of her homeland and the stylistic character of her music.

There are widely divergent opinions among Bajan artists on the extent to which a national recording industry truly exists, underlining an urgent need for major development and re-examination. In early 2012, the self-contained Bajan group Cover Drive topped the charts in Britain with their single "Twilight" on the Polydor label, thereby highlighting the existence in Barbados of a deeper pool of talent beyond Rihanna, though the emergence of major-label interest in such acts is largely the result of her success.

In 2001, a 121-page study titled *The Caribbean Music Industry Database*[2] only mentioned Barbados three times and in incidental contexts. However, events in the decade that followed demand much closer and more serious consideration for the country. Until the twenty-first century, popular music from Barbados had comparatively little impact on the world's major markets, and while that perception has changed in some respects, the existing situation remains complex. The current collective, international sound of high-profile Bajan artists underlines the extent to which commercial influences, both musical and otherwise, impact on creative identity. Beyond image projection, the sonic distinctiveness of Barbados – or the lack thereof – is a central factor in the island's musical future. The omnipresence of physical and digital piracy threatens all recording artists, especially those in small markets like Barbados.[3] This circumstance makes the international dimension more crucial, as the best prospects for long-term survival in the industry usually exist beyond the island's shores. In addressing the post-Rihanna potentialities, this chapter will also examine past and present aspects of Bajan musical internationalization to underscore and recontextualize the extraordinary nature of the singer's career.

There has been a general critical tendency to focus on Rihanna's consciously sexualized image projections in music videos and their feminist implications. The emphasis on the singer's visual personae and gender-related resonances often occurs at the expense of music industry and sonic contexts encompassing the political economies of record production, songwriting and instrumental performance. Indeed, Rihanna's expletive-laden assault thrust at her own band onstage during the notorious 777 tour in 2012 implies a disregard for non-vocal musicians and an unprofessional marginalizing of performance decorum,[4] thereby making holistic critique of the Rihanna sound more imperative. These channels on the cultural console represent crucial phases through which the recorded artefact is created, preceding the photo shoots, album covers and music videos and in effect making their existence possible. Utilizing her many media associations with Barbados, this essay attempts to remix aspects of the Rihanna debates, shifting primary emphasis towards considerations of creativity and commercialization, and towards elements of the business infrastructure that envelops the singer's voice and her cross-cultural identities. Though not foregrounded, this essay's analysis does encompass still photos directly associated with product (musical and otherwise) in order to explore extra-visual dis/connections.

IDENTITY AND RIHANNA

In a 1996 interview in *Reggae Report* magazine, singer/songwriter John King accurately observed that "Barbados has not had a specific genre of music. Barbados has always enjoyed a variety of sounds."[5] The notable historical exception is the spouge rhythm which flourished in Barbados and the eastern Caribbean for a few years after the March 1970 demise of its creator, the renowned singer/songwriter Jackie Opel, who established his reputation in Jamaica in the 1960s. But its decidedly marginal status since then suggests extremely limited commercial viability. Definition of Bajan musical identity is further complicated by its multi-genre musical flexibility, which is simultaneously a commercial advantage and a potential cultural liability. If, for example, effective tourist marketing of the nation's collective identity relies on clarity about its artistic imprint in popular music – an aspect which Jamaica and Trinidad have successfully exploited with reggae and calypso, respectively – then Barbados has significant issues to resolve.

Rihanna's current superstardom provides a highly relevant analytical axis point, as the commercial success of her career has taken Barbados to several international crossroads. As her North American booking agent noted in a *Billboard* magazine interview, "We worked on developing her internationally and not just domestically [in the United States], and I think that's a key to why she's an international icon."[6] Her stardom has generated a large array of stunning statistics, only a few of which will be revisited here. Rihanna was positioned at number twenty-two on *Billboard*'s list of "Music's Top 40 Money Makers of 2012" (calculating 2011 revenue), with net income of over US$7.6 million.[7] She had sold more than a million copies of six of her seven albums in America by the middle of 2013, with the sole exception being her gold debut.[8] Her 87-show world tour grossed over $137 million, making it fifth on the list of top-grossing tours in 2013.[9] Her late 2012 release, *Unapologetic*, also won a 2014 Grammy Award for Best Urban Contemporary Album.[10] However, the focus in this analysis goes beyond the forest of flattering figures.

The predictable national euphoria surrounding this unprecedented global chart conquest by a Bajan performer must also be informed by a reality-based pragmatism that recognizes the innately colonizing nature of the international recording industry. These cautionary observations emphasize the complications involved in achieving longevity in the music business and avoiding creative confinement leading to excessive reliance on commercial trends. In the midst of national debate in Barbados about developing and exploiting the cultural industries (although I prefer the broader term *creative industries*), the dialogue perhaps lacks acute awareness that collisions of culture and commerce are frequently inextricable from conditions of compromise. It is vital to recognize which components represent culture, versus those that are inherently industrial and which bear little or no direct relationship to artistic creativity, particularly where the music business is concerned. UNESCO suggests that, among other things, cultural industries "embody or convey cultural expressions, irrespective of the commercial value they may have",[11] and it is distinctly likely that those less obviously commercial branches need to be more actively nurtured.

With such considerations in mind, we can explore some fundamental questions arising from Rihanna's success. If Rihanna's sound is a generic form of international pop without a unique overall cultural imprint, then this precedent has implications for other Barbadian artists who tackle the global market in the wake of her success.[12] Furthermore, there is considerable doubt surrounding the extent to which this type of success is actually economically fuelling the local industry. One of the more obvious artistic consequences for Barbados has been a cloning effect, duplicating Rihanna's proven formula with other artists. In a 2009 *Billboard* magazine article prophetically titled "Replicating Rihanna",[13] journalist Patricia Meschino notes that Barbados is now seen as an active site for sourcing globally marketable artists in the urban R&B mould. The article also correctly implies that there's little scope for committed major-label record company support outside of this very specific genre model.

Major-label signings of Bajan artists in recent years have demonstrated that what I describe as the "localized global" model is likely to persist, a circumstance in which external stylistic influences largely overshadow local elements of creative expression in the recorded output of a country's artists. Syndicated Rhythm Productions (SRP),[14] which discovered and successfully moulded Rihanna, also signed Hal Linton, Shontelle and Vita Chambers to develop the acts and their product in conjunction with Universal, the record industry's corporate giant. Rihanna's breakthrough also creates the illusion that the major-label model automatically represents the best path for developing artists. However, shifting industry circumstances and global economic crises have made record deals more all-inclusive – for example, the so-called 360 deal that allows the label to share merchandising revenue and income from ancillary sources. From both economic and creative autonomy perspectives, this early twenty-first-century phase might actually be the *least* favourable time to pursue major-label alliances, despite the potential access to enormous distribution networks and promotional capital.

Most major-label artists no longer have the luxury of developing and consolidating their craft over a series of albums in order to achieve creative growth and make commercial success sustainable. The idea of maturity signified by the artist's direct involvement in every stage of making recordings is not yet fully emergent in Barbados's presence on the international stage. The power trident of production, instrumental performance and songwriting capability should be the artist's ultimate objective in order to maximize creative influence on his or her output. However, in the existing pop-music marketplace, such notions of artistry carry limited value, as major record labels have become more reliant than ever on hit production and songwriting teams whose stylistic originality is questionable.

Components of the songwriting process behind Rihanna's success were laid bare in the 2011 NPR story "How Much Does It Cost to Make a Hit Song?"[15] and the 2012 *New Yorker* magazine article "The Song Machine: The Hitmakers behind Rihanna".[16] NPR's exposé revealed that the cost of constructing the single "Man Down" (2011), including the various producers, songwriters and engineers, was $78,000. This, however, did not include the so-called song roll-out expenses of $1 million to ensure simultaneous blanket media exposure upon the single's release. Despite the capital outlay – which was average in major-label terms – the song was not a hit in the United States (the prime expenditure target), only peaking at number fifty-nine after fourteen weeks on the *Billboard* Hot 100.[17]

The disparity between the label's costs and the low return sheds light on the seldom discussed issue of recoupment – the process whereby the label recovers its expenses before the artist derives any profit – and the fracture between financial reality and an artist's veneer of success.[18] Rihanna's cumulative American album sales of over 10 million copies[19] ensure that profits are earned by all entitled participants, but the recoupment scenario reaffirms the idea that success has to simultaneously permeate several dimensions of an artist's career to be legitimate.

Press reports in early 2014 suggested that Rihanna aimed to bridge the gap between performance and authorship by agreeing to write and record a concept album for a children's animated film from Hollywood's goliath DreamWorks company.[20] By also providing the voice for the feature's lead character, she would be undertaking the multilevel creative involvement advocated in this chapter, which both Rihanna's career and those of other international Bajan acts have generally lacked.

With business matters obscured by the aura of stardom, it is also frequently forgotten by the public that the standard language of typical recording contracts exempts record companies from obligation to release material in which they have invested. Rihanna's attainment of gold status with her debut album ensured her immediate future with the gigantic Universal Music Group.[21] Conversely, despite issuing a handful of singles, Universal Motown's release of Hal Linton's international debut album – reported as being imminent in

2009, 2010 and 2011 – never materialized. Instead, the singer/songwriter independently released a free fourteen-song collection titled *Technicolour* in 2012. In a circumstance further symptomatic of the problematic nature of major-label operations, then teenage female singer Vita Chambers released the EP *The Get Go* (2010), also with Universal, but her debut album was never released. Only the electronic dance single "Fix You" had emerged from the label by December 2012, and by 2013, Chambers too was independently releasing her music through her own company, Gold Note Productions Limited.[22] In an inevitably scathing critique of an unremittingly harsh business, she asserted that "I honestly feel better now. It is a machine, but they don't do what they are supposed to do. They look at you as a funnel for money. I went through all of that, I saw it, I didn't want it anymore and I created a new alternative."[23]

R&B/pop singer Jaicko's album with Capitol Records was digitally released in the United States in 2010, but its physical version was only available there as a highly priced Japanese import. While that Bajan artist's album may have suffered from inadequate label support, its situation may also be indicative of a generic pop sound competing with too many similar-sounding products, and this is a dilemma at the core of Barbados's current international presence.

Livvi Franc's initial signing to the now closed Jive Records in 2007 metamorphosed into an affiliation with Warner Brothers. Records after her debut album was shelved. Once again, though, while singles and videos tested the market temperature, taking her to various British and American charts during her tenure with Jive, album product remained absent almost three years after she had first signed a major-label deal. Franc has since consolidated her career with songwriting and background vocal credits on releases by several prominent female pop artists, notably including contributions to Rihanna's 2012 album *Unapologetic*.

The examples of Linton, Chambers and Franc demonstrate that while the Rihanna major-label template has commercial validity, attempts to replicate it also suggest that other Bajan artists need to explore alternative distribution channels to reach global audiences on their own terms. Universal Motown singer Shontelle has at least released two albums, but her career is challenged by a very tangible market saturation of stylistically similar female pop and R&B vocalists whose songs frequently originate from the same Scandinavian sources, as outlined later in this chapter.

Geographical issues are also highly significant, as the germination of a globalized pop sound was a major factor in Rihanna's success. Not every Bajan act with an international following has adopted the same corporate pop path, though singers such as soca queen Alison Hinds have not yet fully converted ongoing commercial potential to cross over from global West Indian communities into the pop mainstream. Almost all of the current crop of internationally positioned performers fit a template which may genuinely reflect the artists' musical influences but which also effectively distances them from the Caribbean, dislocating any readily identifiable Barbadian stylistic and creative contexts. Some have stated that the popular music of Barbados is now too eclectic to have a single, definitive international identity.

All of Barbados's twenty-first-century major-label acts had to physically relocate to further their careers, and their geographical repositioning is quite symbolically significant: their music is equally if not more at home in the major markets, compared to within Barbados. However, under the existing international popular-culture conditions, in which only a limited stylistic lexicon receives adequate promotion, such literal placement within core markets has clear commercial logic. Unfortunately, the sound of cultural neutrality has become the global music-business norm for the newly emergent artists in question, and this should be a stark warning to all concerned with issues of identity and representation, and the frameworks within which international recording industry commerce occurs. The same historical moment within which little-known artists from Barbados have been catapulted into the major-label spotlight also contains the threat of an ominous digital cloning whereby replication negates innovation.

PRE-RIHANNA HISTORICAL BACKGROUND

The international popular-music press essentially has no active consciousness of Barbados predating Rihanna's emergence. Indirectly, further light was shed on Barbados's historic role in shaping popular music with the 2013 death of American acoustic folk singer Richie Havens, who famously opened the legendary 1969 Woodstock music festival in New York. In his 1999 autobiography, Havens notes the pivotal influence of his British-born grandmother, Beatrice Elizabeth Gay, who exposed him to a wide range of music, including "playing old recordings of Caribbean island music she had carried with her from Barbados".[24] As early as the 1960s, Bajan artists had had releases issued in Britain, including Jamaica-based singer Jackie Opel (Island, R&B, Ska Beat) and the calypso group the Merrymen (Island, Trojan, EMI's Columbia label), with occasional singles also licensed to American labels. Neither that decade nor the 1970s witnessed significant commercial progress for Bajan acts with international record companies, but the 1980s and 1990s ushered in the significant rise of UK-based artists either from Barbados or of Bajan descent scoring both European and American chart success on major labels.

Jimmy Haynes was the guitarist and producer of Steel Pulse's Grammy Award–winning album *Babylon the Bandit* (1986), making him the first Bajan musician to achieve such high-level industry recognition for his work, and one of the few behind the scenes to be known at all. The eponymous band of multi-instrumentalist Andrew Roachford scored a transatlantic hit single with "Cuddly Toy", which reached number four in Britain in 1989. One of the frequently overlooked major Bajan hits pre-Rihanna is "Soca Dance" by Charles D. Lewis. That song topped the French charts for six weeks in 1990 while also becoming a big seller in Belgium, Germany, Holland and Austria, and it still has recurrent airplay and income across Europe, where it is frequently licensed for inclusion on hit compilations. Perhaps because the record was not a hit in major English-speaking markets, it has become historically less visible. One of the key commercial turning points was the half-Bajan singer Des'ree's 1994 album *I Ain't Movin'*, featuring the inspirational hit single "You Gotta Be", which reached number five in the United States; shortly thereafter, Barbados-raised, Sweden-based Herbie Crichlow (whose work has even been discussed in *Time* magazine) co-wrote two of the Backstreet Boys' major hits: "Quit Playing Games (with My Heart)" (1996) and "Show Me the Meaning of Being Lonely" (1999). Crichlow was an ASCAP songwriting award winner for three consecutive years in the late 1990s. In 1994, Barbadian multi-instrumentalist Nicholas Brancker had writing and production credits on Jamaican dancehall singer Patra's album *Queen of the Pack*, released by Epic Records, which went gold in the United States.

While this chronology is certainly not all-inclusive, it clearly challenges historical mythologies that Barbados never wielded musical influence beyond its shores before Rihanna. A central feature and distinguishing factor in

Rihanna's case is her total adoption by the recording industry's star-making machinery and the concentrated support of global capital for almost a decade promoting her as an international commercial music commodity.[25]

Despite the aforementioned series of intermittent flirtations with pop success, no Bajan artists had achieved sustained international impact, and an identifiable Bajan sound remained virtually imperceptible. Barbados-based Guyanese artist, producer and entrepreneur Eddy Grant promoted a percussively propelled soca offshoot in the 1990s known as ringbang. Although his Ice Records studio is located in Barbados, Grant has made comments suggesting that ringbang was conceived as a trans-Caribbean musical vehicle rather than necessarily as one centred either on or in the island.[26] The 1995 ringbang showcase compilation *Fire in de Wave* certainly featured Bajan acts, but it still remains debatable whether a uniquely Bajan cultural imprint resulted to fully individualize the style's identity beyond the shadow of soca, and whether its domestic and regional prominence will fully translate into global mainstream success beyond the 2001 UK top-ten placing of Grant's 1983 single "Electric Avenue" in remixed form.[27] The argument here, then, is that Barbados lacks a separate, easily identifiable musical inscription readily evident beyond its geographical or cyber-virtual borders. Rihanna's ascension, often viewed as imbuing Bajan music culture with a missing identity, has in fact further complicated the process of discerning and defining the island's international musical identity.

RIHANNA'S RISE

Rihanna emerged from virtual obscurity, being practically unknown within the Barbados music scene when she was signed to the SRP Music Group. Barbados's best-known artist is a product of the nation's fragmented musical identities, but not part of the island's live or recording scenes through which those identities are most frequently manifested. While this circumstance certainly does not disqualify her from being a voice for and from Barbados, it provides an interesting commentary on the politics of an industry propelled by a capitalism that is often detached from ideals of cultural authenticity. Considerations of what constitutes musical authenticity reside within a vortex of ideological quicksand too vast for extensive discussion here. However, there is incisive validity in Shuker's observation that an "uneasy alliance between art and commerce is frequently placed at the heart of the history of popular music".[28] It may further be argued that textual divergences (the "inauthentic") from approximate stylistic norms (the "authentic") are often more readily identifiable than the bases of consensus about what is considered "real" and upon which criteria such judgement should normally rely. The eventual global success of Jamaican reggae superstar Bob Marley was built on several pre-existing artistic and cultural foundations, but in industry terms, the Wailers' *Catch a Fire* album, released in America in 1973, represents the start of Marley's international journey on Chris Blackwell's Island Records label.[29] That record has been the object of considerable contention since it featured a carefully calculated superimposition of rock elements, ostensibly to enhance the Wailers' commercial appeal.[30] The dilution of *Catch a Fire*'s roots reggae sound, inclusive of performances from an artist now most commonly associated with notions of Afro-Caribbean musical authenticity, echoes long-term industry practices of perceived pragmatism.

The 2005 summer success of Rihanna's million-selling debut single "Pon de Replay", which peaked at number two in both America and Britain, did not lead to equally large album sales, as *Music of the Sun* only attained gold status in both territories. The single was inauspiciously described by one American radio programme director as "kind of mindless, you don't have to think about it".[31] Her distinctly pop-mainstream musical identity continued with her global 2006 hit single "SOS". Apart from her performance persona, perceptibly influenced by contemporary American acts such as Destiny's Child, "SOS" recycles the central riff from British group Soft Cell's 1982 international chart hit "Tainted Love", which was itself first recorded by American singer Gloria Jones in 1964. The adaptation in Rihanna's cover version is almost solely embodied in new lyrics, so the liberal sampling of Soft Cell's version underscores a strategy of commercial safety which has governed most of Rihanna's career, in which components of pre-existing hits by other artists have been incorporated into her recorded material. This commercial strategy can hardly be described as unusual in the digital age of increasing homogeneity and aural intertextuality, but in the context of Barbadian musical identity, the predominance of emulation rather than invention has notable erosive implications.

In the current commercial reality of the recording industry, Rihanna's own prodigious pop/R&B American sales peak of 2.8 million copies for her third album, *Good Girl Gone Bad*, in 2007 is itself unlikely to be replicated by any reggae or soca release in the near future.[32] This raises questions about the extent to which Barbadian and other Caribbean artists can effectively utilize a broader, more culturally resonant musical vocabulary in major markets, in addition to constructing performance images that transcend the kinds of sexualized stereotypes arguably exemplified by Rihanna on her album covers and in her ubiquitous music videos. Operating under the umbrella of the world's largest record company, Universal, Rihanna spoke of her artistic reinvention and growth on her 2010 release, *Loud* – the seventh best-selling album in the world that year – during a *Billboard* magazine interview.[33] However, the development to which she refers is difficult to locate within the actual *sound* of the record, which takes much of its duplicative shape from international pop production and songwriting teams whose work often makes artists anonymously interchangeable.

With sales of over 1.8 million copies in the United States, *Loud* returned Rihanna to a sonic comfort zone with which her audience could more easily identify, as opposed to the more stark and idiosyncratic *Rated R* (2009), which has since been certified platinum but which remains her lowest-selling album since her gold debut release. Conversely, 2012 comments from her record label's personnel suggest an altogether different perception of Rihanna's degree of innovation, proposing that she constantly transcends her previous artistic boundaries.[34] It is ironic that *Rated R*, arguably still her most conceptually ambitious and psychologically exploratory album to date, featuring her largest number of co-writing credits – nine songs – and the least glamorous cover art of all her albums, has also been one of the least commercially successful. With its foreboding, bland and grey façade, it is the only album that slightly diverges from her established stylistic career formula, and also her first with a Parental Advisory logo – now accompanied in that respect by 2011's *Talk That Talk* and 2012's *Unapologetic* – due to Rihanna's increasingly controversial choices of language. In sharp commercial contrast, Rihanna has *no* writing credits (either individually or as co-writer) on her wildly successful *Loud* or *Unapologetic* albums. Her 2015 DreamWorks children's movie concept album will likely redress this type of creative imbalance, but meanwhile, there's an inescapable, abrasive correlation here between altered image, creative growth and commercial stasis. In a virtual directive towards genre conformity, a representative of New York radio station Hot 97 tellingly asserted, "When Rihanna makes music that fits the appeal of hip-hop, we play it."[35] Evidently, then, there's little obvious existing scope for bringing some form of unique Bajan sonic identity to the mainstream, unless it is so diluted as to be culturally indistinct.

The sphere of artist product endorsement and advertising iconography also plays a key role here, inclusive of Rihanna's visually inextricable relationship to the image of Barbados through popular music via her promotional deal with the Barbados Tourism Authority.[36] For effective promotion, the synergies between sales pitch and subject need to be completely synchronized and credible, since effective long-term celebrity endorsement value is best achieved when few contradictions exist between image, reality and the product's marketing.

As an example of inconsistency, there's some irony in Rihanna's endorsement of Vita Coco coconut water, with its slogan, "From a tree, not a lab", with all of its evocations of an organic and all-natural product, and of course the tropical stereotypes of sun, sea and sand that appear in the colour print advertisement's background. Yet Rihanna's records are almost comprehensively the exact opposite, as technology-intensive artefacts from the recording studio lab. This is neither an argument against digital music technology, by any means, nor an explicitly anti-Rihanna position, but simply a commentary on the juxtaposition of her endorsement branding against the sonic reality of her records. Rihanna's wider commercial image is also inseparable from the performance identity that is the very source of her economic market value. On the most fundamental level, it has become increasingly clear that any of her perceived indiscretions – either in her image or in her use of expletives in interviews or social media – now potentially impact both the national and international identities of Barbados, within and beyond popular music.

Media psychology and manipulation are tools of the trade when promoting an artist in the context of a specific product. A two-page Nivea skin cream advertisement featuring Rihanna and appearing at the start of the 2011 Billboard Music Awards supplement was notable for several reasons. In conjunction with the comparable skin tonality of the three depicted participants (the singer on one page and an embracing white couple on the other), there are layers of irony embedded in Rihanna's statement for the campaign, "I think if you feel comfortable within your skin, it shows." Yet despite the apparent relevance of this statement to the artist, the visual continuity of the photographed subjects almost implies that the *advertiser* is only comfortable with Rihanna's skin when it is suitably illuminated. In the advertisement, Rihanna is accurately described as a global icon, but in this visual context, the phrase also demonstrates a form of cultural neutrality that mirrors the general sound of the music. Ultimately, the degree of the singer's comfort within her own skin was too great for Nivea, which terminated her endorsement deal in August 2012, following Rihanna's ongoing lyrical and social media improprieties.[37] There are naturally other noteworthy contexts within which the singer's race functions actively, but this is one which simultaneously projects an exterior persona that explicitly foregrounds her skin and its commercial agency in a music-business publication. It is also an endorsement role which her aura of rebellion, exploited by Rihanna with her designer fragrance names such as Rogue, Rebelle and Nude, has utterly undermined.

It was also interesting that the Barbados Tourism Authority's full-page advertisement in *Billboard* magazine in February 2011 promoting its alliance with Rihanna was on the other side of a cover featuring Bob Marley, which accompanied a story discussing the significance of Marley's posthumous music merchandising. Whether by accident or design, this circumstance invites a variety of comparisons in terms of certain key issues relevant to both artists, ranging from international commercial presence and artist commodification to assimilation of recorded music into a fabric representing national identity, the latter being especially underlined by the Jamaica Tourist Board's use of Marley's "One Love" song in its worldwide TV promotional campaigns. Through its voluntary affiliation to Rihanna, the Barbados Tourism Authority is also implicitly making a statement about the (dis)location of Barbadian musical identity. In this national context, it is quite notable that Rihanna's album releases since (and including) *Rated R* in 2009 have all occurred in November,[38] the very month when Barbados celebrates its political independence. This may be largely coincidental, with the fourth quarter traditionally being targeted by labels for major artists' releases in order to capitalize on consumer Christmas spending. However, the fact that four consecutive Rihanna albums – more than half of her recorded repertoire to date – have made November debuts inevitably invites ideas about her own assertion of independence in the aftermath of her much publicized 2009 assault at the hands of R&B singer and then boyfriend Chris Brown. *Rated R* was the first album on which she was credited as executive producer (as has been the case with her subsequent album releases), although this role cannot necessarily be equated with hands-on creation of the finished product.[39]

THE CONTRASTING CASE OF SHONTELLE

Inevitably, the impulse to clone Rihanna affects the ways in which current aspiring vocalists from Barbados are perceived, as suggested by a September 2011 story in Barbados's *Nation* newspaper in which the host of an annual local talent contest claims that his aim is "to produce another Rihanna".[40] However, the moderate sales of Bajan female vocalist Shontelle's two albums with Universal Motown may be another indicator suggesting that replicating Rihanna has its limitations. Operating through the same production company – Syndicated Rhythm Productions – has not necessarily enhanced the creation of distinct individual identities for the two singers.[41] Shontelle's 2008 debut album, *Shontelligence*, only reached number 115 on the *Billboard* 200 (selling just over thirty thousand copies), spending only a single week there, largely due to the absence of a blockbuster hit single. That situation was remedied by her 2010 sophomore album *No Gravity*, with the Top 20 chart impact of "Impossible" in both the United States and Britain, which certainly raised her commercial profile without quite emulating Rihanna's sales success.

As previously suggested, geography and the globalization of pop are crucial factors in the twenty-first-century market. Reflecting Scandinavia's songwriting and production dominance in the contemporary pop world, spearheaded by Sweden's Max Martin, Ina Wroldsen, the Norwegian co-writer of Shontelle's "Impossible", has also had her songs recorded by other top female pop singers, including America's Britney Spears and Britain's Leona Lewis. Unsurprisingly, then, the actual result on Shontelle's hit single is a generic pop sound, one that is globally marketable but that literally could have come from anywhere. This is also true for most content on Rihanna's records, which have included songs written and produced by the Norwegian, New York–based duo Stargate since her debut album.[42] This pop globalization shaping the sound (and, by implication, the identities) of the Barbadian divas underscores a clear commercial prioritization of an aural transnationalism that requires no passport to achieve its border crossings. The homogenized styles characterizing the immersion of Rihanna and Shontelle within the pop landscape are actually antithetical to the assertion of distinctive national identity, though the situation is in full confluence with the pervasive neutrality associated with selling Caribbean music and tourism to the foreign mainstream. The suggestion here is not that artists should automatically become symbols of a stereotypical, static or perhaps even mythical national identity, but that when the nation, through its government, *officially* identifies with the artist, as in the case of Rihanna, the synergy or lack thereof automatically becomes an object of magnified cultural analysis. A potential counterpoint to the identity scenarios featured in this chapter arises with the emergence of the group Cover Drive, whose second single, "Twilight", topped the British charts at the end of January 2012. Though their sound also strongly reflects significant pop and R&B influences echoing Rihanna (for whom they were the opening act at her Barbados concert), the title of their debut album, *Bajan Style*, appears to conceptually project indigenous rhythmic elements into the sonic foreground, while also consciously signifying and underscoring the Barbadian relationship between artist and nation in a manner previously unseen via an album title on the international stage.

CONCLUSION

From an industry development perspective, Barbados has gained little significant economic benefit from the profile and sales of its major-label artists. Much emphasis has been placed on the economic impact of Rihanna's 2011 live concert appearance in Barbados, estimated by some unverified sources to have generated millions of dollars,[43] but there's no concrete indication that any of this income has filtered into the local music industry. There also appeared to be little focus on the irony that the 2011 concert was the superstar's first public performance in her homeland, reinforcing her status as a commodity constructed outside of an immediately Barbadian sonic context. While her concert appearance (notwithstanding the cancellation of a planned 2013 reappearance) effectively enacted her claim to Barbados and reaffirmed the island's claim to her, it remains uncertain as to what specific components in her sound, if any, qualify as Bajan. The construction of both the singer's career and aspects of her identity as Bajan have occurred with Barbados largely in the narrative periphery. This is in notable contrast to yet another Bajan artist who achieved mainstream international chart success in the twenty-first century.

In late 2004, male singer Rupee's hit "Tempted to Touch", on Atlantic Records, edged into the *American Top 40* before Rihanna's first hit, setting the stage for major-label acquisition of Bajan performers. However, Rupee's album *1 on 1*, from which the single came, is the one album discussed in this chapter which features the participation of Bajan musicians, producers and studio facilities. The Bajan presence on the album is photographically reinforced in the CD gatefold insert by the superimposition of a bus-stop sign over part of a dilapidated chattel house, within which the singer is also depicted. Sadly, the record's absence from major charts at the time of its release suggests it was also one of the least promoted of the albums under discussion. It was also an anomaly because it was released by Atlantic *after* becoming a local finished product rather than being crafted outside of Barbados primarily for the pop mainstream from the outset. Genuine development of a music industry relies on the effective utilization of local creative resources; so far, although Rihanna and Shontelle have both occasionally incorporated Bajan facilities and personnel on various songs and remixes, recent international releases from Bajan artists have incorporated only marginal local involvement to fuel the local industry economy, in order to globalize the local in a manner which is empowering rather than limiting. In any event, the Bajan recording industry cannot and should not rely solely on the country's international stars to generate the year-round activity it so urgently needs, nor can it depend solely on the annual summer Crop Over festival to ensure its survival and growth, given the festival's inherent seasonality. Space must be negotiated and made for locally created music which neither confines artists within stereotypical Caribbean moulds nor condemns them to pop and R&B replication.

Rihanna's success with her seven studio albums should signify the opening of a gateway to many different commercial and creative paths rather than an entrance to a single economic route which consolidates long-held major-label hegemonic power, in an era of potential digital diversity, multimedia opportunity and postcolonial cultural originality. While the Internet readily facilitates crossing national borders, it is also equally capable of neutralizing Barbadian national identity, or at least its representation through popular music targeting the international marketplace. Rihanna scored massive success in late 2012 with the single "Diamonds", but the fact that she held neither production nor songwriting credits for this global hit actively reinforces the arguments surrounding recording industry commerce, artistic creativity (despite the songwriting success of Cover Drive)[44] and its extended implications for Bajan popular music. Her early 2014 collaboration on Shakira's hit single "Can't Remember to Forget You" (on which both singers are co-writers with five others) and the studied eroticism of its video have solidified Rihanna's pop-superstar credentials. Some might question whether the song's titular emphasis on memory unwittingly highlights a lost moment during which her identity might have been more meaningfully amplified and expanded. Barbados's stylistic eclecticism has the potential to open global marketplace doors, but the lack of distinctive sonic identity may ultimately determine its global path.

NOTES

1. Mike Alleyne, "The Digital Imprint on Caribbean Music", in *Culture and Mass Communication in the Caribbean*, ed. Humphrey A. Regis (Gainesville: University Press of Florida, 2001), 135.
2. Vanus James, ed., *The Caribbean Music Industry Database (CMID)*, report prepared for the United Nations Conference on Trade and Development (UNCTAD) and World Intellectual Property Organization (WIPO), October 2001, www.wipo.int/about-ip/en/studies/pdf/study_v_james.pdf.
3. Jess Denham, "Rihanna and Bruno Mars the Most Pirated Artists of 2013", *Independent*, 30 December 2013, http://www.independent.co.uk/arts-entertainment/music/news/rihanna-and-bruno-mars-the-most-pirated-artists-of-2013-9030553.html. According to this and other reports, Rihanna was ranked second in the annual list. Although the scale of her piracy-popularity far exceeds that of any other act from Barbados, and although Rihanna still sells millions of records, the survey's findings underline the ever-present economic threat of copyright insecurity.
4. Bené Viera, "Rihanna Curses Out Her Band in London During 777 Tour", VH1.com, 20 November 2012, http://www.vh1.com/music/tuner/2012-11-20/rihanna-curses-out-her-band-in-london-during-777-tour/.
5. Jonas Sears, "John King: Soca Bajan Style", *Reggae Report* 14, no. 5 (1996): 32.
6. Mitchell Peters, "Rising Stars: Trio of Talents Up for the Breakthrough Award", *Billboard*, 12 November 2011, 42.

7. "Music's 40 Top Money Makers 2012", *Billboard* online, 9 March 2012, http://www.billboard.com/articles/list/502623/musics-top-40-money-makers-2012.
8. Keith Caulfield, "Rihanna Earns Sixth Million-Selling Album", *Billboard* online, 31 May 2013, http://www.billboard.com/biz/articles/news/chart-alert/1565549/rihanna-earns-sixth-million-selling-album.
9. "Top 25 Tours of 2013", *Billboard* online, 21 December 2013, http://www.billboard.com/articles/list/5820092/top-25-tours-of-2013.
10. "56th Annual Grammy Awards: Full Winners List", *Billboard* online, 26 January 2014, http://www.billboard.com/biz/articles/news/tv-film/5885361/56th-annual-grammy-awards-full-winners-list.
11. "Cultural Industries", UNESCO information sheet, 27 February 2006, http://www.unesco.org/bpi/pdf/memobpi25_culturalindustries_en.pdf.
12. From a Caribbean musical perspective, Rihanna's albums have sometimes incorporated reggae, though only in a marginal way. Those efforts have been stylistically typical of a generic R&B/dancehall crossover sound, and rarely have more than two songs per album been allocated to reggae (with 2006's *A Girl Like Me* as a notable exception). Her hit singles have almost uniformly veered towards a mainstream pop/R&B amalgam, a sound that may reflect an aspect of the modern Bajan musical reality but that does not delineate a discrete identity.
13. Patricia Meschino, "Replicating Rihanna", *Billboard*, 5 December 2009, 12.
14. The company is run by the songwriting and production team of Carl Sturken and Evan Rogers. The team's Top 40 hits began in the late 1980s with artists such as Gavin Christopher ("One Step Closer to You" in 1986) and Donny Osmond ("Sacred Emotion" in 1989). In 1991, they released their first album under the group name of Rythm Syndicate, scoring two Top 40 hit singles before altering the band name's spelling to the more conventional Rhythm Syndicate for their 1992 follow-up album. Having attained little album success, the group was then dissolved to allow its creative nucleus to focus on the songwriting and production skills that had made Rhythm Syndicate possible in the first place, leading to a string of hits with high-profile female pop singers, including Christina Aguilera and Kelly Clarkson. According to the company's website, Syndicated Rhythm Productions was formed in 2005, and Rihanna was its first signing, though other sources suggest that both events occurred in 2004. It was SRP that brought Rihanna to rapper/entrepreneur Jay-Z, affiliated with Def Jam Records at that time. Jay-Z assumed executive producer status on Rihanna's first four albums under the banner of the Carter Administration, and then on *Talk That Talk* and *Unapologetic* using the RocNation name. See SRP Music Group, "About Us", http://srpmusicgroup.com/about-us.
15. Zoe Chace, "How Much Does It Cost to Make a Hit Song?", NPR online, 30 June

2011, http://www.npr.org/blogs/money/2011/07/05/137530847/how-much-does-it-cost-to-make-a-hit-song.

16. John Seabrook, "The Song Machine: The Hitmakers behind Rihanna", *New Yorker* online, 26 March 2012, http://www.newyorker.com/reporting/2012/03/26/120326fa_fact_seabrook?currentPage=all.

17. *Academic Charts Online*, 6 March 2014, http://ipm.academiccharts.com.ezproxy.mtsu.edu/releases/324683.

18. Donald Passman, *All You Need to Know About the Music Business*, 8th ed. (New York: Free Press, 2012), 83–84.

19. Keith Caulfield, "Rihanna Hits 10 Million in U.S. Album Sales", *Billboard* online, 16 November 2013, http://www.billboard.com/articles/columns/chart-beat/5793204/rihanna-hits-10-million-in-us-album-sales.

20. Tshepo Mokoena, "Rihanna to Make Concept Album for DreamWorks Animated Film", *Guardian*, 27 February 2014, http://www.theguardian.com/music/2014/feb/27/rihanna-concept-album-dreamworks-animated-film. It is also notable that the announcement was part of the CEO's conference call to shareholders announcing "fourth-quarter and 2013 year-end results". This confluence firmly reinforces the idea of the artist's economic utility, though in this instance it affords Rihanna an unprecedented opportunity to holistically represent herself as an artist rather than just a performer.

21. It should be noted that the Bajan group Cover Drive, signed to Polydor Records and mentioned earlier in this essay, is also part of Universal's subsidiary label apparatus.

22. "Vita's Destiny in Her Own Hands", *Midweek Nation* (Barbados), 4 December 2013,http://www.nationnews.com/nationnews/news/23986/vita-destiny-hands. The newspaper story mistakenly refers to the singer's production company as "Goldnut Productions".

23. Ibid.

24. Richie Havens with Steve Davidowitz, *They Can't Hide Us Anymore* (New York: Spike, 1999), 6.

25. Almost inevitably, each of the pre-Rihanna acts mentioned also achieved their success by direct or extended affiliation to and/or distribution through major labels. British reggae act Steel Pulse was signed to Elektra during Jimmy Haynes's production involvement with the group, both Andrew Roachford and Des'ree were signed to subsidiaries of Sony Music, and Charles D. Lewis's "Soca Dance" appeared in some markets on the Polydor label. Although Herbie Crichlow's impact as a solo artist has been mostly limited to generally modest sales in continental Europe, he has been signed to the BMG conglomerate, later merged with Sony.

26. Curwen Best, *Barbadian Popular Music and the Politics of Caribbean Culture* (Rochester, VT: Schenkman, 1999), xi; Curwen Best, *Roots to Popular Culture: Barbadian Aesthetics, Kamau Brathwaite to Hardcore Styles* (London: Macmillan, 2001), 167–68.
27. Curwen Best, *Culture @ the Cutting Edge: Tracking Caribbean Popular Music* (Kingston: University of the West Indies Press, 2004), 132–46. Best refers to the 2001 popularity of the ringbang remix of "Electric Avenue" by Miami DJ Peter Black that brought both Grant and the song renewed notoriety (143). Despite this commercial impact, ringbang's overall international visibility since then appears marginal.
28. Roy Shuker, *Key Concepts in Popular Music* (New York: Routledge, 1998), 21.
29. It is somewhat ironic that Rihanna's Universal Music releases have been issued by the incongruously amalgamated Island Def Jam Music Group, given Island's historical role in popularizing and commoditizing reggae and Caribbean artists.
30. Mike Alleyne, "Positive Vibration? Capitalist Textual Hegemony and Bob Marley", in *Caribbean Romances: The Politics of Regional Representation*, ed. Belinda Edmondson (Charlottesville: University Press of Virginia, 1999), 92–104.
31. Michael Libby, "Rihanna Makes 'Play' for Stardom", *Billboard*, 13 August 2005, 45.
32. Caulfield, "Rihanna Hits 10 Million". The cited sales figure was the latest available at the time of writing. It should also be considered in the context of the remarkably poor performance of reggae releases in America, as outlined in the *Jamaica Observer* newspaper story "Sean Paul Tops Chart Despite Weak Sales", which reports that the number one *Billboard* reggae record sold a mere 2,160 copies. *Jamaica Observer*, 1 March 2014, http://www.jamaicaobserver.com/entertainment/Sean-Paul-tops-chart-despite-weak-sales_16166543.
33. Monica Herrera, "The Happiness Project", *Billboard*, 16 October 2010, 19–21.
34. Andrew Hampp, "Unstoppable", *Billboard*, 24 November 2012, 14–17. In this article, Island Def Jam's A&R (artists and repertoire) representative Abou Thiam comments on the then imminent release of *Unapologetic*. He asserts that "she's the type of artist that makes everybody go outside their comfort zone – she's not trying to do a song that's already been done." This viewpoint represents the polar opposite of this chapter's premises regarding the artist's commercial identity.
35. Herrera, "Happiness Project", 20.
36. Giles Fitzgerald, "Rihanna Signs Up as Barbados Tourism Ambassador", *Music Week* online, 17 June 2011, http://www.musicweek.com/news/read/rihanna-signs-up-as-barbados-tourism-ambassador/045975.
37. Kory Grow, "Rihanna Loses Nivea Deal After Year-Long Sexiness Campaign", *Spin* online, 8 August 2012, http://www.spin.com/articles/rihanna-loses-nivea

-deal-after-year-long-sexiness-campaign/; Laura Stampler, "Nivea Axed Rihanna for Being Too Sexy", *Business Insider* online, 9 August 2012, http://www.businessinsider.com/controversial-celebrity-endorsements-2012-8.

38. Hampp, "Unstoppable", 16; Sarah Maloy, "Rihanna Announces 'Unapologetic' Album, Debuts Cover Art: Photo", *Billboard* online, 11 October 2012, http://www.billboard.com/articles/news/474702/rihanna-announces-unapologetic-album-debuts-cover-art-photo.

39. Richard James Burgess, *The Art of Music Production: The Theory and Practice*, 4th ed. (New York: Oxford University Press, 2013), 187. Burgess carefully separates the executive producer role from that of album producer. The executive producer is described as "usually someone in a position of power who has some responsibility for the project". They may be involved in "creating the concept for the project, financing or sourcing the funds", and their "day-to-day involvement ranges from nonexistent to active monitoring of the project". He further notes that the executive producer category is "not Grammy-eligible", further underscoring its distinction from the more actively vital role of the album producer.

40. "Potential Record Deal", *Daily Nation* (Barbados), 22 September 2011, http://www.nationnews.com/nationnews/news/1957/potential-record-deal.

41. By early 2014, Shontelle was no longer listed among the client artists of Syndicated Rhythm Productions on the company's website. In 2013, she was a guest on the single "Critical Condition", independently released by fellow Bajan artist Hal Linton, taken from his *Technicolour* album.

42. Seabrook, "Song Machine". The description of Stargate's roles demonstrates a variance in the modern pop market from the more broadly encompassing production responsibilities formerly associated with the position: "The producers compose the chord progressions, program the beats, and arrange the 'synths', or computer-made instrumental sounds." In this scenario, melodic, lyrical and vocal supervision is abdicated to other specialist parties, often resulting in incredibly long credit lists and a potential lack of clarity in determining whose roles were more crucial to the respective creative success or failure of a given song.

43. Ricky Jordan, "Rihanna Does It All in 2011", *Daily Nation* (Barbados), 1 January 2012, http://www.nationnews.com/nationnews/news/19954/rihanna-2011.

44. The band members were all credited as co-writers on the chart-topping "Twilight" single. Also, in the interest of full disclosure, this author performed keyboards on an eventually unreleased 2012 soca remix of the later single "Explode". The remix was produced in Barbados by guitarist Ian Alleyne (no relation), who has previously recorded with Des'ree, the hit singer of Bajan descent, and it also included keyboard bass from premier musician/producer Nicholas Brancker, who is mentioned earlier in this chapter. Both Brancker and Ian Alleyne are former members of Eddy Grant's live support band.

4

"WHAT'S MY NAME?"

Reading Rihanna's Autobiographical Acts

ESTHER L. JONES

A **little over** three years after the infamous pre-Grammy domestic violence incident of 8 February 2009, Rihanna and Chris Brown revealed their collaboration on two songs, one for each of their respective latest albums, igniting speculation as to whether this professional collaboration also signalled their romantic reunion. In light of Brown's subsequent behaviour, which revealed an apparent refusal to deal with his anger issues,[1] critics' and fans' reactions ranged from shock to approbation, with the bulk of the condemnation directed towards Rihanna as the victim who should know better than to return to an abuser exhibiting no effort to change. Open letters to both performers were penned by pop-culture analysts; fellow celebrities like hip-hop mogul Jay-Z and actress Reese Witherspoon variously expressed their disappointment, touting the responsibility of Rihanna, in particular, to young female fans who may follow her example. There were just as many fans, however, who resisted the very idea that celebrities' lives should be open to critique, defaulting to a position of "Live and let live; it's no one else's business what choices they make."

But beyond whether Rihanna's decision to reunite with Brown is a public or private matter (which is a false binary to begin with; if we can borrow anything useful from second-wave feminism, it is the notion that the personal/private is political and therefore public) lie the following questions: Who has the authority to tell Rihanna's story, and what tools are available to the public in interpreting that story? While the answer to the former question may seem obvious – that Rihanna's story is, quite naturally, hers to tell – it is far from apparent that the nature of her story, or any life story for that matter, is produced and exists in isolation from the communities within which it emerges. Further, the latter concern over how to interpret that narrative seems to lie at the centre of public debate. The viewing public cannot help but attempt to make sense of the actions and behaviours of those who operate in the public eye; indeed, the animus of celebrity virtually demands of popular icons their availability for mass consumption by a simultaneously adoring and derisive public.[2] However, these acts of interpretation as a meaning-making process function as a collective and communal production and suggest an investment in a corollary and equally communal process that contributes to the creation of competing narratives of who Rihanna is and what her choices and behaviours ultimately mean.

In this chapter, I argue that Rihanna's discography and public performances can be read as a form of life-writing – self-narration through a set of autobiographical acts that bring the artist/author and audience/reader into mutual creation and interpretation of the former's artistic identity. Of import to note is the highly collaborative nature of image and identity production, particularly in the music industry. Like those of all public figures, performers' identities are carefully considered productions in which a multitude of factors and behind-the-scenes actors play a part. The host of branding and marketing agents, songwriters, publicists and the like all play a role in the creation of the iconic image that is Rihanna. Many of her songs are co-written with a number of other writers, or written by others altogether. But in the end, it is she who makes the ultimate decisions as to how and in what manner she will present her image to the world. I explore Rihanna's efforts to establish narrative authority over her public persona throughout her celebrity career and the role that audience reception has played in shaping and applying meaning to that process. This narrative control reveals an increasingly personalized depiction of a girl/woman who is simultaneously ordinary and exceptional, intimate and distant, known and inaccessible. Further, Rihanna's celebrity persona walks a delicate line between the perceptions of distinctly public and private selves, a line that was disrupted with the eruption of the abuse event of February 2009. Unlike other female celebrities, such as Tina Turner and Halle Berry, who have also experienced intimate partner violence, Rihanna had no control over when or how to share her experience of domestic abuse. The event was immediately public, rendered a shared event as details unfolded in close to real-time occurrence. As such, the event and its fallout have presented as an ongoing public therapy of sorts, wherein Rihanna's response and the public's responses work together to define and redefine multiple meanings of who Rihanna is and what her behaviours mean in relation to explicit and implicit messages in contemporary culture about violence against women.

NARRATING THE CELEBRITY LIFE

Contemporary critics in the field of life-writing have begun to recognize the widely varying means by which self-narration occurs. Moving beyond the historical definition of autobiography as self-life-writing that privileges primarily written methods of self-reflection, Sidonie Smith and Julia Watson explain that "there are practices of [constructing the self] and framing its [life] that are particular to texts that perform self-reference, be they written, imaged, spoken, and/or figured".[3] They go on to suggest that "emergent theorizing of the autobiographical at interdisciplinary boundaries suggests new ways to engage the canon of autobiography and the larger field of life narrative, including other media of self-representation".[4]

Certainly, thinking about contemporary popular-music performance as a form of self-narration moves us beyond the purely written word of the lyrics to include image (based on album cover art) and the oral/aural (through music videos and stage performances as audiovisual texts). Such strategies reflect a kind of performativity inherent to self-construction that layers the self-narration process with additional, complex meanings.

Considering contemporary popular-music performance by celebrities as being within the frame of autobiographical genre theory enables us to think critically about notions of performativity and dialogism within acts of self-narration. The production of both celebrity and autobiography are "form[s] of self-invention that constitute the self".[5] This performative view of life narrative resists the notion of identities as fixed attributes of subjects. Rather, they are "produced and reiterated through cultural norms, and thus remain provisional and unstable".[6] Therefore, the idea of an "authentic" or "real, true" self that is revealed in autobiography becomes a matter of debate.

Within our understanding of popular performers, this element of the performative – the unstable, not quite "real" representation of a public persona – is widely and readily understood at the same time that moguls of the music industry make certain rhetorical moves that routinely invoke the discourse of authenticity and "realness" in order to market performers. This notion of the "real" is especially central to hip-hop music and culture.[7] And often, the degree of a popular performer's success depends upon the extent to which audiences come to accept the authenticity of that performer's self-narration and representation through his or her music and concomitant performances.[8]

This acceptance or rejection by the audience of a celebrity persona's self-narration based on its perceived "realness" reveals the dialogic nature of self-construction. While traditionally it has been assumed that the author who narrates the self has the ultimate authority and control over this story, contemporary critics of life-writing suggest that there are multiple potential voices beyond the narrator that help to shape the telling of a life story. In other words, self-narration is not a monologic utterance of a solitary, introspective individual; it is created in dialogue with a community of others who mutually frame and constitute the story being told.[9]

In the case of celebrities and popular performers, the audience becomes a co-contributor to the performer's construction and interpretation of the self, rendering the concept of narrative authority as an entirely solitary process untenable. The process of narrating the celebrity self is a communal one, in which the celebrity's audience actively participates.

Further complicating this issue of narrative authority as a communal process is what Steven Connor describes as "the machine of disgrace", ritualized acts of defilement against celebrities that reveal the public's ambivalent adoration: "To be a celebrity is to stand in present need of celebration. Because the celebrity is in need of celebration, the celebrity makes an implicit claim upon us", exercising a power by consent of the adoring, which the public simultaneously assents to and resents.[10] Admiration and degradation become inseparable in the communal production of celebrity,[11] and in actuality these seem to create one of the key conditions in attaining celebrity, the implied requirement of full access to matters both public and private, laudatory and shameful, in the celebrity's life:

> It is important that celebrities not only be disgraced and derided but also that they continue to exist visibly in their humiliated condition: like a hanged man, the celebrity must be brought low on high. It is for this reason that celebrities do not cease to be celebrities after they have been defiled: indeed, one might say that they only really become celebrities once they have reached this point, and not just because they have been inoculated or hardened to their condition. It is the destiny and function for the celebrity to be exposed to scandal and absurdity and to bear its mark forever.[12]

The idea that celebrities belong as much to the public as they do to themselves – especially in their low periods of public scandal – fuels not only the public's ambivalence towards the artist but also the artist's ambivalence in relation to her public. To what extent should an artist allow her ostensibly private choices to be dictated, if not mediated, by a continuously engaged public? Does the struggle for narrative control and authority necessitate a reassertion of the primacy of individualistic rights to privacy? In what ways does the communal nature of identity construction and meaning-making undo the impulse to ridicule, censure, upbraid, defend or protect choices that are implicitly considered a shared, communal experience?

As with the writers of early slave narratives, Rihanna's autobiographical positioning has her simultaneously representing her singular experiences and the communal collective accounts that constitute her narrative. One of the unforeseen effects of Rihanna's abuse incident, for example, was the almost immediate rise in the reporting of intimate partner violence by her primary target demographic, young women between the ages of seventeen and twenty-three. This suggests the sense of identification with Rihanna that young female fans experience as a result of her position both as a singular, exceptional star and as just another ordinary girl. Rihanna's public experience of this situation had the effect of shifting the sense of intimate partner violence as an isolated experience for which the victim shoulders the burden of blame, guilt, and shame privately and alone, to a set of circumstances that requires a community of support to overcome.[13] In the experience of the abuse incident and the interpretation of its meanings, the community – inclusive of the responding authorities for the 911 call, the court of law to which the case was remanded, and all interested parties who followed and weighed in on the incident, fans and detractors alike – worked in concert with Rihanna's own efforts at self-refashioning to engage the complexities and ambivalence of making meaning surrounding domestic violence and victimhood.

This process of life narration reveals the production of Rihanna's identity, both as a young woman coming of age and as a celebrity and pop icon, as continuously in formation. In the sections that follow, I read Rihanna's discography and related public performances, interviews and other modes of expression as a narrative that tells the story of her trajectory into superstardom, mapping the fashioning of her identity in the early stages of her career, followed by her rise to superstardom and international pop-icon status; the moments of "defilement" that serve to solidify this status; and the process by which the public colludes in the ongoing reconstructions of Rihanna's identity and the meaning of certain significant events in her life narrative.

It is important to look at Rihanna's coming of age as an artist in order to engage her identity – that of the top-selling Caribbean international performing artist of all time – beyond her experience of domestic violence. Many have noted the tendency to read (black) celebrities primarily in the context of their misfortunes, and to continuously frame subsequent behaviours solely within that context. I want to emphasize that the scope of this analysis is designed to provide a more expansive vision of the development of the artist that does not limit Rihanna's personal and professional identity to "the Chris Brown incident". Rather, I seek to place her in context of an identity continuously undergoing transformation in order to move beyond the victim status, centring her representational force around her full body of work as a young woman coming of age in the celebrity spotlight.

As theorists of life narrative attest, identities are complex and messy; they rarely conform to a congruent, totally coherent and consistent whole. In autobiographical theory, the elements of authority, authenticity, voice, embodiment, agency, relationality and identity converge to produce an understanding of the complex processes by which acts of self-narration occur. Of these elements that create the autobiographical subject Rihanna, I focus most explicitly on issues of embodiment, authority, authenticity, relationality and agency. It is through the depictions of Rihanna's body that struggles for authority are negotiated and questions of authenticity articulated. Control over the representational force of the body is the battleground upon which issues of relationality are worked out and agency claimed.

"WHAT'S MY NAME?" ESTABLISHING AUTHORITY, ENACTING AUTHENTICITY

Rihanna's discography can be read as a life narrative, a story mapping her journey from her youthful Barbadian origins to her iconic pop-superstar status on a global stage. As a Caribbean woman and artist, one of the most powerful tools available to her is the degree to which she can exercise authorial power over the writing of her own life narrative through her art. Her debut album, *Music of the Sun* (2005), features a young Rihanna paying homage to her Caribbean roots through prominent reggae and dancehall rhythms with a crossover pop and hip-hop edge.

The album's title, while seemingly lacking an individualized self-referentiality, nonetheless places the seventeen-year-old Rihanna as representing not only herself but also an entire culture and heritage. Heather Russell maintains the significance of this representative act for Rihanna's home nation of Barbados, suggesting that Rihanna, as the nation's first international superstar and the Caribbean region's top-selling artist of all time (even surpassing Bob Marley), belongs both to her home nation and to the global community that has embraced her celebrity.[14] This narrative of belongingness generates complex issues surrounding the interplay of personal identity and cultural belonging, which represent ostensibly competing interests. At once claiming Rihanna as its own, the Barbadian nation-state traded upon her popularity as a specifically Bajan commodity[15] to simultaneously market another of its biggest commodities, the tourism industry. Shortly after the release of *Music of the Sun*, Rihanna was featured in tourism advertisements for Barbados, singing the light-hearted single "If It's Lovin' That You Want" as she frolics on the beaches of her native country, inviting her global consumers to come "share her world".

The girlish iconography from the album cover for *Music of the Sun* consists of a headshot of Rihanna with Barbie-pink glossed lips; pink-blushed cheeks; long, loosely waved, natural brown locks neatly arranged to reveal a sun-kissed face; and a gold-sequined blouse that covers her shoulders. The lighting is bright, vibrant and tropical, with sparkling tones of gold, pink and brown.

This demure styling strategy continues in the tourism commercial, where the suggestion of flesh, necessary for enjoying Barbados's beaches, is balanced with a variety of methods for covering up alternating body parts in alignment with an image of innocent propriety; Rihanna thus simultaneously exudes the fun and sensuality to be had on her native island. In the opening shot, a bared back and the suggestion of cleavage are balanced by the length of the white sundress that fully covers her legs; subsequent scenes show long legs extending from beneath a loose tunic that covers most of the derrière and midriff but allows a peek of cleavage. In the final look, a long serape completely covers her legs to balance the exposed upper body of the bikini top. Tastefully sexy and moderately suggestive as Rihanna sings the hook, "If it's lovin' that you want, then come and take a walk with me", the commercial concludes with the invitation, "Barbados: Experience the authentic Caribbean".

This linkage of Rihanna's authenticity as a true Bajan native with the idea of Barbados as representative of that which is most authentically Caribbean solidifies her narrative authority and identity as at once singular and individualized vis-à-vis her pop-star status. However, it also invokes the communal, national identity that she represents in a manner that is both gendered and sexualized. Interestingly, this trading upon Rihanna's sexuality, while simultaneously attempting to contain that sexuality beneath a youthful veneer of innocence, ironically enters into the discourse of an ostensibly less desirable commodity that the Caribbean region struggles to contain as well: the sex tourism industry.

It would seem that the nation-state, in its use of Rihanna as a commodity that "sells" the nation for global consumption, wants to have it both ways: it wants to sell her sexuality at the same time that it tries to control that sexuality by marketing respectability, creating a seemingly paradoxical vision of virginal sexuality. This delicate balancing act requires, however, that Rihanna forever maintain the public image of the "pretty little Bajan girl" whose sexuality can be safely contained and managed in service to the state. In other words, Rihanna's identity – her position as a subject, as reinforced by her first album and the Barbados tourism commercial – speaks for not only the artist as an individual, but also for an entire nation, one which she represents on the national stage. Her identity is constructed in a social and cultural context that claims an equal, if not excessive, role in the production of her identity as Barbados's "pretty little Bajan island girl" whose "sweetness and innocence go a long way" to keep Barbados on top of the world.[16]

In spite of these initial representational claims placed upon her by the nation, Rihanna's next two albums, *A Girl Like Me* (2006) and *Good Girl Gone Bad* (2007), progress to a more self-referential titling, suggesting a more personal, revelatory tone. While the cover art for *A Girl Like Me* reasserts the girlish imagery of *Music of the Sun*, a slightly matured look is revealed. The shading of the image creates a more muted look, and Rihanna wears a deeper shade of pink lipstick; sports long, lightly tousled, highlighted brown locks that fall playfully into her face; and reveals more flesh, as a white lace strap and delicate pearl necklace slip from bared shoulders. Thematically, the album's song selections invoke an intimate look into the singer's life that simultaneously invites identification with her target demographic, girls and young women aged seventeen to twenty-three.

In a 2006 interview for MTV News, Rihanna specifically expressed the intimacy of the album both as an expression of her individual experiences and as a way to connect with her audience: "It's called *A Girl Like Me* because it's a very personal album; it's my baby. It's all about what it's like to be a girl like me, speaking of personal experiences as well as things that girls like me have gone through."[17] The interpersonal, communal construction of identity shifts from the representation of the racialized and sexualized nation-state to a specifically gendered, youthful – but still communal – identity that invokes the criteria of both individual and shared experience to authenticate the construction of her "girl" persona.

As previously mentioned, *Good Girl Gone Bad* continues the strategy of more explicit self-referentiality; however, unlike *A Girl Like Me*, this album simultaneously signals an attempted break from the communal representational claims that Rihanna offers her audiences in the girlhood status of her first two albums. The demure, colourful headshots of those previous album covers are replaced by a more explicitly dark and womanly depiction.

On *Good Girl Gone Bad*, a full-body side portrait of the singer in black and white shows off womanly curves sheathed in a glove of a white dress. Her hair has been dyed stark black and cut into a shorter, severely blunt bob that echoes the angularity of her body posture as she leans backwards in a near-impossible forty-five-degree angle. On the cover of album two, the playful, seemingly accidental lock of hair that falls into her face still allows the audience to see those figurative windows of the soul. On this third album cover, however, her hair is deliberately styled to cover half her face, including one eye, suggesting the beginnings of an intentional assertion of privacy.

The embracing of girlhood in the first two albums assumes an openness and availability, full access to a life presumably uncomplicated by adult concerns and experiences. The imagery of *Good Girl Gone Bad* symbolizes an emergence into womanhood, in which a denial of full access to the self invokes the privileges of adulthood. Yet while a clearly more mature, independent, self-actualized and sexy image emerges, the containment of sexuality and the operation of the sexualized/innocent binary continue as a representational strain. Rihanna's dress, with its white colour, offers echoes of the Victorian virginal purity of white lace and pearls in the cover for *A Girl Like Me*, while simultaneously challenging that purity through its skintight fit. Moreover, this tight fit conceals flesh as it simultaneously reveals the shape of the body underneath, calling attention to it, with the arms positioned in protective cross-body posture and the hands decorously enfolded in front.

Lyrically, the songs for *Good Girl Gone Bad* evoke a new, independent attitude that reflects the artist's emergent adulthood. While it is generally known that Rihanna is not the sole writer of her lyrics, nor does she write a good number of her songs – songwriter Ester Dean is one of the main creative forces behind many of her top-selling tracks[18] – Rihanna plays a critical role in the communal process of determining the overall creative direction of her image and branding. All aspects of image production – from hair and clothing design to song selection, lyrical content and titling, and album cover art design – are part and parcel of the collective construction of the iconic identity for which Rihanna ultimately claims responsibility. Upon the album's release, she shared with *Entertainment Weekly* precisely this effort to reflect her maturation as an artist and as a woman:

> *Good Girl Gone Bad* was an expression of where I am at this point in my life, where I am in my career. It just represents my rebelliousness. I got really rebellious because I was being forced into a particular innocent image and I just had to break away from that. . . . I think every teenager just has a point in their life

when they just get rebellious. They go into their own world, they shut everybody's opinion out, and they don't care. That's when they stick to what they want and that's what I'm doing right now.[19]

In reference to the album's titling, she expressed to MTV News a similar concern with assertion of individuality and independence as well as with control over her sound, look and identity: "*Good Girl Gone Bad* was the perfect title because it showed people I'm my own [person] now. Not doing what anyone wants me to do. I'm not the innocent Rihanna anymore. I'm taking a lot more risks and chances. I felt when I cut my hair, it shows people I'm not trying to look [like] or be anybody else."[20]

Revealing a personal maturation paralleled by the act of "coming into her own" as an artist, *Good Girl Gone Bad* was Rihanna's most successful commercial album up to that point, according to music critics and sales numbers, going double platinum in the United States and five times platinum in the United Kingdom and Canada. With a series of chart-topping singles titled in the imperative mode, such as "Shut Up and Drive", "Don't Stop the Music" and "Take a Bow", Rihanna depicted herself as a woman taking command of her life – and likely other people's lives. For her world tour, she adopted a leather-and-lace aesthetic in a BDSM styling (bondage/discipline, domination/submission, sadism/masochism) that blurred the boundaries of sexual pleasure and pain, softness and hardness, femininity and masculinity, madonna and whore. This emergent womanhood celebrated the complexities of the dualities with which young women, particularly, are faced in the creation of fully actualized identities.

This declaration of independence, however, was met with attempts by some among her audiences to reassert claims not only over her identity as artist and woman but over the very structure of the narration of her life as well. As Rihanna's popular acclaim escalated over the course of her first three albums, her native country of Barbados, in particular, continued to lay claim to the image and personality that would best serve their needs, as exhibited by the naming of Rihanna as "honorary youth and cultural ambassador" by Barbados's then newly elected prime minister, the Honourable David Thompson, in 2008. However, the bestowal of this honour emerged amidst a hotbed of controversy over comments Rihanna had made in her 2007 *Entertainment Weekly* interview with Margeaux Watson, wherein she revealed her frustration with the burden of representing the nation, particularly as it related to her visits home.²¹

The Bajan public's ambivalent reception reflects the process of adoration and defilement that Connor suggests instantiates the condition of celebrity: Rihanna owes an image and ideal to her Bajan public that aligns with their desire for her to remain their pretty little (innocent, desexualized) Bajan girl. However, Rihanna's emerging frustration with the public's claims upon her representational authority became clear when Watson asked her what her return visits home had been like: "[People in Barbados] always have something to say about what I'm wearing, what I'm not wearing, like in the 'Umbrella' video. If I wear a swimsuit to the beach, it's a problem, they put it on the front of the newspaper and call in to programs."²² However, while her resistant commentary in the interview constitutes the proverbial prodigal native daughter casting off her audience's narratives of control over her behaviour, she also asserts certain expectations from her audience as well. In return for "putting Barbados on the map", she expects the freedom to be her own woman:

> It really annoys me when people that I try to represent and I try to put them on the map as much as I can – you know, I didn't have to put tridents in my videos . . . which is the symbol of the flag. I didn't have to talk about them. I didn't have to even mention that I'm from Barbados. But I do and people kind of take it for granted. They hate me. They talk s—— about me all the time. But I'm like, "Whatever. I'm still doing this 'cause I love to do it and you're not going to stop me."²³

Certainly, the combined factors of mounting international stardom, nation-based representational fatigue, and the exigencies of asserting adulthood that are typical among young adults in their late teens converged to mark Rihanna's transition from girl to woman. Such synergies suggestively produce the desire to author oneself authentically: "This [album] is all me. It's something that I just feel like doing. And what you get is exactly me."²⁴ The traces of girlishness found on the album cover for *Good Girl Gone Bad* highlight her evolution from state-sanctioned pretty little Bajan girl to burgeoning independent woman, a process that would be rudely interrupted by the events that transpired in February 2009.

GIRL, INTERRUPTED: RELATIONALITY, CELEBRITY DEFILEMENT AND AUDIENCE BACKLASH

Rihanna's self-narration through her artistry, up to this point, could be described as remarkably effective in its demonstration of an almost naturalized progression and growth towards maturity, from girl to woman, both personally and artistically. However, autobiographical theory complicates the notion of a completely autonomous, individuated identity by emphasizing the processes by which one constructs the self through situations and conditions that actively influence the shaping of identity. These conditions acknowledge and engage the culturally and historically specific situations in which that sense of identity is created and the communal aspects that compel the individual to narrate herself.[25]

The battle for control over identity articulated in the previous section positions the nation-state of Barbados and its citizens as one of the "coaxers" or "coercers"[26] who compelled Rihanna to narrate her identity in a particular way at the beginning of her career, whether in compliance with an accepted set of images, like the innocent girlishness of her first two albums, or as an act of resistance and assertion of independence, as in her subsequent releases. This section turns to yet another pivotal situation and set of actors that constitute a major coercive site that prompted Rihanna's reassertion of narrative authority and control: the February 2009 domestic violence incident with then boyfriend Chris Brown and the whirl of media response thereafter.

While the relatively smooth maturation process of growth and increasing authorial control delineated in Rihanna's first three albums allowed her the space to express an evolving identity at her own pace and on her own terms, this narrative control was violently disrupted in the Chris Brown abuse event of 8 February 2009. The incident, occurring just prior to Rihanna's twenty-first birthday on 20 February and just before the start of production on her fourth studio album, *Rated R*, situated Rihanna in a highly personal yet public violation not only against her body and spirit, as is the case for any domestic violence victim, but against her public image, which was immediately called into question.

In spite of previous interviews wherein Rihanna had positioned her music as increasingly personal and more fully representative of who she truly was with the *Good Girl Gone Bad* album,[27] the public's reaction to the domestic violence incident revealed the extent to which they presumed the deliberate (read: false) construction of celebrity identity. In addition to the many racial and gendered historical and cultural factors that informed how the public understood Rihanna's position as victim and culprit in this event[28] was the public's prevailing assumption that celebrities exist as products of the media industry's creation. This assumption not only cast Rihanna as responsible for the abuse event; it also set her up for the process of defilement and ridicule that Connor describes as "the disgrace machine".[29]

In the early transmission of the details surrounding the nature of Brown's attack, online discussions lit up with various speculations, none of which proved to be true: Was it all just a publicity stunt? If not, what had Rihanna done to provoke Brown? Did she hit him first? Did she cheat on him with Jay-Z? Had she given Brown a communicable disease? While many fans reacted to her experience with sympathy, many more focused on grinding the humiliation axe to a fine, sharp point; in the ensuing months, unauthorized photos of a battered Rihanna were leaked to celebrity gossip engine TMZ, and rumours of sex tapes swirled. Certainly, many members of the media and viewing public used the occasion to amplify the complexly layered attributes of Rihanna's emergent "bad-girl" persona well beyond what was suggested by the lyrical content and visual framing of her emancipatory album *Good Girl Gone Bad*.

Rihanna's silence in the media in the months pursuant to Brown's assault coincided with the development of her next album, *Rated R*, which she started producing in March 2009, suggesting that she would work through and respond to the assault through her art form. And she did. Possibly anticipating that anything produced after the Brown incident would be perceived as speaking to the abuse, Rihanna, in concert with her cadre of industry advisers, appears to have opted to confront the meaning and significance of that event in the shaping of her identity through, yet again, her song selections and album cover art. And true to expectation, Rihanna's subsequent actions and musical releases have been analysed as being in direct dialogue with the event.

The title of 2009's *Rated R* references the release of the album in the year of Rihanna's twenty-first birthday, a significant milestone that signals the full age of legality in the United States. It is also suggestive of the "adult" content of the songs and the cover art for some of the album's singles, which marked a much harder, more risqué image, with more overt hypersexuality than had been depicted to date. The cover art for *Rated R*, once again shot in black and white, offers up an even more dramatic intensity when compared with the softened greyscale image for *Good Girl Gone Bad*, creating an almost film noir effect with its stark lighting contrast.

The headshot on the cover of *Rated R* features Rihanna with a drastically shorter haircut, with shaved sides and a punked-out blonde bang that sweeps away from her face, as her right hand, covered in rings reminiscent of brass knuckles, covers her right eye, an indirect reference to a desire to hide the black eye suffered at the hands of Brown. Hard, sharp angles, from the metallic, sword-like *R* emblem in the corner of the image to the stiff, erect placement of her arm and fingers, characterize the subject of the photo as simultaneously aggressive and vulnerable. Dark lipstick and a heavily rimmed left eye that nonetheless makes direct contact with the audience intimate the darker, more intense tone and content of the album, while the black leather shirt that completely covers the singer all the way to her neck further suggests an imagery of both concealment and confrontation.

However, in spite of the hard, edgy, protective imagery of the main album cover, the liberated yet controlled sexiness of adulthood that emerged in *Good Girl Gone Bad* blazons into a smouldering, danger-tinged hypersexuality in the cover art for four of the six singles to drop from *Rated R*. The images for "Wait Your Turn", "Russian Roulette", "Hard" and "Rude Boy" all reveal Rihanna in various degrees of undress, from topless ("Wait Your Turn") to near-complete nudity ("Rude Boy"), suggesting a refusal to relinquish the woman's right to articulate a sexualized identity in spite of others' efforts to suppress or contain it.

The cover art for the single "Russian Roulette" and Rihanna's collaboration on rapper Eminem's "Love the Way You Lie" in 2010, however, generated the most controversy, as they came to be read as responses to the Brown abuse incident. The "Russian Roulette" cover art, which features the singer wearing BDSM-style clothing and a holed patch over her right eye (again gesturing towards the blackened eye given her by Brown), and the lyrics of the chorus for "Love the Way You Lie", which ironically plays upon the popular but often unstated perception that somehow victims gain some sort of pleasure from abuse, confused much of the viewing public. As previously discussed, BDSM is generally perceived as a set of sexual practices that blur the pain/pleasure threshold; the visual reference to it on "Russian Roulette" complicates the lyrical hook of "Love the Way You Lie", which references the burning and abuse of a domestic violence victim while the victim seemingly – ironically, perhaps – accepts and even "loves" the emotional and physical pain inflicted by her abuser. The emotional complexity and ambivalence of these lyrics come into greater clarity when read in the larger context of Rihanna's full body of work, and particularly as part of a coming of age narrative.

The irresolute treatment of pain as pleasure and pleasure as pain, through the "Russian Roulette" cover imagery and the ambivalent lyrics of the song coupled with the chorus for the Eminem collaboration, set the tone for subsequent alarmed critiques following the release of the "S&M" and "Man Down" singles from the *Loud* album (2010). This time, however, the lyrics for "S&M" – which, read alone, are clearly highly suggestive of the raunchy, illicit sex play of sadomasochism – are translated into a metaphorical turnabout on the media and on the critics who censured Rihanna's previous, seemingly ambiguous positions on domestic violence with "Russian Roulette" and "Love the Way You Lie".[30]

Offering her own critique of those members of the media and the public whom she frames as metaphorical sadists interested primarily in continuing to mire her within the "machine of disgrace", Rihanna asserts her artistic right to explore the tensions and ambiguities surrounding what constitutes a "proper response" to domestic abuse. Thus, "Man Down", heavily criticized by anti-violence groups for its depiction of murder in retaliation for rape (but applauded by some as, finally, an emphatic position that violence against women is unequivocally wrong),[31] appears to, for now, signal the final of many possible positions that a girl (or woman) like Rihanna might take as she finds herself struggling to make sense of the complex emotions of having been abused by a loved one.

On the cover art for *Loud*, the imagery returns to the full-faced beauty shot, emphasizing the use of red – a woman's colour, in contrast to the girlish pink of albums one and two and the stark absence of colour in the black-and-white photos for albums three and four. The softness from the first two albums returns with an added vulnerability that bespeaks a maturity born of having come through. Wafted red waves frame the singer's face; bright red lips seem to part slightly in a weary sigh as her face turns into the curve of a bare, raised shoulder. Notably, her eyes remain closed for the first time on any of her album covers, as if to gently foreclose access to the artist's soul. Connor's "machine of disgrace" seems to have performed its painful function of instantiating celebrity status as she embraces the ultimate autobiographical act of self-naming in the permanence of the tattoo on her neck, which reads, "*rebelle fleur*", or rebel flower.

The "Rihanna" of the first three albums, having undergone a disruption and transformation in the Brown abuse event, emerges as simply an abbreviated *R* on the *Rated R* album, signifying a possible loss but also the dual representation of the public and private selves: the Robyn of the police report filing and the Rihanna of the public image.[32] The *rebelle fleur* tattoo is the only signature on the *Loud* album, suggesting the selection of a name and identity of the artist's own choosing to mark a commitment to literally narrate her identity, career and life through her body, on her own terms.

TALKING THAT TALK TO A GIRL LIKE ME: AGENCY, AUDIENCE RELATIONALITY AND THE CHRIS BROWN REUNION

If one assumes that identity is solely created and controlled by the isolate self, one might read some of Rihanna's artistic representational acts in terms of song selection, cover art design and video production as a deliberate disavowal of popular opinion. Rihanna asserts an independent, complex identity that takes the shape of a narrative that explores the multiple iterations of an identity constantly undergoing transformation – particularly in the face of competing interlocutors for narratives that demand a singular, stagnant depiction, whether it be that of innocent girl, victim, sinner or independent rebel – regardless of whether it is comfortable, generally appealing or neatly conforming to certain of her audience's expectations. But this is not to say that the woman who Rihanna has become has not been shaped by those audience demands that she has resisted. The controversies surrounding Rihanna's artistic expressions and self-representations reveal that the process of identity formation is intercalated by audience demands and the Brown abuse episode, which act as coaxers providing the counterpoint against which the artist defines herself as the *rebelle fleur*.

Talk That Talk (2011) reveals a synthesis of all the albums (and identities in formation) that have come before. The full headshot and bright lighting, along with a return to brown highlighted hair, echo albums one and two. The militant camouflage top and skullcap reflect the dark edginess of album three, and the chunky finger jewellery and stark eye makeup return from album four. Finally, the parted red lips and the concept of a "naming" tattoo echo stylistic strategies from album five, revised this time to name the album rather than the artist, signalling that the artist herself has been transformed into a living work of art. At this juncture, Rihanna has successfully claimed ownership over the construction of her identity; however, it remains to be seen if she will acknowledge and claim the responsibility that comes with the onus of full celebrity maturity.

So who gets to decide when and how to close the book on an incident that was painfully shared with and felt by so many? *Slate* writer J. Bryan Lowder, commenting on Rihanna and Chris Brown's collaboration on the song "Birthday Cake" in 2012, wherein the personas of former lovers fantasize about sharing carnal pleasures once more, provided the following provocative analysis, which brings together the complexities of celebrity identity production, individual agency and social responsibility:

> Even though we know that collaborations like this are almost always commercial in motivation, we like to imagine that the artist's choice of a creative partner gives us some kind of access to their private, emotional world. Collaboration suggests a personal relationship, and our eavesdropping on that interplay conjures up a feeling of intimacy between audience and artist that is very powerful. We feel like we know what's really going on with Rihanna and Chris Brown because we are virtually present in the studio with them, and here, the thing we're meant to know is that everything's OK now. The problem is, the strategy won't work; because of an infamous leaked photograph, we were also virtually present in the car that night three years ago when Brown beat Rihanna till her face was bruised and bloodied. And that kind of terrifying intimacy is not easily forgotten.[33]

In November 2009, just prior to the release of *Rated R*, Rihanna discussed the domestic violence incident in an interview with Diane Sawyer on *20/20*. For the many girls and women who began the process of ending their silent suffering by reporting their abuse in the days after that interview, it is doubtful as to whether the motivations of Rihanna and Brown's collaboration can truly be characterized as innocent, in spite of Rihanna's claims.[34] The many women who watched the 20/20 interview engaged with Rihanna's story of abuse as a teachable moment,[35] one that inspired silent victims to reach out to domestic violence hotlines and seek the help they needed and which Rihanna herself acknowledged as playing an important role in the lives of women and girls in similar situations: "I couldn't be held responsible for going back. . . . If Chris never hit me again, who is to say that their boyfriend won't? Who's to say that they won't kill these girls? . . . And these . . . are young girls. And I could not . . . I just didn't realize how much of an impact I had on these girls' lives until that happened."[36] In this acknowledgement of the shared community that not only helps to produce the celebrity's identity but also helps to make meaning of that life and the concomitant actions that bring the artist into an intimate and inexorable connection with her audience, Rihanna reached a peak moment of maturity that, like the cycles of abuse to which domestic violence victims are so often prey, ebbs and flows with the tide of time.

Rihanna did, in fact, reunite with Chris Brown for a brief period in 2013, shortly after the release of her seventh album, *Unapologetic* (2012), her most successful album to date. The album features a range of ballads, mid-tempo and pop-dance tracks, and collaborations with Eminem and Brown yet again. Its title suggests a connection between her personal life motto – that "there is only one truth, and you can't apologize for that. It's honest"[37] – and the music produced for the album as a reflection of that honesty: "I want [my music] to be real, authentic, raw."[38] Such invitations to elide the public and private boundaries of her life are reflected in the way music critics and audiences continue to read her artistic productions as representative of an increasingly authentic private self. "Nobody's Business", a collaboration with Brown, riffs on the Michael Jackson classic "The Way You Make Me Feel" to assert the singer's autonomy of choice when it comes to her private life, even while it invites viewers to witness these private experiences. Choices such as these reflect the messy, incongruous, complex, yet very real and necessary imperative of reconciling the personal impulses of individualized identity in relation to broader communal commitments.

Yet the personas that emerge in tracks such as "Phresh Out the Runway",

"Numb" and "Pour It Up", in their homage to high times and fast living, subsume the tortured love theme that characterizes the tracks that might typically draw associations with and speculations about her relationship with Brown. In fact, on this album, the most controversial track is not the collaboration with either Eminem or Chris Brown but the strip club anthem "Pour It Up". Widely discussed primarily for its highly sexualized, all-female video featuring Rihanna as both performer and consumer of exotic dance culture, the song has generated debates in some feminist camps as to the manner in which she subverts gender and sexuality codes for black women, especially, as sexual agents absent the male gaze.[39] Such bold artistic choices disrupt the ongoing narrative of the on-again, off-again, could-be romance with Brown, reducing it to but one of many aspects of her persona, a passing, passed-over and passé moment of her personal history that she has since transcended with vastly more interesting things said and done.

As such, the *Unapologetic* album cover art evokes a greater assertion of narrative authority and its role in identity formation than ever before. Similar to the body posture of the controversial cover art for the "Russian Roulette" single, which features a frontal, half-body shot of the singer's semi-nude figure, styled in a way that invokes her beating at the hands of Chris Brown – a holed patch over the right eye, double layers of constrictive wrappings in the form of a corset, leather wrappings designed to look like barbed wire, and blood-red lipstick – *Unapologetic* depicts a frontal, nude, half-body shot, but this time the woman is unabashed, unashamed and unvictimized. She has a short black pixie haircut that enables an unobstructed view of her face. Instead of painful layers of constrictive wrappings and chains binding her body, she is fully – freely – nude and adorned in an overlay of language. Symbolic images do not have the same resonances with the beating that those of "Russian Roulette" did; instead, we see a tattoo of the powerful ancient Egyptian goddess Isis in her spread-winged aspect inked onto Rihanna's ribcage just below the breasts. Words and phrases such as *fun, victory, fearless, faith* and *love* are superimposed over her body, marking a profound shift in the discursive and creative assertion of identity to depict the air of honesty consistent with Rihanna's professed efforts to remain true to herself. There is even a scratched-out "error" which has been overwritten on the right breast to suggest the air of fallacy, the acknowledgement of mistakes having been made and corrected

– rewritten. For Rihanna, this is a revision that acknowledges the self as an ongoing identity in progress, evolving, always aware of what has come before that contributes to who she is today, but never overburdened by a past that no longer serves nor overly determines who she is becoming.

As events, choices and decisions continue to unfold, the complexities of human behaviour continue to reveal as much about Rihanna's autobiographical acts, her narrative authority and her control over her life as they do about her audience's investment in them. As such, these acts signal no definite conclusions; rather, they allow us all the opportunity to reflect upon the transient moments in this process of becoming that constitutes the life of the *rebelle fleur*.

NOTES

1. Brown stole and smashed a fan's cellphone on one occasion and stormed out of a *Good Morning America* interview with anchor Robin Roberts, leaving a trashed studio dressing room in his wake, because she inquired about the domestic violence incident. Mikaela Conley, "Chris Brown Throws Anger Progress to the Sidewalk", ABCNews.com, 23 March 2011, http://abcnews.go.com/Health/chris-brown-trashes-gma-dressing-room-throws-anger/story?id=13197090.
2. Steven Connor, "Defiling Celebrity", in *Modernist Star Maps: Celebrity, Modernity, Culture*, ed. Aaron Jaffe and Jonathan Goldman (Burlington, VT: Ashgate, 2010), 221–35.
3. Sidonie Smith and Julia Watson, *Reading Autobiography: A Guide for Interpreting Life Narratives* (Minneapolis: University of Minnesota Press, 2001), 137.
4. Ibid.
5. Ibid., 140; Nancy Armstrong, "Afterword", in Jaffe and Goldman, *Modernist Celebrity Maps*, 237.
6. Smith and Watson, *Reading Autobiography*, 143.
7. Jeffrey O.G. Ogbar, *Hip-Hop Revolution: The Culture and Politics of Rap* (Lawrence: University Press of Kansas, 2007).
8. Emilie Zaslow, *Feminism, Inc.: Coming of Age in Girl Power Media Culture* (New York: Palgrave, 2011).
9. Smith and Watson, *Reading Autobiography*, 146.
10. Connor, "Defiling Celebrity", 226.
11. Ibid., 229.
12. Ibid., 232.

13. Juju Chang, Michelle Major and Jennifer Pereira, "Rihanna Interview Inspires Domestic Violence Conversation", ABCNews.com, 9 November 2009, http://abcnews.go.com/GMA/Entertainment/rihanna-interview-women-react-dating-domestic-violence/story?id=9031571.
14. Heather D. Russell, "Whose Rihanna? Diasporic Citizenship and the Economies of Crossing Over", paper delivered at the annual Caribbean Studies Association Conference, St Peter, Barbados, 24–28 May 2010, available at http://casgroup.fiu.edu/pages/docs/3490/1307032072_Heather_R_Whose_Rihanna.pdf.
15. Ibid.
16. Ibid.
17. Gil Kaufman, "Rihanna Hooking Up with Ne-Yo When She's Done Crying 'S.O.S.'", MTVNews.com, 4 April 2006, http://www.mtv.com/news/articles/1527788/20060404/rihanna.jhtml.
18. John Seabrook, "The Song Machine: The Hitmakers behind Rihanna", *New Yorker* online, 26 March 2012, http://www.newyorker.com/magazine/2012/03/26/the-song-machine.
19. Margeaux Watson, "Caribbean Queen", *Entertainment Weekly* online, 22 June 2007, http://www.ew.com/ew/article/0,,20043298,00.html.
20. Shaheen Reid, "Rihanna Loses Good Girl Image, Thanks to Jay-Z, Justin, Timbaland, Ne-Yo", MTVNews.com, 1 May 2007, http://www.mtv.com/news/1558496/rihanna-loses-good-girl-image-thanks-to-jay-z-justin-timbaland-ne-yo/.
21. Watson, "Caribbean Queen".
22. Ibid.
23. Ibid.
24. Ibid.
25. Smith and Watson, *Reading Autobiography*, 49–50.
26. Ibid., 50.
27. Watson, "Caribbean Queen".
28. I explicitly engage, at length, the socio-historical matrix of black Caribbean women's political sexual histories in my article "On the Real: Agency, Abuse, and Sexualized Violence in Rihanna's 'Russian Roulette'", *African American Review* 46, no. 1 (Spring 2013): 71–86.
29. Connor, "Defiling Celebrity".
30. For a lengthier analysis on the possible multiple meanings and complexities surrounding the abuse incident, and on the usage of BDSM imagery in "Russian Roulette" as a response, see Jones, "On the Real".
31. See "Man Down: On Rihanna, Rape and Violence", *Crunk Feminist Collective*

32. (blog), 2 June 2011, http://crunkfeministcollective.wordpress.com/2011/06/02/man-down-on-rihanna-rape-and-violence/.
32. Rihanna is the middle and stage name of Robyn Rihanna Fenty. The police report of the abuse event used Rihanna's first name, which is one of the ways in which the public and private personas became elided and disrupted. See Jones, "On the Real", for a fuller discussion.
33. J. Bryan Lowder, "Why the Rihanna and Chris Brown Reunion Collaborations Won't Erase the Past", *Slate*, 23 February 2012, http://www.slate.com/blogs/xx_factor/2012/02/23/why_the_rihanna_and_chris_brown_reunion_collaborations_won_t_erase_the_past.html.
34. Ryan Seacrest, interview with Rihanna, *On Air with Ryan Seacrest*, KIIS FM, 15 March 2012.
35. Chang, Major and Pereira, "Rihanna Interview Inspires Conversation".
36. Ibid.
37. "Rihanna Explains 'Unapologetic' Album Title and Confirms New Fragrance 'Nude'", Capital FM online, 18 November 2012, http://www.capitalfm.com/artists/rihanna/news/unapologetic-album-title/.
38. Jay Bulger, "Rihanna: Obsession of the Year", *GQ* online, December 2012, http://www.gq.com/moty/2012/rihanna-cover-story-gq-men-of-the-year-2012?current.
39. See Evette Dion, "The Twerking Feminist", *Mic*, 25 October 2013, http://mic.com/articles/69657/the-twerking-feminist; Melissa Bradshaw, "All I See Is Controversy: Rihanna's 'Pour It Up'", *Red Bull Music Academy* online, 12 October 2013, http://www.redbullmusicacademy.com/magazine/all-i-see-is-controversy.

5

SHE DANCES ON THE HOLODECK

CURWEN BEST

Just after the release of her third album, *Good Girl Gone Bad*, in May 2007, Rihanna, responding to a set of questions concerning her fascination with movies and the roles she would like to play, revealed: "I've read a few scripts. I haven't gone for anything yet, but I'd really want to do an action movie. Like an *Aeon Flux* or *Matrix* or *Underworld*. I love those movies.... *300* is one of the best movies I have seen. The choreography, the fighting, the costumes, the production – phenomenal. I make everybody watch it."[1]

Rihanna's hunger to cross over into the dedicated arena of bodice-ripping blockbuster film was again brought up around the time of the release of her fourth studio album, *Rated R*, in November 2009, when she playfully declared, "I'm a bad girl and I like dangerous stuff."[2] In these and other interviews, she both teased and informed her fans, in the manner that megastars often do while responding to eager interviewers who want to get ahead of the game, predict the future, look beyond the visual/material sphere and into the event horizon.[3] Much earlier in her career, Rihanna's expression of fascination with daring characters and personas might not have sparked interest beyond the ordinary, but as her own persona has morphed over the years of her involvement in the entertainment industry, her comments about imagined film and stage roles invariably take on more significance.

This has to do with the fact that for artists like Rihanna, whose presence is sustained by and heavily reliant on acts of technology, it is increasingly challenging to differentiate real from fanciful desires, both hers and our own. In the 1990s, digital culture began to engulf entire areas of the world. As computer technology and cyberculture advanced, they were able to simulate the subject matter of the real world and to project even newer spheres of possibility. In the current era, technology places us much closer to the world of science fiction than in past decades. Because powerful tech gadgets are so embedded in our daily lives, many of the desires that we express about the future are based on the fact of the proximity and awareness that the world of, say, *Aeon Flux* and *The Matrix* is a real possibility. By late 2009, when the album *Rated R* was released, Rihanna's own on- and offstage personas, as well as her virtual online simulations, were not far removed from the mystifying hyperreality that undergirds the blockbuster films of which she had dreamt.

These interviews, a sample among many circulating the Internet, provide a useful starting point for more in-depth enquiry into the complex issues surrounding the evolution of this Barbadian/world sensation. The specific films to which Rihanna refers are, for the most part, science fiction, action, thriller and fantasy. They explore and foreground the intersection of "the real" and "other" worlds. They are violent. They are blockbusters. They create an artificial space which is so powerfully and technically constructed that it promises to envelop all else, threatening the primacy of conceptualizations of the real world. The overriding question that this chapter addresses, therefore, is: What is the nature of the relationship between real and virtual projections in the expanding arena of cyberculture, an arena inhabited by artists of Rihanna's stature and generation, but a sphere in which countless other "ordinary" people worldwide are also embedded?

I begin this exploration by suggesting that, being the creation of a post-analogue Barbadian culture, Rihanna was already connected to the digital matrix at the moment when influential interests decided that she was a marketable product. Next, I give a sense of where some Barbadian (and, by extension, Caribbean) citizens were situated in relation to digital culture around and after the turn of the twenty-first century. Finally, I suggest a few reasons why the academic literature on the emerging digital culture of the Caribbean is in need of constant updating, and I discuss how updated and upgraded metaphors, methodologies and critical tools can assist with defining what we are becoming in the age of hyperreality. To this end, I find the idea of the holodeck to be a richly suggestive metaphor. In science fiction lore, the holodeck is a virtual-reality room where people can vicariously experience other worlds, conditions and situations. Because of its dynamic function, it can help give perspective to frontier artists of our time, like Rihanna, while getting a lock onto the fluid nature of the relationship between reality and hyperreality.

Jean Baudrillard, in his seminal work *Simulacra and Simulation*, discusses how far we have advanced in modern society, to the point where our contact with the real world is challenged by *representations* of the very world. He suggests that we have become so dependent on replicas and maps that we have begun to lose connection with the world that came before the map: "The territory no longer precedes the map, nor does it survive it. It is nevertheless the map that precedes the territory."[4] Hence, he suggests that reality itself, or what we have conventionally constituted to be reality, merely imitates the model which now goes before and shapes the real world. In *The Gulf War Did Not Take Place*, Baudrillard further highlights the expanding role of technology in shaping our reality and establishing the hyperreal by arguing, for one thing, that the first Gulf War of 1991 (as seen in and by the West) was a carefully scripted and produced media experience rather than a "real" war.[5]

While Baudrillard and critics such as Umberto Eco[6] refer to concoctions like Disney and Western media culture as prime agencies and spaces for the playing out of relations between reality and hyperreality, relatively little is known (via academic literature) about how these two concepts interplay in the Barbadian and Caribbean arena – that affected region from which Rihanna emerged and which she left behind, as it were. For many decades, it has been the Caribbean artists, particularly the creative writers of the region, who have creatively engaged the future. Caribbean authors have been at the forefront of the project of imagining the future while exploring its relationship with the past and examining its relevance to the present. A selective, but by no means comprehensive, listing of creative artists who have crafted powerful insights and images in the formulation of a Caribbean vision of the future includes Wilson Harris, Kamau Brathwaite, Jamaica Kincaid, Oscar Hurtado, and more recently Tobias Buckell, Nalo Hopkinson and Anthony Joseph.

Harris's work, for example, the earliest of which dates back to the 1940s, has provided intriguing, complex ways of conceiving the Caribbean and the world. Drawing substantial influence from his own encounter with native

Guyanese symbols, icons and technologies, his outlook has challenged observers of Caribbean and other cultures to behold and reconsider the relationship between civilizations, societies and individuals across time and space. He shares this advanced thinking with scores of contemporaries, who have been traversing supposedly liminal dimensions for a much longer time than we tend to acknowledge. Interestingly, in Harris's work, as in that of Kamau Brathwaite, the individual's "desire of becoming" is foregrounded as a way of revealing both the possibility and impossibility of sustaining any single, self-contained state. Personas like Harris's Mariella and Brathwaite's X/Self reflect the pressures brought to bear on the ambitions of the individual in a world already ordered by history, a history coded with a range of technologies.

One recurring truth revealed in the work of Harris, Brathwaite and others is that the Caribbean (like those characters who stand in for it in creative literature) is a much more advanced frontier space than people tend to think. According to Brathwaite's thinking, the region was "post-modem" even before the West's mainstream became aware of digital technology in the 1980s and 1990s.[7] Caribbean subjects therefore inhabit a space where they are endlessly connected to new dimensions, where they influence and are influenced directly by people of various cultures and realities. Rihanna's dreams and her proximity to various real and virtual icons of the past, present and future are therefore hardly new if viewed through the lens of Caribbean creative writing and its embedded philosophy of limitless reach.

VIRTUAL DEFINITION

Rihanna was not the first and is not the only Barbadian artist or citizen to experience firsthand the transformation brought on by digital media. Like other Caribbean and developing nation-states, Barbados underwent substantial changes within its communication and entertainment sectors throughout the latter decades of the twentieth century, particularly during the 1980s and 1990s. In the recent book *The Popular Music and Entertainment Culture of Barbados: Pathways to Digital Culture*, I contextualize these transformations.[8] Such analyses build upon my earlier work, *The Politics of Caribbean Cyberculture*, in which I conclude that "Caribbean culture, as we knew it traditionally, died in the decade of the 1990s. In the late twentieth century, the rise of the machines signaled the progression of a new set of relations within cultural, social and economic activity."9

But how far-reaching really was the shift in the arena of information communication and technological application? Towards the end of the twentieth century, Barbados's control and ownership of its geo-cultural space was severely challenged by a new technological encirclement. The effective loss of control of the nation's communications space to external media and interest groups meant that Barbadian citizens, particularly youths, were increasingly under the controlling influence of external forces. The space was encircled by satellite television, including Multi-Choice TV and DirecTV. The persistent uncritical reliance on leading Western media sources (CNN, the BBC and affiliates) helped to shape the dominant thinking in corporate and governmental quarters. Top 40 music and dancehall culture were the driving engines on Bajan FM radio. Though the annual Crop Over festival provided an opportunity for a small sample of local content to gain radio rotation for a few weeks, this was very seasonal and was largely drowned out by an expanding Western pop-culture machinery. Many persons of Rihanna's generation were nurtured by the satellite culture promoted via American and Western popular media.

Barbadian youths were no longer primarily citizens of the local state; they were also freestyle participants in the digital revolution. They shape-shifted across identities. Their world was local inasmuch as they interacted within the geographical, topographical place that is Barbados (that is, they lived in actual houses and were palpably situated in the island), but their experiences with technology, communications media and Western entertainment culture meant that their lives were also acted out in another sphere of augmented and virtual displacement. They were wired to hi-def culture via the Internet, mobile phones and a shared understanding with countless other fellow citizens of the world, of the matrix. They were keenly dexterous. They knew of the traditional computer keyboard. They could use older digital input systems, as found on calculators, boom boxes and the Discman, but they were even more adept at manipulating Qwerty, half-Qwerty and displaced Qwerty keypad devices. Edward Tenner refers to this kind of transformation as a "curious cyborgian shifting of the balance of power in the human hand from the index finger to the thumb".10

By the early twenty-first century, large numbers of Barbadian youths had become potential port replicators for the expanding Western pop cyberculture industry, as they connected their very consciousness into the matrix of digital culture. This process of cultural progression is prefigured in the creative work of the Barbadian poet Kamau Brathwaite, particularly in the 1987 collection *X/Self*, in the poem "X/Self xth letter from the thirteenth provinces". In this poem, the offspring protagonist X/Self (somewhat like Rihanna) excitedly and nervously types back home to his mother to declare his entry into the world of capitalism, mercantilism and virtuality:

> Dear mumma
> uh writin yu dis letter
> wha?
> guess what! Pun a computer O
> kay?[11]

More conventional definitions of the nation refer to a territorial division containing a body of people who share a common history, culture, language and general aspirations. During the decade of the 1990s in particular, many Caribbean people, youths especially, aspired to new and different kinds of groupings and associations. They pledged more and more of their time to personal technological transactions. They became knowing and unknowing members of other kinds of alliances. Because they lived, moved and had much of their being in cyberspace, they became members of a virtual-def culture. The term *high-definition* became a buzzword for marking the superior sound and video quality of media systems during the latter decades of the twentieth century, when standard-definition systems were being widely replaced. Arguably, the next stage of content relay will be defined by the effacement of the medium, where we are less aware that there is a gadget between ourselves and the material being transmitted. The term *virtual definition* can therefore refer to the culture that supports this procession towards virtual reality.

The "hi-def community" of Barbados consists of many people who came to technology by way of the computer during the 1990s. Prior to this group, however, there were other tech-savvy individuals who first entered this space. Here, I am talking about people working in multimedia, film, video, music and music technology, who through their understanding of the evolution of sound and video became fully immersed in a world of ambitious desires to make these technologies even better and more robust. Many of these founding members of the hi-def community in Barbados owned computers and computer-like systems even before it was popular to do so.

Although members of this grouping have commonalities with other cyber and virtual communities abroad, over time they have established some of their own unique spaces that set them apart from others. Two of the more potent and popular of these are the sites Bajandancehall.com (now defunct) and Bajantube.com. These sites reflect connections with other nations, as their names would attest, but they are also fiercely insular, inasmuch as they have guarded their content and privileged the work of a group of people who have a Barbadian passport or some other close affiliation with the country. Bajandancehall.com at times promoted artists from elsewhere, especially when they were due to perform locally; but in its heyday, around the early to mid-2000s, its thrust was attracting an expansive community of Barbadian Internet users.

Bajantube, in particular, embodied the soul of many youths who in cyberspace found an outlet for their creative energies, at a time when traditional media houses were establishing even more rigid playlists and were on the verge of going out of style. On their "About Us" page, the owners of Bajantube declare, "Bajantube.com was launched on the 4th of November 2007. It was created for [the] sole purpose of promoting Bajans and Barbados by hosting various types of video content which are exclusive[ly] Bajan."[12]

As a result, many youths turned increasingly to Bajantube and similar websites to stage their presence and participate along with others, regardless of whether their creative contributions matched the "broadcast quality" of the heavily politicized traditional media houses. These online spaces had gatekeepers and controllers like the more traditional outlets, but at least they promised to give near-equal facility to a wider constituency. During the twenty-first century, these sites featured Rihanna and less well-known acts (globally) like Crimeson, Fari and Crab Soldier. Over the years, they have expanded to allow users to connect with an even broader community of users worldwide. These digital connections transgress more conventional notions of what it means to be Bajan. The popularization of social media websites and facilities such as Facebook and, more recently, WhatsApp and Snapchat means that subscribers to Bajantube segue between that location and more globally known social media sites with ease, confidence and a sense of being simultaneously situated within and outside the nation.

During the late 1990s and onwards, when the computer, the Internet revolution and digital machine culture thrived, many more citizens entered the matrix. Many of the full-blown cybercitizens of the early twenty-first century were participants in an arena whose impetus for advancement was founded on shared cultural trends and movements located in a range of high-tech facilities and phenomena. In fact, many Barbadian and Caribbean citizens, especially youths, were more intricately connected in cyberspace than their counterparts in the so-called industrial world were.

So even as Rihanna played out her professional and private life in cyberspace, many other Bajan youths of her generation, and some people much older, have also been found living their lives on MSN, Facebook, Twitter, Myspace, Mininova, YouTube, Google, LinkedIn, the Pirate Bay, ESPN, Badoo, Cricinfo, Kazaa, LimeWire, blogs and Skype, and endlessly connected to BlackBerries, laptops and all manner of peripherals. The symbols, totems and popular metaphors that circulated around these citizens and the culture that impacted them from the 1980s onwards were very often rooted in entertainment, technology and popular culture. Film and video gave this movement much of its inspiration and impetus. If books and "older" technologies helped to shape ideas about the Caribbean region's relationship with the external world, then digital media and iconic, blockbuster television shows like *Star Trek* had an equal – if not more substantial – impact on the consciousness of Caribbean culture as compared with their impact on Western culture.

CYBER METAPHORS

Caribbean theorists, critics and commentators are conscious of the myths, models, tropes, allegories, symbols and metaphors that reflect and represent the nature of power relations within Caribbean culture and global culture. Caribbean critical thinkers have actively employed cultural phenomena and symbols as part of a systemic matrix for understanding and indeed problematizing the relationships which cultures like those of the Caribbean share with others, especially colonial and imperial powers. Lamming has, for example, for some time now foregrounded the Caliban and Prospero story as part of a system of interrogating the confrontation, contestation and negotiation between "local" and foreign cultures.[13] The Crusoe and Friday encounter is another relationship that has been serviceable to articulating the anti-colonial project.

Although these long-established allegories and metaphors never fully lose their core relevance, it is possible that they cannot tell us all about the present and future, especially in light of the fact that a rapidly transformed world and an even more uncertain future, with its uncharted spaces, beckon us to new sites of critical reference. New and evolving digital and cyber metaphors can lend further assistance in articulating social, cultural, political and economic relations between peoples in a highly technologized, fluid yet fractured space. Given the realities of the current world, it is possible that contemporary citizens require newer, more techno-culturally relevant types of reference points and critical tools for coming to terms with how our world and its relations are situated. Rihanna's own fascination with pop-culture blockbusters and icons is not a casual one; it is rather a candid revelation of the reference points to which younger people refer in the twenty-first century.

In a sense, Caribbean criticism also requires an upgrade, so to speak, in order to address the changing culturo-technological environment. Given this need, I employ the notion of the holodeck by way of presenting an alternate pathway for coming to terms with the intersection of the real and its simulation in relation to the frontier figure Rihanna.

THE HOLODECK

A holodeck is a virtual-reality facility found on starships and starbases in the fantastic world of *Star Trek*.[14] An episode of *Star Trek: The Animated Series*, "The Practical Joker", helped to introduce the notion in the 1970s, when it presented a leisure room capable of holographic simulations. The term *holodeck*, however, was arguably first presented in *Star Trek: The Next Generation*, in the lead episode, titled "Encounter at Farpoint", which aired in 1987, some five months prior to the birth of Robyn Rihanna Fenty. Upon entering the holodeck, participants can command the computer to recreate any time period and location, along with their accompanying objects, symbols and characters. The computer then recreates that reality through beams and force fields within the room, where the individual can interact face-to-face with holographic characters or merely observe the actions of others in that space. To end the experience, participants can command the computer to close the program, at which time the holodeck returns to its prior state. It is a sterile, characterless room.

There are, of course, holodeck-type facilities in other works of pop culture. The 1974 Japanese TV series *Space Battleship Yamato* (called *Star Blazers* in its adapted, US form) aired in Barbados during the 1980s and featured a recreational "resort room". In the *X-Men* comic book series, the X-Men train in the "Danger Room"; in the film *X-Men: The Last Stand*, this holographic space is created by way of light projection and solid objects. The television series *Stargate SG-1* and *Stargate Atlantis* also reveal the presence of this technology among advanced cultures within *Stargate* lore. The notion of the holodeck also has a life in video games such as *Perfect Dark* and *Madden NFL 09*. In fact, in some Electronic Arts cricket video games, a player within the program and the game's manipulator can better their skills by practising outside the context of the match in a controlled environment. Codemasters' *Brian Lara Cricket* video game franchise enhanced these interactive capabilities over the years, beginning around 1995. This is a measure of the reach of the holodeck concept in contemporary pop culture. These have all played out in full view of Caribbean citizens, at home and abroad. Caribbean people have participated both vicariously and actively in such hyperreality enterprises. The holodeck, then, as both imagined, imaginary space and conceptual reality, transcends the specific arena of *Star Trek*, though it finds substantial grounding there.

In *Star Trek: The Next Generation*, season 6, episode 12, titled "Ship in a Bottle", while enjoying a Sherlock Holmes mystery, Geordi and Data discover a glitch in the holodeck program. On investigation, Professor James Moriarty, fictional arch-enemy of Sherlock Holmes, turns up and reveals that the program created him so well that he has come alive. He has seized agency by willing himself life, performing the scientifically impossible act of leaving the artificial world of make-believe and walking off the holodeck into reality. He leaves the imaginative world of fiction and enters the material world by declaring the words, "I think, therefore I am." To the amazement of Captain Picard, Lieutenant Commander Data, and Lieutenants Barclay and La Forge, Moriarty strides off the holodeck and does not disintegrate forever, but instead enters into the real space of the starship *Enterprise*. This episode, like so many others that feature the holodeck, raises philosophical issues about reality, life, purpose, power, humans' place in the universe and the existence of God. As such, it is an apt metaphor through which to glean deeper meaning regarding Rihanna's aesthetic concerns and articulations of desire and fulfilment.

In this vein, Rihanna's ambition of entering other worlds and becoming other personalities echoes Moriarty's desire for longevity, agency and crossing seemingly impossible thresholds. For instance, a July 2011 report on the website *Digital Spy* quoted an interview with Rihanna in which she expressed her admiration for Madonna. In particular, she pointed to Madonna's flair for reinvention and her longevity.[15] Madonna and Rihanna are, notably, both similar to and different from each other. Madonna, who was born in 1958, came to stardom in the mid-1980s with the albums *Like a Virgin* and *True Blue*. She pushed the boundaries of pop music, especially in the area of lyrical content, in which she explored sexual and taboo themes and subject matter. Arguably, Rihanna has continued in this vein. Madonna also wowed and shocked the world with her costumes, and lack thereof, and with the evocative imagery within her music videos. She became a fixture on MTV. She has owed much of her status and enduring power to this foundational medium of music television.

But whereas Madonna is a pop icon of the MTV generation, Rihanna's iconography is post-MTV. She rose to global prominence at a younger age than Madonna. She would have been influenced in some way by MTV, but her current status has less to do with the kinds of production aesthetics that defined 1980s pop culture than with the fact that she entered the entertainment arena in the era of digital interactivity. Rihanna's overt expression of admiration for Madonna is an important and telling declaration. She shares this fascination with her handlers at Def Jam Recordings, who fully understand key aspects of the history of the music industry, including Madonna's role in exploiting and transforming the mediums of her time. Pop-music discourse has held up Madonna as one of the two individual artists who did the most to exploit music culture in the late twentieth century. With Michael Jackson, Madonna is arguably the most enduring artist in Western pop-music culture of the late analogue age. There is no doubt that Rihanna's controllers at Def Jam see Madonna as her foremost model as they seek to exploit the market, make the most money and keep Rihanna relevant.

While one is sure to evoke grave concern by audibly willing him- or herself life and longevity, it is much more accepted to trust in advanced machines to help achieve these human desires. For futurists like Ray Kurzweil, this is an approaching possibility, with the rise of smart machines and technological singularity.[16] While the world of *Star Trek* is some ways off, the strategists at Def Jam are using technology to manage Rihanna's campaign towards greater popularity, financial rewards and maybe longevity (possibly even greater than Madonna's) as well. Their investment and trust in the technology of our age is well known. The entertainment industry has its life in this sector. Rihanna's proliferation on the major tech platforms and within virtual sites online reflects the phenomenal diffusion of her presence.

The search engine Bing listed Rihanna at number three in its most popular searches for 2013, signifying the expansive display of her image and content. Like so many other pop stars of her generation, Rihanna can be found in an official capacity on the major social networks, but she is also located there in hashtags and public discussions, and from time to time as the subject of hot and trending topics, such as in September 2011 when she was ordered by a farmer in Northern Ireland to cover up her nudity, a story aired widely on YouTube and elsewhere.[17]

She also appears on Twitter, IMDb, Instagram and countless other websites across the parameters of cyberspace, promoting her wares or drumming up hype, such as when she displayed her new New Zealand Maori hand tattoos and nails painted with the South African flag during the October phase of her 2012 world tour. In early May 2014, it was widely reported that her account had been deactivated by Instagram because she had posted topless photos from her shoot with French magazine *Lui* that violated the site's policy. Her fans were vocal on a range of platforms in support of her actions. Though Instagram explained it as an automated technical glitch (recognizing the traffic that her presence attracts), the account was yet again deactivated, much to the disappointment of her loyal worshippers, who nonetheless knew they could consume these images elsewhere online. They went to *TMZ*, Twitter, *Gossip Cop*, *Huffington Post*, *Idolator* and countless other sites for full display and to gain access to her most recent manifestations. Rihanna is in virtual reach of all those who are similarly connected or who are in proximity to the digital matrix. For all intents and purposes, she, like Moriarty (who challenges the parameters of the holodeck), can consider herself one step away from defying the gap between reality and hyperreality.

The question of perspective is critical here. The holodeck's perspective is often first-person, though at times third-person perspective is possible, such as when individuals walk around in that world unobserved by the simulated holographic characters. But at the conceptual level, this question is critical as well. In *Star Trek*, the characters leave the simulated world on the holodeck by uttering the command, "Computer. End program!" Such a declarative utterance from the space of the holodeck might lead us to question: Who commands perspective? How embedded are specific individuals in the digital matrix? Do we see them more accurately or acutely than they see themselves, such as what might occur when we stand back a little? Are some people more embedded than others? Are there several layers of embeddedness? Who determines where one person stands in relation to the others? Are we all implicated anyway? All of these are vital questions raised by *Star Trek* and other mainstream films and pop-culture simulation games, and, by extension, are useful markers for our interrogation of the ways in which Rihanna navigates space.

In the end of the aforementioned *Star Trek* episode, members of the crew discover that Moriarty never really left the holodeck. Instead, he had created a copy of the holodeck, and when he appeared to leave the simulated world, his departure was an illusion. His was a simulation of a simulation. In order to circumvent Moriarty's schemes, which are fuelled by his desire to live in the real world, the crew programs the holodeck's holodeck to convince Moriarty that he and his loved one, Regina Bartholomew, are ultimately being freed and beamed into the open spaces of the real world. In fact, they are only "beamed" into the holodeck's holodeck. But at the end of the episode, the scene features the two lovers floating off happily into what appears to be an infinite space, feeling liberated in their own minds, even though in effect they are still trapped in the boxed confines of a memory cube extracted from the holodeck.

The crew members' reflections on the outcome of their Moriarty-containment project are intriguing:

> *Barclay:* As far as Moriarty and the Countess know, they're halfway to Meles II by now. This enhancement module contains enough active memory to provide them with experiences for a lifetime.
> *Picard:* They will live their lives and never know any difference.

Troi: In a sense, you did give Moriarty what he wanted.
Picard: In a sense. But who knows? Our reality may be very much like theirs. All this might just be an elaborate simulation running inside a little device sitting on someone's table.

This dialogue, which concludes the episode, calls our attention to long-standing philosophical questions about the thin membrane that lies between reality, fantasy and truth. But the ending also recognizes the immense role that perspective can play in our determination of reality and hyperreality. Sometimes, all one has to fall back on is perspective.

RIHANNA ON THE HOLODECK

Although we cannot know for sure the true nature of Rihanna's world, we can identify and describe some of the cultural layers of replicated matter, tractor beams, shaped force fields and holographic images that encompass Rihanna as she performs in the wide, if confined, arenas and spaces on which virtual culture is staged for consumption beyond the first decade of the twenty-first century. When she dreams of starring in specific kinds of films and assuming the personae of other fictional characters within her holographic universe, she is, one supposes, like most individuals who dream of and long for an opportunity to become someone or something else. Her desire and virtual entry into the arena of *Aeon Flux* provide some insight into her wishful imagination.[18]

Aeon Flux was originally an avant-garde animated series that aired on MTV starting in 1991, initially as a set of film shorts on the animation showcase *Liquid Television* and later as a stand-alone series. These were followed by a film version, produced by MTV Films and released by Paramount Pictures in December 2005, starring Charlize Theron and Marton Csokas.

The world of *Aeon Flux* is a dystopian future world. The series is set in the year 2415, and the title character is an assassin. She is fiercely independent, and her actions are highly stylized. The animated shorts on MTV are characterized by graphic violence, gritty, edgy characters, sexuality, fetishism and domination. The series is marked by a disjointed visual narrative, and the episodes lack continuity. In the MTV shorts, Aeon dies at the end of every instalment, through fate or some act of negligence. In the stand-alone series, she dies once and is replaced by an identical clone. The 2005 film contains some elements of the MTV version, though it is overall less graphic and intense.

Does Rihanna's desire to play a character like Aeon Flux mean that she has a fascination with the future, strong women, bravery, tragedy, heroism and fierce individualism in the face of death? Does this mean that she wants to be that kind of personality off-screen as well? Should we even assume so? Where do Rihanna's off-screen and on-screen personalities reside? Is she so embedded in the arena of simulation that it is compulsory for fans and others to imagine her only as a creation of digital tools and cyberculture, so that when she declares an innocent wish along the pathway of her artistic and creative development, we consider it a premonition of some kind?

To some commentators, Rihanna's deep entrenchment in the arena of virtual simulation reflects a loss of identity and a potential loss of her soul. Throughout the decades of its modern development, the entertainment industry has been suspected of concealing a covert agenda. Some influential players and artists have been accused of being members of secret societies, being involved in hidden plots to infiltrate the corridors of political power, and hijacking the minds of youths and the impressionable within society. Hidden messages within phonographic recordings, coded lyrics, promotion of devil worship, and commodification of symbols and signs associated with the occult and the Illuminati are seen as representing the sinister underbelly of the industry.

The Illuminati is commonly described as an ancient secret society comprising influential political and cultural figures. Some of the world figures and institutions said to be part of this movement include the Pope, the Queen of England, and presidents of the United States of America, the Federal Reserve and the World Bank. Jay-Z has repeatedly been accused of being a key figure in hip-hop's wing of satanic worshippers. His sphere of influence is said to have expanded to include artists like Kanye West, Beyoncé and Rihanna, among others. Internet conspiracy buffs have widely declared that artists like Madonna, Lady Gaga and Rihanna have only modest singing talent but have elevated themselves to superstardom by signing a pact with the devil. Some leaders and members within the Barbadian and Caribbean religious community have interpreted Rihanna's unprecedented evolution as a descent into an obscure, dangerous space.

Some of the debates about the employment of occult symbols in her music,

music videos and stage performances derive from this position. For instance, in some readings of the song "Umbrella", being under her umbrella has nothing at all to do with platonic camaraderie, or even pleasurable sex; instead, the song and its video are seen as having to do with supernatural phenomena, self-erasure and becoming possessed by evil forces:

> The vocabulary used in this song is not about a relationship between two lovers. The fact is, "Umbrella" is about a subject matter that is sinister, dark and disturbing: becoming possessed by evil. . . . Rihanna sings the whole song but she actually takes on two roles. During the first half of the song, she plays the role of an evil entity that is trying to seduce and possess Rihanna. . . . The second role she plays is herself. So the song is basically a dialogue between the Devil and Rihanna. The video of the song makes this very clear.[19]

The large volume of online accusations levelled at her mentor, Jay-Z, regarding his alleged membership in the Illuminati has resulted in numerous close readings of Rihanna's videos, stage performances, attire and dance for symbols confirming her concomitant involvement. Jay-Z and Rihanna are not the first or only artists whose work has been scrutinized for subliminal occult material, but among some Barbadians much of the uneasiness surrounding Rihanna's visual and temperamental transformations has to do with the fact that she is Bajan and has been declared a national ambassador of youth and culture. As a consequence, there is underlying anxiety that what she develops into over time, whether a respectable lady, an evil vixen, a mixture of both, or neither, could be a sign of what the fans who adore and worship her, especially those from the youth population, might also aspire towards. The world of the occult, like the world of cyberspace, is vast. Whereas the occultic space tends to be shrouded in secrecy, the arena of cyberspace is touted as a democratic space, open to the full view of users and limited only by the kinds of searches and questions that we pose within it. So as Rihanna dreams, so too do so many other human beings.

Part of the irony surrounding Rihanna, though, has to do with the realization that the universe and experience that she imagines and suggests she longs for in her many interviews, a world of uninhibited experimentation and freedom, is often already created within her own stage performances and music videos. Two examples of such imaginative longings are perhaps evident in her performance during the 2010 Nickelodeon Kids' Choice Awards routine with Titan the Robot (who can only be controlled, it is said, by players who are good at playing Xbox) and her location in the *Aeon Flux*-esque "Only Girl (in the World)" music video. In her performance with Titan, she dances to the song "Rude Boy". There are two versions of the robot on stage with her, which operate in tandem. Their stiff movements contrast with her free and fluid actions, but the huge video screens that form the backdrop add to the spectacle of human and machine in consummate synchronicity. The crowd reacts wildly to those moments when Rihanna taunts the robots by gyrating with her Playboy-style bunny tail. In the "Only Girl (in the World)" music video, directed by Anthony Mandler, Rihanna walks, sings, dances, swings and floats in the open spaces of an unreal-looking field. The altered reality is suggested by the video's excessively bright colours, especially red.

As a result of these earlier cyber-technological performances, the green-screen technology used during the filming of the 2012 blockbuster film *Battleship*, in which Rihanna appeared, would not have been foreign to her. As she stood on the deck of a version of the battleship USS *Missouri*, the reminder that "the [ship's] firing systems are all analogue" would have reinforced for her the distance between old technologies and more modern machinery. In the movie, her character, Cora Raikes, has an uncanny relationship with the invading aliens from another world, as revealed in her line, "My dad said they would come." As the crew's weapons specialist, she also pulls the trigger to destroy the first alien outpost on earth.

Cora Raikes comes face-to-face with the unknown world, and in the face of danger she carries out her duty with gusto. For the actress who plays her, life's choices, regarding what is good, what is bad and how to achieve final victory, are not as clear-cut. The act of filming is circumscribed by tight parameters. The script is already written and the roles are assigned. Although the business of being a pop star also has its parameters, these are more fluid and demand sustained effort to negotiate where the real world and the virtual or imagined intersect. As Rihanna navigates her world, it is not as straightforward as identifying a plot and holding steady to a role. The world outside feature blockbusters is not fixed and ordered with dexterous thumb on the lever, a tight camera angle and utterance of the word "BOOM". Where *Battleship* presents the other world as a pernicious force to be guarded against and destroyed, there exists a more ambiguous construct in the life of megastars. The technology that they sometimes abhor is the technology that also popularizes them.

What Rihanna may or may not realize is that her audiences, fans and the many others who seek her out have themselves become embedded in a world that is no less fantastical than the world of *Aeon Flux, Matrix, Underworld* or *Battleship*; each of these movies contains traces of Rihanna. Of all the versions and simulations of Rihanna that exist, the most powerful are those in which she speaks with echoes of her Bajan intonation, sheds a tear, sings, screams, acts and dances in our living spaces, or is caressed in the palms of our hands (on cellphones and tablets) on our own hardware, our personal holodecks. Those who see and hear her react to her in different ways based largely on their own experiences, preferences, politics and outlooks, and according to the powerful mediums that relay versions of her to us. But perhaps sometimes, when we don't have the hardware, we fall back on the realization that holodecks might also be less solid constructs than we think, and that the mind is also a holographic space.

We are hardly ever free from the proximity of the holodeck. Maybe some are further removed than others. Given our uncertainty, we become like the character Barclay at the end of the *Star Trek* episode "Ship in a Bottle" – not trusting where we stand in relation to the holodeck, to reality and its simulations, we test the matrix by issuing a command:

"Computer. End Program."

NOTES

1. Mary H.K. Choi, "Rihanna: Good to the Last Drop", *Complex* online, 11 May 2011 (originally printed in June/July 2007 issue), http://www.complexmag.ca/music/2011/05/rihanna-2007-cover-story-gallery.
2. Jessica Brown, "Rihanna: Megan Fox is Hot", *Daily Star*, 8 December 2009, http://www.dailystar.co.uk/playlist/view/111704/Rihanna-Megan-Fox-is-hot/.
3. The term *event horizon* carries the layman's meaning of "the point of no return", but as used here, it also hints at the term's deployment in the field of astrophysics, where it refers to the point beyond which nothing, including light, can escape from a black hole due to the intense bending of the gravitational field. The 1997 movie of the same name, directed by Paul W.S. Anderson and starring Laurence Fishburne, also explores this phenomenon.

4. Jean Baudrillard, *Simulacra and Simulation*, trans. Sheila Faria Glaser (Ann Arbor: University of Michigan Press, 1994), 1.
5. See Jean Baudrillard, *The Gulf War Did Not Take Place* (Bloomington: Indiana University Press, 2005).
6. See Umberto Eco, *Travels in Hyperreality* (New York: Mariner Books, 1990).
7. Nadi Edwards, introduction, *Caribbean Culture: Soundings on Kamau Brathwaite*, ed. Annie Paul (Kingston: University of the West Indies Press, 2007), 1–36.
8. Curwen Best, *The Popular Music and Entertainment Culture of Barbados: Pathways to Digital Culture* (Lanham, MD: Scarecrow Press, 2012). In this work, I give a sense of the historical development of Barbadian music and entertainment culture. This analysis places contemporary developments in historical perspective.
9. Curwen Best, *The Politics of Caribbean Cyberculture* (New York: Palgrave, 2008), 1.
10. Edward Tenner, "Thumbs Up: A New Digit, Digitally Empowered", *Free Inquiry* 24, no. 4 (2004). Margaret Talbot restates the inner reach of this phenomenon; see Talbot, "My Son, the Cyborg", *New York Times* online, 15 June 2003, http://www.nytimes.com/2003/06/15/magazine/15WWLN.html.
11. Kamau Brathwaite, *X/Self* (Oxford: Oxford University Press, 1987), 80.
12. Bajantube.com, "About Us", http://www.bajantube.com/about-us.
13. See George Lamming, *The Pleasures of Exile* (Ann Arbor: University of Michigan Press, 1992).
14. Some of the information in this section is drawn selectively from several popular online sources, including StarTrek.com, *Wikipedia* and IMDb. But see also Sarah Hardy and Rebecca Kukla, "A Paramount Narrative: Exploring Space on the Starship Enterprise", *Journal of Aesthetics and Art Criticism* 57, no. 2 (1999): 182; Paul J. Ford, "A Further Analysis of the Ethics of Representation in Virtual Reality: Multi-User Environments", *Ethics and Information Technology* 3, no. 2 (2001): 113–21; Thomas Richards, *The Meaning of Star Trek* (New York: Doubleday, 1997), 108–9.
15. Lewis Corner, "Rihanna: 'Madonna Is My Biggest Inspiration'", *Digital Spy*, 21 July 2011, http://www.digitalspy.co.uk/music/news/a330967/rihanna-madonna-is-my-biggest-inspiration.html.
16. Raymond Kurzweil, *The Singularity Is Near* (New York: Viking, 2005).
17. See "Half-Naked Rihanna Told Off by Farmer in Bangor", *ODE*, 27 September 2011, http://www.youtube.com/watch?v=yWZZZF2DVuU.
18. Some of the information in this section is derived from popular online sources including AeonFlux.com, IMDb and Rotten Tomatoes.
19. See, for instance, "Occult and Prophetic Messages in Rihanna's Umbrella", *Vigilant Citizen* (blog), 14 December 2008, http://vigilantcitizen.com/?p=175.

6

FROM "F LOVE" TO "HE IS THE ONE"?

Rihanna, Chris Brown and the Danger of Traumatic Bonding

DONNA AZA WEIR-SOLEY

> The American Medical Association reports that *one woman out of three* will be a victim of violence by a husband or boyfriend at some point in her life. The emotional effects of partner violence are a factor in more than one-fourth of female suicide attempts and are a leading cause of substance abuse in adult women. Government statistics indicate that 1,500 to 2,000 women are murdered by partners and ex-partners per year, comprising more than one-third of all female homicide victims, and that these homicides always follow a history of violence, threats or stalking.
>
> —Lundy Bancroft, *Why Does He Do That?*[1]

Rihanna's position as a megastar is unquestionable. So is her status as a battered woman who, though not by choice, has joined the ranks of those listed in the statistics quoted above. However, the purpose of this essay is neither to situate the superstar as hapless victim nor to vilify her for not responding to domestic abuse in ways we consider to be "empowering" or worthy of a feminist icon, a mantle Robyn Rihanna Fenty has never publicly claimed. According to many of her critics, Rihanna's responses to domestic violence – her return to attacker Chris Brown shortly after the incident and her appearance in music videos that at once glamorize and critique violence against women – have been variously troubling, contradictory and complex. The aim of this essay is to analyse Rihanna's public responses to her assault by Chris Brown as a way of understanding the effects of what expert Lundy Bancroft refers to as "traumatic bonding" between victims of domestic violence and their abusers. Traumatic bonding is a phenomenon that may be as common as domestic violence itself and is impervious to class, ethnicity, culture, megastardom or anything else we may believe should set Rihanna apart from other survivors of intimate-partner abuse.

The practice by too many second-wave feminists of "slut-shaming" Rihanna and other young female performers whose public behaviour and performance do not conform to traditional feminist notions of female empowerment, often comes in for harsh backlash from younger feminists who identify with these iconic figures through their music, fashion sense and sexual expressivity.[2] Invariably, cultural critics who identify as third-wave feminists ably situate so-called provocative sexual performances within a theoretical framework that is recuperative of female agency and is sexually and commercially empowering.[3] While some among the more traditional feminist camp hold that icons such as Rihanna are flawed role models for young girls, whether they like such status attribution or not, some more recent feminist conceptualizers argue that since these performers eschew the imposed status of role model, they should not be held to a standard that is, at best, paternalistic.[4]

In the end, what both camps share are sometimes trenchant, sometimes superficial examinations of the way in which Rihanna is portrayed and discussed in the media, and of what her performances and collaborations with various artists "say" about female agency and empowerment. Rarely do they bother to examine Rihanna's own words on the subject of her abuse, and even more rarely do they place those words against her public actions and images and the self-fashioning in her music videos.

Some critics, for instance, argue that continued focus on the domestic abuse Rihanna suffered not only pathologizes the megastar but fixes her in the static role of victim, despite her attempts to transcend this image. However, to ignore that Rihanna is a survivor of domestic violence is to miss the opportunity to educate women who have a lot to lose by silence on the issue – namely, their very lives. Intimate-partner violence is a common societal ill. Victims and survivors of domestic violence are mostly women. No woman is immune to it, and no victim manages to escape the psychological trauma it imparts. Not even Rihanna. For many, Rihanna is already the face of domestic violence. Discussing the issue of intimate-partner violence in a sensitive but candid way, and situating the problem as a common societal ill rather than as a personal failure on Rihanna's part, may prove more helpful than harmful for the young megastar and her fans. Even more significantly, using Rihanna's story in service to the education and potential survival of other women is a self-consciously political act of empowerment, not an act of vilification or further victimization.

To these ends, this essay examines Rihanna's own words in two separate interviews (one with Diane Sawyer in 2009, shortly after the widely publicized incident, and the other with Oprah Winfrey in 2012), some of her video appearances after the abuse, and her projected public persona, in order to place Rihanna's own response to the abuse against and within critical research on a subject that has devastating consequences for the lives of women. My hope is that this juxtaposition – which will privilege Rihanna's own thoughts on the subject and read her words and public actions in relation to commonplace analyses from experts who study domestic violence – will help to shed light on the psychology of intimate-partner abuse. As one still-relevant second-wave feminist, Audre Lorde, reminded us over thirty years ago, our silence will not protect us.[5] It was true then. It is truer today.

During most of 2012 and 2013, Rihanna and Chris Brown's turbulent, on-again, off-again relationship was fodder for tabloid and respected publications alike. In that period, they were photographed together in intimate poses at several public events. On 10 February 2013, they were photographed sitting together at the Grammy Awards ceremony. Brown danced in the aisle as Rihanna paid tribute in song to reggae icon Bob Marley. Later that month, according to the ABC News entertainment blog, Chris Brown told a reporter that Rihanna was "the most beautiful girl in the world", that she had forgiven him, and that they were back together.[6] Just prior to these events, Rihanna had confirmed that indeed they were back together when she told a reporter from *Rolling Stone* magazine, "Even if it's a mistake, it's my mistake."[7] Her words suggested that she fully intended to see the relationship through. She was not going to allow public opinion to stand in the way of what she considered to be "true love". It is clear here that Rihanna believed she was exercising agency over her own life, performing an act of self-authorization that underpins feminist articulations of a woman's right to choose. That being said, the choice was troubling for many. Still, I wonder if there is a way to understand the cycle of abuse within which Rihanna is imbricated without branding her a perpetual victim, feeling sorry for her or vilifying her for not doing what we *think* we would have done in a similar situation.

Although the reunion itself was short-lived, the fact that it occurred in early 2013 may have come as no surprise to those who saw Rihanna's August 2012 interview with Oprah on the Oprah Winfrey Network.[8] In that interview, Rihanna spoke candidly about her relationship with Brown, the 2009 battery that made headline news all across the world, and her forgiveness of the man who had brutally assaulted and publicly humiliated her. Rihanna also revealed to Oprah that she still had feelings for Chris Brown. She admitted to partying with him on a friend's yacht in San Tropez in 2012. Photos of that meeting had been leaked to the press amidst rumours of a reunion, and Rihanna made no attempt to deny it. But she stated that although they had managed to "rebuild trust" and had become good friends again, they were not together as a couple at that time. Brown was in a relationship of his own, and she was single. However, when Oprah asked her what it was like to be in his presence, she made no bones about the fact that she was a woman still in love: "My stomach drops. I have to maintain this poker face and not let it get to the outer part of me."[9]

Rihanna further admitted to Oprah that she was lonely and that lonesomeness was the hardest thing about being a star. She added that the loneliest aspect of stardom was not being able to share intimate matters with the people in her life because she did not like to be seen as or treated like a victim. In these paradoxical statements lie the key to Rihanna's bonding with Brown. No one else understood her. And at the same time, no one else could, because she could not let anyone else be privy to what was really going on.

Denial. As revealed in Rihanna's 2009 interview with Diane Sawyer on 20/20, denial was the coping mechanism that Rihanna had relied upon since she was a child.[10] Denial continued in her troubled relationship with Brown. The cycle of loneliness was exacerbated by the abuse she encountered at his hands, and the harsh judgements from the court of public opinion only made matters worse. The only way for her to regain control of her life was to defy public opinion and do what she felt was right for her. However, when one has been subjected to abuse over time, the trauma it causes can have long-term psychological effects. As a result, doing what is perhaps in one's best interest can prove challenging.[11]

In 2013, Rihanna told a writer from British tabloid the *Daily Mirror*, "He's giving and loving. And he's fun to be around. That's what I love about him."[12] Clearly, Brown's charm was part of the hold he had over Rihanna. Domestic-violence experts identify charm as one of the main arsenals an abuser has in his bag of tricks. Lundy Bancroft, author of *Why Does He Do That?*, has been working with abusive men for over fifteen years. What he describes as "traumatic bonding" seems, in many ways, to provide a context for understanding Rihanna's deep attachment to Brown:

> One of the greatest tragedies of all forms of abuse is that the abused person can become emotionally dependent on the perpetrator through a process called traumatic bonding. The assaults that the abuser makes on the woman's self-opinion, his undermining of her progress in life, the wedges he drives between her and other people, the psychological effects on her when he turns scary – all combine to cause her to need him more and more. This is a bitter psychological irony.[13]

Through the process of traumatic bonding, the abuser (in this case, Brown) becomes the person to whom the abused feels most close. She may see him even as a soulmate. Rihanna alluded to this bond when she repeatedly told Oprah that Chris Brown was her best friend. Lundy Bancroft observes, "Almost no abuser is mean or frightening all the time. At least occasionally he is loving, gentle and humorous and perhaps even capable of compassion and empathy. This intermittent and usually unpredictable kindness is critical to forming traumatic attachments."[14]

Throughout much of the interview with Oprah, Rihanna had difficulty controlling her tears. The singer revealed that her grandmother, Clara Brathwaite (affectionately called Gran Gran Dolly), to whom Rihanna was very close, had recently died after a protracted battle with cancer. Clara Brathwaite's death seemed to have rendered Rihanna more open and vulnerable than usual, and may help to explain why she wanted to turn to Brown for comfort. Rihanna appeared young and fresh-faced, wearing very light makeup, in a loose floral sundress with a turquoise background as bright as the waters of her Caribbean sea. She tried hard to stem the flood of tears and worried about appearing "too soft". From this viewer's perspective, the scene felt genuine and the emotions real. Finding it hard to keep her composure under Oprah's friendly but incisive questions, Rihanna, through her tears and her ready laughter, made her professions of love for Brown seem innocent and guileless – at least, until the viewer remembered the graphic and viscerally disturbing photo of her battered face that had been leaked by TMZ. Still, her grief over losing her other mother figure and her sheer joy in being back home in Barbados (the one place where she says she truly feels safe) were refreshing to many viewers, particularly in light of some of the videos and songs she had made after the battering incident, which showed a darker side to this Caribbean princess of pop.

Once Rihanna was out of the formal interview setting, her tears gave way to youthful exuberance at the prospect of showing off her island home to Oprah Winfrey. As she drove Oprah through the streets of Barbados in her Jeep, Rihanna cheerfully called out to people with whom she grew up and people who watched her grow up, and they returned her greetings elatedly, calling out, "Robyn!" Watching the segment, it comes as no surprise that Barbados is the place Rihanna still calls home. Whatever issues some Barbadians may have had with her sexual expressivity, it is clear that many more, perhaps the majority, are proud of their girl Robyn and her tremendous success.[15] Rihanna's mother later told Oprah that what made her most proud was that her daughter was still humble, still acknowledged her roots, and was still just "Robyn" to so many.

The 2012 Oprah interview seemed vastly different from the one Rihanna had given Diane Sawyer for *Good Morning America* and 20/20 in November 2009, roughly nine months after the battery. In the Sawyer interview, Rihanna openly admitted to what Brown did to her and indicated that she was coming forward because she wanted to raise awareness about domestic violence in order to save her young fans from going through the horrific ordeal she herself had experienced. The sober-faced Rihanna seemed hurt, betrayed and angry, but she allowed no tears to fall in that interview. She told Sawyer, "The more in love we fell, the more dangerous we became for each other. . . . It was a bit of an obsession." Now that she had ended it, she wanted Brown to "accept the responsibility and not find a way to feel sorry for himself". She spoke eloquently about the emotional pain that remains with victims long after the physical scars have healed. "It's the scar inside you. You flash back. You remember it all the time. It comes back to you and it's very painful. I don't know if he understood that. They never do. They don't know that. They can't know that."[16]

When asked why she had gone to see Brown in Miami only weeks after the beating, Rihanna stated that she had been concerned for his mental state and wanted to make sure he did not harm himself. She explained that it was a very confusing time for her and that she had been trying to work out her ranging emotions in her own head. She admitted having gone through a depressive period, in which she just sat for hours watching television. According to her, in those moments she felt that if *she* was going through such a deep depression, she could not help but wonder what *he* was going through: "Again, lying to yourself. I had to protect him. The whole world hates him now. His fans – his career – he lost me. I just had to let him know, 'Don't do anything stupid.'" Although he had beaten her badly, Rihanna still felt protective of Brown. Strong feelings of attachment are not easy to turn off under normal circumstances, and they are even more difficult when such relationships involve traumatic bonding.

Rihanna explained to Sawyer that it was when she realized that she could not stand being around Brown, could not even stand to hear his voice, that she realized the depths of her anger. She told him, "I can't do this. . . . We can't do this", shortly after returning from Miami. Sawyer reminded her that on average, it took seven attempts before a battered woman was able to leave her abuser, and Rihanna corrected her: "Eight or nine, actually." She had obviously done her homework. Rihanna understood that she had been caught up in a common psychological drama and was taking pains to understand her conflicting emotions and reactions in the aftermath of the beating. The one thing that she did not seem conflicted about during the Sawyer interview, however, was her decision to leave Brown. Her clarity and conviction on this point were as believable to this observer as her candour and transparency about helplessly loving him were in the later interview with Oprah. How, then, to understand the divergent conclusions at which she arrived in the two interviews?

Not insignificantly, Rihanna told Diane Sawyer that she was humiliated and ashamed. Sawyer asked her why she would be embarrassed and she replied, "That's embarrassing that that's the type of person that I fell in love with." Although she vehemently denied that she did anything to cause Brown to hit her and suggested that she did not fight back because she wanted the hitting to stop, the foregoing statement betrays the internalization of shame and guilt felt by many abused women who believe the abuse is their fault for loving the wrong man. These feelings of worthlessness and guilt are only exacerbated by the societal judgement, blame and shaming to which the abused is subjected once the violence is made public. Heather Russell contends that although the response in Barbados to Rihanna's abuse was mostly "outrage, protectiveness and organization around domestic violence issues", even at home, some critics could not resist a "veiled, paternalistic, 'I told you so'", as if to suggest that Rihanna had brought the violence on herself by not conforming to certain standards of socio-sexual propriety.[17]

Despite the statistic, alluded to by Sawyer, that most abused women make multiple attempts to leave before they actually succeed, many people think they are experts on what they would do in such a situation. However, the real experts who have studied the phenomenon maintain that it is much harder to leave an abusive lover than a non-abusive one. Abusive lovers are skilled in the art of manipulation and in fearmongering. They use whatever psychological tools they have at their disposal to maintain control: sex, fear, charm, threatening the children or making the woman feel guilty about the prospect of raising them in a broken home, denying access to money, alienating the woman from friends and family who might support her and give her refuge – whatever works in a given situation. In Rihanna's situation, some of these clearly did not apply. Money was not an issue, and there were no children involved.[18] Nevertheless, her own words to Sawyer reveal that the intimate bond she shared with Brown felt like "an obsession", one that Bancroft and other experts would argue is a result of traumatic bonding.

In the interview, Sawyer linked Rihanna's response to Chris Brown's abuse to the fact that she was raised in a home where there were frequent incidents of domestic violence. Rihanna's father had habitually beaten her mother while she was growing up in Barbados. When asked about the two police reports indicating that Brown had bashed her SUV on one occasion and repeatedly shoved her into a wall on another, Rihanna seemed confused. First, she denied it: "He did not repeatedly shove me into a wall." But when pressed by Sawyer, she admitted, "He shoved me into a wall." Rihanna then related many incidents in which her mother had been beaten by her father and had not sought help. She told Sawyer, "He broke her nose one time, but she would never go to the hospital. Domestic violence is not something that people want anybody to know. So she just would hide it in the house."

Rihanna seemed to clearly understand the complex psychology of domestic violence. Most interestingly, in the interview, she seemed to collapse her mother's response and her own into one seamless narrative. This was particularly evident when she candidly said to Sawyer, "Denial is, you start lying to yourself. . . . The minute the physical wounds go away . . . you start lying to yourself." Discussing her childhood confusion and difficulties processing her own pain as a child of abuse, she said, "I felt really lonely. There were times when I cried." Her admission of loneliness was tied to silences she felt compelled to uphold, family secrets she felt bound to guard. Ironically, she could just as well have been speaking about her own abuse at the hands of Brown. Rihanna's emphasis on the denial inherent to the cycle of domestic violence may very well hold the clue to her decision to return to Brown, four years after the incident that left her bruised and battered. The physical wounds had gone away. Rihanna was again, according to Brown and many of her adoring fans, "the most beautiful woman in the world". In January 2013, Rihanna was unapologetic about being back with Brown. She told *Rolling Stone* magazine, "It's different now. We don't have those types of arguments anymore. We talk about s———. We value each other."[19]

Compare the above sentiment to what she told Sawyer in 2009: "I am strong. This happened to me and it can happen to anyone. . . . I'll say that to any young girl going through domestic violence: 'Don't react off of love. F love!' Come out of the situation and look at it third-person . . . because love is so blind – so blind." By her 2012 interview with Oprah, Rihanna seemed to have forgotten that love could not be trusted in domestic-violence situations. By February 2013, she had eschewed her statements to Sawyer, and she appeared to be able to see only through the lens of a blind love.

Despite what he has said publicly about how much he has grown since the 2009 incident, Chris Brown's actions following the incident have not been those of a changed man.[20] At the time of this writing, Brown has recently completed serving time in jail for violating the terms of his probation from the 2009 case.[21] He has asked for Rihanna's forgiveness publicly: once in a video posted online on 20 July 2009, and again in September of that year on *Larry King Live*, where he appeared with his mother (who was herself a victim of domestic violence). Although he may have been reading from a teleprompter in his posted video, Brown seemed sincere enough. He accepted full responsibility, stating that he wished he had handled the situation "differently and better". Was this merely a publicity stunt? It would be impossible to say definitively one way or the other. Still, Brown seemed to want to blame his violent behaviour on growing up in an abusive home, an allegation which is only partially supported by studies on domestic violence. Lundy states, "A bad childhood doesn't cause a man to become an abuser, but it can contribute to making a man who is abusive especially dangerous." He continues, "If abusiveness were the product of childhood emotional injury, abusers could overcome their problem through psychotherapy. But it is virtually unheard of for an abusive man to make substantial and lasting changes in his pattern of abusiveness as a result of therapy."[22]

Whatever the underlying reasons, violence seems to follow Brown wherever he goes. This makes him unsafe for Rihanna, love or no love. Rihanna understood that in her 2009 interview. She did not seem to understand it in 2013. On 5 March 2013, the *Daily Mirror* linked Rihanna's comments (made in *Elle* magazine) about her new single, "Stay", to her reunion with Chris Brown: "It's a story about having love that close and wanting it to last forever. You don't have that feeling with everybody – so when you have it you don't want to let go of it. I'd definitely say that he is *the one* I have that kind of relationship with."[23]

Chris Brown's public behaviour suggests that he still has violent tendencies that could prove harmful to Rihanna. It is not impossible for an abusive man to change, but it is rare. Lundy Bancroft observes, "The majority of abusive men do not make deep and lasting changes even in a high-quality abuser program."[24] The reason they do not succeed, according to Bancroft, is that "there are no shortcuts to change, no magical overnight transformations, no easy ways out. Change is difficult, uncomfortable work."[25] So as narratives about agency and survival go, the fact that Brown and Rihanna are not together at the time of writing spells progress for Rihanna. Because even more troubling than Rihanna's aforementioned contradictory statements is the fact that by February 2013, Brown seemed to be minimizing the domestic-violence incident that had made international news in 2009. Bancroft identifies minimizing as a common tactic used by abusers, one that often allows them to successfully avoid prosecution in the courts.[26] After all, it is his word against hers. At a party for the Elton John AIDS Foundation held after the Academy Awards in 2013, Brown was quoted as saying, "Sometimes you fight with the one you love and things get said, stuff spirals."[27] Given the extent of Rihanna's injuries on the night of the assault, that statement is more than a little scary. Brown seemed to have normalized the event in his own mind, firmly locating it within a narrative of normative relations between loving couples. Although he later told the reporter that that fateful night was "the deepest regret of my life" and that he had "worked hard" to win Rihanna's forgiveness, it was clear that Brown believed he had transcended his violent past.[28] It was also clear that he thought the violent incident of 2009 had not been such a big deal, after all.

Brown's history following that assault tells a different story. His smashing of a window after his *Good Morning America* interview with Robin Roberts in March 2011 (after Roberts pressed him about the 2009 incident), his nightclub brawl with Drake (reported by the *New York Daily News* as Drake's fault) in June 2012, his fight with Frank Ocean over a parking space in February 2013, and several other public fracas, as well as parole violations leading to court appearances and one recent incarceration in 2014, all mark him as someone who attracts danger, whether wittingly or unwittingly. A series of nasty verbal conflicts on Twitter with various celebrities in 2013 demonstrated an alarming lack of maturity. Brown seems to believe that he should not have to face questions from reporters or criticism from the public for his brutal attack on Rihanna. As Lundy Bancroft observes, "Freedom from accountability means that the abusive man considers himself above criticism."[29] Brown does not come across as someone who has learned from his mistakes. I think most observers can agree that Rihanna would be well advised to keep her distance from him – a course of action to which she seems committed at this writing.

In her essay "Whose Rihanna? Diasporic Citizenship and the Economics of Crossing Over", Heather Russell compares the Caribbean pop princess to her predecessor Grace Jones. Russell argues, "Self-possessed and self-generating, surely Jones remains a powerful, alluring icon and symbol of Caribbeanity, whose nonconformist deconstruction of traditional sex and gender roles, invocation of phallic power and hard, edgy sexuality explodes fully the dichotomy between victim and perpetrator into which Rihanna had been read in 2009."[30] Russell continues by declaring that Rihanna's career trajectory has already surpassed Jones's, despite its infancy, and that the young star is not merely mimicking her predecessor but is appropriating her image in a subversive, empowering and recuperative narrative. Similarly, recent bloggers and critics have positioned Rihanna's "Man Down" and "Pour It Up" (both of which contain female-dominant, aggressive and hypersexual images) as affirmations of raw, edgy female power independent of patriarchal framing, and have declared Rihanna's "solidarity" with female rape victims, sex workers and strippers as a powerful affirmation of sisterhood that transcends victimhood, collapses the boundaries between fantasy and realism, and invokes female agency in ways that may appear counter-intuitive to second-wave feminism yet remain powerfully subversive.[31]

But these latest videos are not the first manifestations of Rihanna's capacity to reinvent and refashion her image for public consumption. In fact, the contrast between Rihanna's powerful incarnations in videos that came out immediately after the abuse and the thoughts she expressed about Brown in the Oprah interview less than four years later seems to mirror one of the classic features of domestic violence: leaving and then returning, vacillating between opposing positions vis-à-vis the relationship. Not long after the 2009 incident, Rihanna performed the duet "Love the Way You Lie" with Eminem, which could be read as a response to the battering and the public onslaught that came in its wake. Eminem's hardcore lyrics and hard-driving beats provide the perfect score to dramatize the dangerous pattern of violence followed by guilt, regret and recriminations that characterize the vicious cycle of domestic abuse.

When asked by Oprah about this video, Rihanna responded that after the 2009 battery she was in a "dark place", and it was coming out in her songs and in her dress. Some of the lyrics in the verses, which were written and performed by Eminem, include, "She f——ing hates me and I love it"; "We said things, did things that we didn't mean"; "I apologize, even though I know it's lies"; and "If she ever tries to f——ing leave again, [I'll] tie her to the bed and set this house on fire." In the video, a man is seen alternately caressing and beating a woman. The pattern of fighting and making up includes scenes where she's crying and he's apologizing with a rose and a teddy bear. Eminem's brilliant portrayal of this vicious cycle of domestic violence brings to life many of the features of traumatic bonding that experts discuss.

Rihanna's contribution to the song is the refrain, which in the video she sings with lips curled in a sneer:

> Just gonna stand there and watch me burn
> But that's alright because I like the way it hurts.
> Just gonna stand there and hear me cry
> But that's alright because I love the way you lie, love the way you lie.

Rihanna's short red hair and black hoodie are the perfect complements to her bad-girl persona in the video. The refrain's suggestion that Rihanna's persona likes the abuse mirrors, mocks and reproduces societal misunderstandings of the psychology of abuse, which may make a person stay in a relationship that he or she knows is unhealthy. It is an ironic statement, not meant to be taken literally. Victims of abuse do not like getting beaten. Their reasons for staying are myriad and are socially and psychologically complex. It is not just the abuser who gets maligned when the truth surfaces; the abused comes in for his or her share of public scorn as well. As Heather Russell observes, Rihanna was vilified and excoriated by Brown's fans in the wake of the 2009 abuse: "Those who did not want to imagine their native son, the clean-cut poster boy of contemporary R&B, as violator, immediately began blaming the victim. In their Web posts, Rihanna's critics asserted everything from the idea that she had provoked Brown by hitting him first, she had been cheating on him with Jay-Z (long-standing false rumour), and she had given Brown a communicable disease: herpes."[32] Rihanna's refrain in the Eminem duet is meant not just for Brown but for the society that watches, condemns and alienates victims of domestic abuse, thereby increasing their pain and humiliation.

Similarly, Rihanna's "S&M" video, released two years after the assault, directly targeted one societal group who had actively participated in exploiting her after that incident: the media. In the video, Rihanna is wearing a dress made of newsprint and is being dragged out of a room kicking and screaming by two well-dressed men in black suits who represent members of the press. Next, we see her stuck to a wall behind a transparent sheet of plastic, still wearing the newsprint dress. She is at a news conference and is surrounded by reporters taking notes. Words such as *Barbados, slut* and *Daddy issues?* flash across the screen. Rihanna is squirming and resisting, but she cannot escape her plastic prison. Her voice rings out in song:

> I may be bad
> But I'm perfectly good at it . . .
> Sticks and stones may break my bones
> But chains and whips excite me.

In an interview in *A Burst of Light*, feminist poet and critic Audre Lorde points out that the role playing associated with sadomasochism is a response to the larger society's preoccupation with dominance and power: "Sadomasochism is an institutionalized celebration of dominant/subordinate relationships. And, it prepares us either to accept subordination or to enforce dominance. Even in play, to affirm that the exertion of power over powerlessness is erotic, is empowering, is to set the emotional stage for the continuation of that relationship, politically, socially, and economically."[33]

Rihanna's employment of sadomasochism to speak her resistance to the media's degradation of her after the assault is double-voiced and subversive. Chris Brown's attack was physically, emotionally and psychologically damaging, but the media's public battering of her after the incident was hurtful, cynical and profit-based. The following statement by Lorde is borne out in the "S&M" video: "The linkage of passion to dominance/subordination is the prototype of the heterosexual image of male-female relationships, one which justifies pornography. Women are supposed to love being brutalized. This is also the prototypical justification of all relationships of oppression – that the subordinate one who is 'different' enjoys the inferior position."[34] Rihanna's "enjoyment" of the public flagellation with words and accusations is her attempt to speak back to the larger forces of dominance and power, forces that uphold Chris Brown's assault on her by prolonging it for their own entertainment and profit.

Brown's actions cannot be divorced from the larger profit-based motives behind oppression nor from the larger profit-based motives behind the media and the music industry's exploitation of Rihanna's private tragedy. The greater question we need to ask ourselves is, Who benefits from Rihanna's abuse? The media, Rihanna's label, Chris Brown (who is even more popular and edgy now than before, parlaying his bad-boy image to full advantage)? Rihanna, who is smart enough to figure out that "if you can't beat them", it is better to "join them", seems to be fully cooperating in this scheme to make money from her tragedy, and why not? Perhaps, ultimately, that is her only triumph

– money is the only thing she stands to gain from the abuse. That is more than most abused women can say. Money "run tings" in a capitalist society. Nobody knows this better than working-class Caribbean people, and Rihanna comes from working-class Bajan roots. Because Caribbean societies are so class-stratified, even the least educated Caribbean person understands the dynamics of power and profit and how they often operate at the expense of the powerless. The "S&M" video represents Rihanna's attempt to reclaim her power, her acknowledgement that the media is getting off on demonizing her, and her own cynical decision to profit from her abuse, which has made so much money for so many.

Although Rihanna's face and words in the video suggest that she is enjoying being dominated, her body, tightly wrapped in plastic, is immobile. Her sneering face and alert eyes flash with a fire of resistance that says she will use this degradation to her advantage. The difference between sexual ownership and sexual dominance is the difference between sexual freedom and integrity and sexual exploitation. Rihanna's simulation of a sexually dominant image to replace the inferior/submissive image that plagues victims of domestic violence is just one step on the road to her freedom and ownership of self.

The Rihanna that is projected in "S&M" and "Love the Way You Lie" is very different from the Rihanna in the Oprah interview and much closer to the Rihanna who tells Diane Sawyer, "F love!" How, then, do we explain her sentiments about the relationship as related to Oprah long after the Sawyer interview, especially in light of the fact that she reunited with Brown shortly after the Oprah appearance, but the reunion did not last to the end of 2013? Both Sawyer and Rihanna concur with experts that it takes multiple attempts to leave before a victim of domestic violence succeeds in making a break from the abuser. It is that final separation that marks the trajectory from victim to survivor. My contention is that the contradictory imperatives that we see in the videos and interviews are public expressions of a private struggle, carefully marketed for commercial consumption, but possibly no less real for Rihanna despite their profit motive.

Thus, her Oprah interview, occurring in a moment of vulnerability (immediately after her grandmother's death), followed by a short-lived return to Brown, then topped off by the recent videos "Man Down", in which she kills her rapist, and "Pour It Up", in which she poses as both a powerful stripper and a consumer of the striptease, replicate and mimic the pattern of leaving and returning that commonly characterizes domestic violence. In "Pour It Up", Rihanna poses like the queen of all strippers and rains money (printed with the image of her face) down on herself and the other strippers. Her refrain "still got more money" suggests that she is basking in her hard-won success – hard-won because she has subversively parlayed one of the most painful episodes of her life into further successful commercial ventures. In noting Rihanna's "solidarity" with marginalized women who also parlay their feminine assets into one form of power (money), younger writers associate Rihanna with third-wave feminist thinking that rejects the notion that women should *not* "sell" or barter their sexuality in exchange for money. Many see Rihanna as the ultimate example of a woman who uses everything she has – negative experiences such as abuse, her ability to self-fashion, sexiness, as well as undeniable talent and beauty – to snatch power from the hands of men in the music industry (and in the world) who unapologetically exploit female sexuality to enrich themselves. In "Chatting About the 'Pour It Up' Video" (4 October 2013, *Hairpin* [blog]), bloggers Susan Elizabeth Shephard and Sarah Nicole Prickett comment on the absence of men in the "Pour It Up" video, which gives the impression that the female strippers are performing for the enjoyment of themselves, each other, and for other women instead of exclusively for male consumption. These bloggers clearly view this focus on the female gaze as an empowering gesture, despite what detractors condemn as gratuitous sexual display in the video.

Despite her youth, Rihanna projects a powerful image that identifies her as someone who has agency enough to shape her own self-fashioning, in spite of the music industry's image manipulation, and to ultimately orchestrate her incarnation of the powerful woman she allows us glimpses of in her videos. To fix her image in the narrative of powerless victimhood would be both cynical and simplistic. However, to deny serious critical attention to the issue of domestic violence as crucial to her journey into selfhood would be disingenuous, at best. For, as Rihanna moves further and further away from the 2009 incident, we tend to block out the battered face shown on TMZ and replace it with the striking beauty who is the Rihanna millions adore. The danger here lies, as Rihanna explained in the Sawyer interview, in denial. Denial is an insidious part of the cycle of abuse, and societal denial is no less problematic for the collective. While we are busy forgetting, many more women will die.

The truth is that the face of domestic violence is not the battered face of Rihanna that we saw after the 2009 incident. It is, instead, the face that is cleaned up, fully made up, complete with stiff upper lip. As Rihanna told Sawyer, she is strong, and abuse still happened to her. It can happen to anyone. Similarly, to deny that Rihanna may have suffered from traumatic bonding and that it took her some time – years, in fact – to work through these issues is to distance her from other women who also suffer the long-term effects of abuse.

Domestic-partner abuse is not a personal problem of weak-willed, ineffectual women who enjoy performing the role of victim. It is a serious, complicated societal issue that even the US court system has trouble getting a handle on. In fact, in *When Dad Hurts Mom*, Lundy Bancroft points out that there is a marked bias in the court system against women who allege and are seeking protection against abuse.[35] The 2012 Florida case involving Marissa Alexander demonstrates that this bias may be even more pronounced against women of colour.

Alexander is an African American woman who tried to defend herself from further intimate-partner violence. A legally licensed firearm holder, she fired a warning shot in a moment of extreme threat to try to stave off further abuse from her estranged husband, against whom she had already obtained a restraining order. For her attempt to protect her life, she was sentenced to twenty years in prison.[36] Although her husband had a documented history of abusing her, Marissa Alexander was not given the benefit of the doubt when she tried to invoke the Stand Your Ground law, which allows a person to justifiably use force to defend themselves without having to first retreat. Her case has been taken up by the NAACP and other groups to help expose the racial bias inherent in the way the Stand Your Ground law is applied in Florida, especially in the aftermath of the controversial Trayvon Martin and Jordan Davis murder trials. In the Martin case, George Zimmerman was acquitted of murdering an unarmed black teen, Trayvon Martin, on the grounds that he felt "threatened" by him. In the case of Jordan Davis, who was killed by Michael Dunn because of an argument over what Dunn believes was loud "thug music", there was a mistrial because the jury could not agree on a verdict, followed by a retrial in 2014 in which Dunn was later convicted and sentenced to life in prison. However, the original mistrial reflects the controversy over "Stand Your Ground" and its differential application in cases involving racialized subjects.

Most germane to my point here, however, is that the Marissa Alexander case not only demonstrates the variation in women's responses to intimate-partner violence, but it also highlights the ways in which such victims, even when they stand up for their lives, become doubly victimized. The remarks of US Representative Corrine Brown in the aftermath of the verdict remain disturbingly accurate: "The Florida criminal justice system has sent two clear messages today. . . . One is that if women who are victims of domestic violence try to protect themselves, the 'Stand Your Ground Law' will not apply to them. . . . The second message is that if you are black, the system will treat you differently."[37]

The fact that Marissa Alexander stayed with her abuser and had a child with him before she gathered the strength to walk away did not help to make her case for self-defence. However, it does show that having the courage to leave or to fight back does not protect women from further abuse by the assailant nor from prosecution by the court system.[38]

Rihanna's recent video appearances situate her as a sister in solidarity with women who are usually marginalized and exploited – among them, abused women, strippers and exotic dancers. Still, few women who work in the sex industry manage to subversively snatch agency and feminine power from the domain of alpha males in decidedly patriarchal settings. Despite Rihanna's current status as what one critic dubs an "affirmative . . . self-love femme power icon",[39] she (or any woman, for that matter) is insulated neither from intimate-partner violence nor from the commodification of female sexuality that is endemic to patriarchal capitalist ventures such as the music and sex-trade industries.

To juxtapose the image of Rihanna in her most powerful incarnation against and alongside the image of her as a survivor of intimate-partner abuse is to establish that the victims and survivors of domestic violence are not losers, are not women who are too weak to take a stand for themselves, are not hapless, helpless victims, but are our mothers, sisters, daughters, neighbours, friends, favourite rock stars and power icons. Perhaps now is exactly the time to establish that healing from intimate-partner violence is a process, one that takes time, and that in moments of vulnerability (such as when Rihanna was losing her Gran Gran Dolly and gave that tearful interview to Oprah), even the strongest among us may take a step backwards before moving forward. Perhaps the face of Rihanna – not the bruised and battered image of it, but the one befitting "the most beautiful woman in the world" – is the face to establish this fact once and for all: women who are abused are like Rihanna, women who are abused are like you, like me, like your mother, sister, aunt, and like Marissa Alexander. There is no one face of domestic-abuse victims. All faces, any face, can be the face of domestic-violence survivors. And women who are victims and potential survivors of domestic violence *need* from the courts and from society support and understanding, not condemnation and judgement.

NOTES

1. Lundy Bancroft, *Why Does He Do That? Inside the Minds of Angry and Controlling Men* (New York: Berkeley Books, 2002), 7–8.
2. Evette Dionne, "The Twerking Feminist", *Mic*, 25 October 2013, http://mic.com/articles/69657/the-twerking-feminist.
3. Cate Young, "Sexualization, Exploitation, and Black Female Celebrities: On the Subtle Womanism of Rihanna and Nicki Minaj", *Batty Mamzelle* (blog), 18 November 2013, http://battymamzelle.blogspot.com/2013/11/Sexualization-Exploitation-And-Black-Female-Celebrities-On-The-Stripper-Anthems-Of-Rihanna-And-Nicki-Minaj.html#.U1RxoqJ7TB9.
4. See Sarah Ditum, "Should Feminists Lay Off Rihanna?", *New Statesman* online, 11 March 2013, http://www.newstatesman.com/culture/2013/03/should-feminists-lay-rihanna/.
5. Audre Lorde, *Sister Outsider* (New York: Ten Speed Press, 2007), 41.
6. Luchina Fisher, "Chris Brown Says Rihanna Has 'Forgiven' Him", ABCNews.com, 26 February 2013, http://abcnews.go.com/blogs/entertainment/2013/02/chris-brown-says-rihanna-has-forgiven-him/.
7. "Rihanna on Chris Brown: 'We Know Exactly What We Have Now'", *Rolling Stone* online, 30 January 2013, http://www.rollingstone.com/music/news/rihanna-on-chris-brown-we-know-exactly-what-we-have-now-20130130#ixzz3A2Nzuzsb.
8. At current writing, Brown and Rihanna are said to have split up and gone their separate ways.
9. Rihanna, interview with Oprah Winfrey, *Oprah's Next Chapter*, OWN, 19 August 2012.

10. Rihanna, interview with Diane Sawyer, *20/20*, ABC, 6 November 2009.
11. See "Battered Women's Syndrome" at Rape, Abuse and Incest National Network (RAINN), https://www.rainn.org/get-information/effects-of-sexual-assault/battered-woman-syndrome.

    I am not suggesting that Rihanna has or has had battered woman syndrome fully blown at any point. This is a determination that can only be made by someone who is trained in that field and has had Rihanna as a patient. I mean to imply that many victims of domestic violence suffer psychological effects in differing degrees and manifestations. See Joseph M. Carver's analysis of Stockholm Syndrome, "Love and Stockholm Syndrome: The Mystery of Loving an Abuser", n.d., http://drjoecarver.makeswebsites.com/clients/49355/File/love_and_stockholm_syndrome.html.
12. Fisher, "Chris Brown Says Rihanna Has 'Forgiven' Him".
13. Bancroft, *Why Does He Do That?*, 220.
14. Ibid.
15. See Heather Russell, "Whose Rihanna? Diasporic Citizenship and the Economies of Crossing Over", in *Archipelagos of Sound: Transnational Caribbeanities, Women and Music*, ed. Ifeona Fulani (Kingston: University of the West Indies Press, 2012), 308.
16. Rihanna, interview with Diane Sawyer.
17. Russell, "Whose Rihanna?", 322.
18. British tabloid the *Daily Mirror* claimed that Rihanna had disclosed in *Elle* magazine that she wanted to have a baby for Chris Brown. Stephanie Wood, "Rihanna Says 'I Will Have a Baby', Channels Catwoman, a Dominatrix and a Chessboard in New Magazine Shoot", *Mirror Online*, http://www.mirror.co.uk/3am/celebrity-news/rihanna-elle-magazine-shoot-sexy-1738255#.U-gLxkhRFmo. Rihanna appeared on the cover of *Elle*'s UK edition in April 2013.
19. Ray Rahman, "Rihanna Talks Chris Brown in *Rolling Stone*: 'He Doesn't Have the Luxury of F——ing Up Again' ", *Entertainment Weekly* online, 30 January 2013, http://music-mix.ew.com/2013/01/30/rihanna-chris-brown-rolling-stone/.
20. Fisher, "Chris Brown Says Rihanna Has 'Forgiven' Him".
21. Associated Press, "Chris Brown Trial to Start on Monday: Faces Jail Time if Convicted", *Fox 411* (blog), 19 April 2014, http://www.foxnews.com/entertainment/2014/04/19/chris-brown-trial-to-start-on-monday-faces-jail-time-if-convicted/.
22. Bancroft, *Why Does He Do That?*, 25.
23. Wood, "Rihanna Says 'I Will Have a Baby' " (emphasis added).
24. Bancroft, *Why Does He Do That?*, 335.
25. Ibid., 334.

26. Ibid., 71.
27. Fisher, "Chris Brown Says Rihanna Has 'Forgiven' Him".
28. Ibid.
29. Bancroft, *Why Does He Do That?*, 58.
30. Russell, "Whose Rihanna?", 316.
31. See "Man Down: On Rihanna, Rape and Violence", *Crunk Feminist Collective* (blog), 2 June 2011, http://crunkfeministcollective.wordpress.com/2011/06/02/man-down-on-rihanna-rape-and-violence/; Susan Elizabeth Shepard, Ayesha A. Siddiqi and Sarah Nicole Prickett, "Rihanna On My Mind: Chatting About the 'Pour It Up' Video", *Hairpin* (blog), 4 October 2013, http://thehairpin.com/2013/10/rihanna-on-my-mind; Muna Mire, "Talkback: In Defense of Rihanna", *Feminist Wire* (blog), 16 October 2013, http://thefeministwire.com/2013/10/rihanna/.
32. See Russell, "Whose Rihanna?", 320.
33. Audre Lorde, *A Burst of Light: Essays* (New York: Firebrand Books, 1988), 14.
34. Ibid., 17.
35. Lundy Bancroft, *When Dad Hurts Mom: Helping Your Children Heal the Wounds of Witnessing Abuse* (New York: Berkley, 2005), 242–44.
36. See Jamil Smith, "Marissa Alexander Gets 20-Year Sentence", MSNBC.com, 11 May 2012, http://www.msnbc.com/melissa-harris-perry/marissa-alexander-gets-20-year-sentence.
37. Ibid.
38. Mitch Stacy, "Marissa Alexander Gets 20 Years for Firing Warning Shot", *Huffington Post*, 19 May 2012, http://www.huffingtonpost.com/2012/05/19/marissa-alexander-gets-20_n_1530035.html.
39. Ayesha A. Siddiqi makes this observation in Shepard, Siddiqi and Prickett, "Rihanna on My Mind".

7

RIHANNA AND BAJAN RESPECTABILITY

AARON KAMUGISHA

On Sunday, 20 November 2011, at a church service hosted by Barbados's ruling party and designed to mark the beginning of independence anniversary celebrations, Bishop Marlon Husbands launched a verbal salvo against Barbadian-born international pop star Robyn "Rihanna" Fenty. The immediate object of Husbands's ire seemed to be her well-publicized risqué performance in a field in Northern Ireland, but his wider target was the "level of indiscipline, immorality and homosexuality" in Barbados.[1] Accusing the star of "always doing foolishness", Husbands reportedly declared her not only an inappropriate role model for Barbadian youth, but unfit to be a cultural ambassador for Barbados. This speech represents probably the most coherent attack on Rihanna by an establishment figure in Barbados since her meteoric rise to fame, and it should not be dismissed as merely a Christian conservative reaction to her music, performances or global image. It might be seen better as an expression of the ambivalent appreciation with which many in Barbados regard her, a dubious affection containing both embrace and aversion that demands further engagement, exploration and consideration.

In this chapter, I wish to explore the contours of Barbadian respectability and the extent to which Rihanna's disruptive performances help us understand its current state as well as arguments for self-legitimation. The claim here is not in any sense that Rihanna is a fundamentally transgressive figure, posing questions about sexuality and enjoyment on the local or global scene that have gone hitherto unremarked. While Rihanna is not transgressive, the ambivalent reaction to her *is* fascinating, revealing much about political economy, power and social relations in contemporary Barbados. It also clarifies much more about Barbados than is generally perceived in the popular Caribbean and global imaginations, and highlights its important role in the hemispheric reproduction of that contradictory and much-maligned group – the black middle class.

THE CARIBBEAN MIDDLE CLASSES

> I do not know any social class which lives so completely without ideas of any kind. They live entirely on the material plane.
> —C.L.R. James, *Party Politics in the West Indies*[2]

In 1961, a hemisphere apart, two Caribbean intellectuals made powerful statements about the historical conjuncture their communities inhabited, statements filled with desperate urgency for the future of the anti-colonial revolution to which they had devoted their lives, and the future of the world in general. The status of these two radicals, C.L.R. James and Frantz Fanon, as the exemplary political thinkers of the Caribbean's twentieth century is scarcely in doubt. In their respective texts *Party Politics in the West Indies* and *The Wretched of the Earth*, both advanced critiques of the new elites then poised to guide Third World countries to independence, critiques that remain unsurpassed in their prescience about the persistence of colonial arrangements in the post-independence state.

Fanon's well-known critique of the then newly emerging national elites reaches its zenith in his warning about what he terms "the pitfalls of national consciousness", in chapter three of *The Wretched of the Earth*, but his conclusions about the limitations and corruption of the middle class begin in his celebrated first chapter, on violence. "Spoilt children of yesterday's colonialism and of today's national governments", he writes, these "wily intellectuals" emerge to organize the tremendous upheavals against colonialism from below.[3] For Fanon, unlike the bourgeoisie of Europe, these new elites are not a true bourgeoisie, but a "little greedy caste" on "its historic mission: that of intermediary" between metropolitan power and the postcolonial masses.[4] Beyond their parasitic irrelevance, the national middle classes are to blame for the absence of a truly purposeful national consciousness, the fruits of their "intellectual laziness", "spiritual penury" and "profoundly cosmopolitan mould" of existence.[5] Imitation here weds bourgeois ideology to coloniality's dehumanization: "Bourgeois ideology . . . , which is the proclamation of an essential equality between men, manages to appear logical in its own eyes by inviting the sub-men to become human, and to take as their prototype Western humanity as incarnated in the Western bourgeoisie."[6]

C.L.R. James, writing against the encroaching lethargy and betrayals of the People's National Movement of Trinidad on the cusp of independence, in concert with Fanon stresses the intermediary position of the middle classes, a people with status but "no knowledge or experience of the productive forces of the country".[7] James's lament concerns the role of this class as a facilitator of colonial governmentality and its lack of a historical imagination, ideas of its own, or indeed *anything* beyond a desire for acceptance by the ruling elites. Perhaps the one perspective, crystallizing into almost an ideology, that James would suggest the middle classes possess is an "unshakeable principle that they are in status, education, morals and manners, separate and distinct from the masses of the people". James's analysis of the new elites closes with the ominous observation that "the ordinary people of the West Indies . . . do not want to substitute new masters for old. They want no masters at all . . . history will take its course, only too often a bloody one."[8] Over thirty years into a global neoliberal project that has seen appalling levels of material impoverishment for citizens of the global South, and soaring rates of violence in these societies, James's warning appears more prescient than he could have imagined.

These texts by Fanon and James constitute the most searching critiques of the new postcolonial elites by Caribbean intellectuals writing at the moment of anglophone Caribbean independence. They represent a wider critical body of work by African diaspora intellectuals on class formation beyond the reduction of people of African descent in the Americas to an undifferentiated mass by colonialism. The work of African diaspora sociologists, pioneered by W.E.B. Du Bois in the late nineteenth century, constantly faced the problem of racist caricatures and distortions of their communities' lives. Du Bois described this well as the treatment of black people as the problem rather than as a people with problems.⁹ In the mid-twentieth century, the African American sociologist E. Franklin Frazier's classic monograph *Black Bourgeoisie* (1957) sounded a warning about this class's conspicuous consumption and genuflection to Euro-American tastes, styles and ideals. Greg Thomas summarizes this text as follows:

> This "lumpen-bourgeoisie" is characterized not only by racial subordination and socio-economic dependence, but also by systematic political collaboration, a deep-seated inferiority complex, a compensatory set of self-righteous mythologies, and a profound self-hatred exceeded only by an intense loathing of the black masses on top of flagrant, idolatrous imitation of whites, or an abject conformity to white Western ideals. In short, a comprehensive material and subjective investment in the domestic and global status quo is in evidence.¹⁰

In an intricate dissection of E. Franklin Frazier's career, Greg Thomas has shown that despite his undoubtedly progressive denunciation of the national elite, Frazier remains a "sociologist of integration" who perceived that the future of African Americans lay not in "self-determination" but in "mass assimilation led by an elite which should be as genteel as culturally possible".¹¹ The prominent Trinidadian Marxist Oliver Cox shared a similar concern about *Black Bourgeoisie*, claiming that Frazier "hardly confronted even tangentially a real power structure".¹² In this reading, Frazier's focus on the foibles of the black upper class comes at the price of an absence of criticism of white supremacy in capitalist America.

In the anglophone Caribbean, intellectual labour, whether as sociological study or radical critique, on the question of black middle-class formation lies enmeshed within the debates about social stratification, pluralism and creolization that have been argued by Caribbean theorists for the last sixty years. Historians of the anglophone Caribbean have noted that the defining features of the black middle class in the post-emancipation era were their occupational status (namely, that they held jobs not involving manual labour), a functional level of literacy and an investment in European cultural styles, behaviours and attributes; however, these were interpellated by a complex series of social prohibitions and exclusions premised on race and colour.¹³

Black middle-class respectability was thus secured by literacy and professional success and by a conservative view on social change, with educational accomplishment being the most highly prized single attribute distinguishing the middle class from the poor and the peasantry. Yet this same class produced a number of prominent figures who advocated race pride in a vindicationist spirit, including J.J. Thomas of Trinidad and Robert Love of Jamaica, who stand as major figures in the genesis of a tradition of anti-colonial thought and political theorizing in the anglophone Caribbean. Here, even at the height of the colonial era, the difficulty involved in flattening the complexity of this class becomes clear, for as Belinda Edmondson has shown, from the nineteenth century, its members were never solely reduced to being an imitative rendition of British culture.[14]

The development of sustained intellectual labour on the question of anglophone Caribbean social structure in the 1950s twinned questions of class with those of race, which led to a particularly theoretically inventive era in Caribbean social thought. The theories of this era are known to Caribbeanists under the nomenclature of the plantation school, pluralism and creolization. Lloyd Braithwaite's pioneering study of 1953, *Social Stratification in Trinidad*, with its demonstration of social and racial hierarchies, colour, shade and kinship, shows well how an ethnically diverse society remained captive to systems of domination established under slave society and economy.[15] In his ethnographic approach to middle-class tastes and assumptions, Braithwaite illustrates how the heraldry of whiteness permeates social and economic relations, from the intricate assessment of potential marriage partners to the prospects of a career in colour-coded fields of employment. The intermediary middle class in this colonial arrangement is not reactionary in any easy manner for Braithwaite; rather, he describes a "tendency to radicalism", along with one towards "compulsive conformity", within them.[16] Writing twenty years later, in the development of a theory that was meant to serve as a forceful counterpoint to the social stratification and plural society models, Kamau Brathwaite would adopt a somewhat related tack, referring to the middle classes as the "most finished product of unfinished creolization", obsessively concerned with a mimicry with little subversive potential, and thereby making an apt description of the ascriptive value of whiteness in their lives.[17]

Arguably, the post-independence critique of the middle class reached its zenith in the outpouring of leftist activism in the region beginning in the late 1960s, two decades before Rihanna's birth, and continuing to the late

1970s. Here, the Caribbean state became figured, to gloss Marx's famous lines, as merely a management committee for the affairs of a local bourgeoisie and international capitalist interests. Thus, when we examine contemporary middle-class "anxieties" regarding Rihanna, it becomes necessary to fully situate them within this complicated and dynamic history.

A highly significant but generally unheralded article by Walter Rodney, "Contemporary Political Trends in the English-Speaking Caribbean", is one of the best examples of the thought of this period.[18] Rodney commences with the observation that most anglophone Caribbean states have now achieved constitutional independence, tying this historical development to the dramatic collapse of European empire in the thirty years following the Second World War (the article was published in 1975). The limited character of that independence is a central part of Rodney's considerations, and he stresses the importance of distinguishing colonialism from neo-colonialism as "the patterns of politics continue to change after the initial transfer of power to a local ruling class".[19] The consolidation of a new form of rule in the postcolonial Caribbean represents the continued march of Western imperialism, but the emergence of new forms of politics requires the use and clarification of the term *neo-colonialism*. For Rodney, "neo-colonial politics are those that derive from the consolidation of the petty bourgeoisie as a class around the state".[20] The appearance of this class over and over again across various Caribbean territories, and in regimes that claim political orientations that should be radically different – from liberal democratic and democratic socialist to authoritarian – leads Rodney to the declaration that "to speak of petty bourgeois dictatorship in the English-speaking Caribbean is no play with words".[21]

Rodney was writing before the full advent of neoliberalism, charted by many as emerging along a US-British axis with the electoral triumphs of Margaret Thatcher in 1979 and Ronald Reagan in 1980. A generation later, with the collapse of state socialist alternatives throughout the world and the harsh conditionalities of structural adjustment, a different accent has emerged in debates about the role of the middle classes in Caribbean society by members of the Caribbean left. Two articles, by Don Robotham and Rupert Lewis, respectively, both prominent former members of the Workers Party of Jamaica, demonstrate this shift from the analyses of the 1960s and 1970s.[22]

Robotham's essay, "Blackening the Nation", follows the P.J. Patterson administration's attempt to create a black capitalist class in Jamaica rather than the standard Caribbean post-independent arrangement of black political power and cultural leadership with minority (largely white) economic dominance. For Robotham, the "black bourgeoisie has the potential, but only the potential, in the course of its attempt to gain and consolidate power, to implement reforms of critical benefit to the majority of the people".[23] There is more than a suggestion here that capitalism is the only game in town, and the sole question for the state becomes merely how well one can "walk the tightrope" between satisfying a populace's demands and the acquisitive, accumulative imperatives of capitalism.[24]

Rupert Lewis's "Reconsidering the Role of the Middle Class in Caribbean Politics" travels a different, though not completely dissimilar, terrain. Lewis starts by suggesting that "social-democratic and Leninist ideas [in the region] . . . have run their ideological course". He argues that past criticism of the middle classes – James is specifically mentioned – needs updating in order to account for the significant class mobility we have seen in the last generation, and to comprehend the constitution of this middle class, which is drawn far more from entrepreneurial groups than from the civil service and the professions. Lewis thus eschews the tendency of the Caribbean left to dismiss the middle classes, stating that the study of Caribbean politics teaches us that after "any wave of social upheaval, mass protest or revolutionary transition, new forces from the middle strata arise to implement and direct alternative policies in the process of institutionalizing change".[25] His hope rests in the creation of a new entrepreneurial class which will be constitutively different in its vision and social outlook than the predatory minority colonial elites of the last few centuries.[26] This privileging of entrepreneurship within a developmental vision for the Caribbean state sits uneasily with the previous hard-won gains of generations of trade unionism. It is also key to comprehending the Barbadian state's response to Rihanna's overwhelming success not merely as a musical artiste but in terms of the industry that has come to surround her – and the state's quest to gain access to it.[27]

Yet simultaneous to these changing perspectives on the middle class by the region's political theorists, another pathway was being forged through the discipline of anthropology that sought to consider and explain class stratification in the Caribbean. This track relied more on manifestations of social difference in the realm of popular culture and on more consciously thematized questions of gender and power in the public sphere. Peter Wilson's essay "Reputation and Respectability: A Suggestion for Caribbean Ethnology" and his subsequent book *Crab Antics* are arguably the most influential works in this area, and they are essential works in what is now termed masculinity studies in the Caribbean.[28] Wilson's thesis – that the crucial organizational tension in Caribbean society is the dichotomy between reputation and respectability, spheres inhabited by men and women respectively – has been subjected to searching commentary by a generation of Caribbean scholars.[29] Perhaps the greatest weakness of Wilson's approach, however, is exposed by Jean Besson's critique, which claims that Wilson's thesis is painfully unaware of the "unequal and exploitative gender relations" that structure his case study. For Besson, Wilson forgets that women compete for status too and thus have their own forms of "reputation", and his schema suggests that "Afro-Caribbean women are . . . bearers and perpetuators of the Eurocentric colonial value system".[30]

Despite this, Wilson's reputation/respectability dichotomy, along with the conundrum it seeks to articulate, has remained an important touchstone in Caribbean cultural criticism, in work as diverse as Shalini Puri's vision for a new Caribbean cultural studies and David Murray's ethnography of homosexuality in Barbados.[31] For Puri (following Daniel Miller), the emphasis in studies of Caribbean culture on carnival versus Christmas is symptomatic of a privileging of reputation over respectability and is the Caribbean version of the "fetishization of resistance and transgression in cultural studies".[32] David Murray's ethnography shows the complex ways in which performances and disavowals of same-sex relationships are captive to the mesmerizing power of respectability, which often bedevils his informants' attempts to secure true erotic autonomy and freedom.

The respectability portion of the reputation/respectability divide in the Caribbean is thus premised on a very different version of the latter than that which has been classically understood to secure middle-class hegemony in Western societies since the nineteenth century.[33] Its raison d'être is to secure middle-class rule, but it has an odd relationship to discourses of middle-classness because it is suffused with coloniality. This, Peter Wilson understood well, and he clearly outlined it in "A Polemic by Way of Conclusion", the final chapter of *Crab Antics*. For Wilson, "respectability is the moral force behind the coercive power of colonialism and neo-colonialism".[34] The tragedy of the new West Indian middle classes at independence is the dawning realization within them that the values they have sought, their "straining ambivalently toward respectability", has been for naught, as it is built on a series of pleasures and prohibitions created in a foreign land. Their hegemony can only remain weak, and in a quest to solidify it, the lure of colonial authoritarianism is likely to be too great to disavow. Wilson acknowledges that despite his call for a Caribbeanization of the social values now claimed by respectability, some "new legitimation of authority" will hardly be uniformly progressive.

Writing a decade later, Diane Austin showed the shifts caused by the search for new forms of legitimation in her observation that the Jamaican middle-class elite "has shifted its ideological emphasis from colour to education, from birth to socialization, from 'manners' to social competence, [while] retaining . . . their privileged class position" – a discerning and generalizable insight on middle-class hegemony in the contemporary anglophone Caribbean.[35] The denouement of all this is our current moment, alternatively described as an era of hegemonic dissolution, in which new forms of domination are being actively reproduced on Caribbean populations by its elites.[36]

Bringing together the threads of the different discourses I have been charting on the Caribbean middle classes, I would propose the following. Despite the peculiarities of the Caribbean – its intensely modern location within the West, its small geographical size and its multicultural communities sutured together by coloniality – the expansion and rise to power of a post-independence upper middle class in the region should not be of any great surprise, nor does it require an elaborate explanation. Rather, it is closely allied to a global historical event since the late 1960s which Neil Lazarus has termed "a *consolidation* of the historical patterns of bourgeois class domination".[37]

And it is here that Rihanna's home, Barbados, occupies a peculiarly important space in the Caribbean. Though the country was once derided as an imitative backwater of England, the quintessence of conservatism in a rapidly decolonizing Caribbean, perceptions of Barbados in the region have undergone a shift in the last two decades.[38] One reason for this change is a retreat from prescriptions of radical social change by the Caribbean left following the disillusionments caused by the collapse of socialist experiments in Grenada and Jamaica, and a subsequent shift to a more cautious social-democratic vision of the polity. The other, arguably more pressing, reason is the considerable success that post-independence Barbados has enjoyed compared to its anglophone neighbours.

Typically the top-ranked Latin American or Caribbean country in the United Nations Human Development Index, in 2010 Barbados was listed as "developed" by that index, the only country from the region thus categorized.[39] Its achievements in areas linked to both human development (life expectancy, infant mortality, health-care spending per capita, number of years of education) and middle-class consumption habits (car ownership, technological access) are undeniable.[40] In the contemporary anglophone Caribbean, which is marked by growing income inequalities and spiralling rates of violence, with out-migration at one of its historical peaks and with resource-rich Trinidad and Tobago the only country on a secure economic footing, Barbados's success seems extraordinary, and has been subject to a number of commentaries.

Some of these are relatively easily dismissed as displays of showy self-congratulation, full of ahistorical statements, made by local elites invested in the country's progress over the last generation.[41] However, the more fascinating conversation here surrounds two islands paradoxically seen as opposites, yet strangely twinned in the Caribbean: Jamaica and Barbados. In these discussions, Barbados, previously dismissed as the conservative side of the revolution/reaction polarity between these two countries, is now perceived to be a society that has reached a laudable consensus and social peace.

This view, trumpeted from time to time on Jamaican talk shows, has found some academic allies. In his comparison of sugar production in nineteenth-century Jamaica and Barbados in the first generation after slavery, Don Robotham states that the reason for the decline in production in Jamaica versus its increase in Barbados was the inability of contending factions in Jamaica to compromise and reach a consensus, as they supposedly did in Barbados.[42] This comment is so absurd and ahistorical that it deserves no further comment. Nor is it an isolated perspective of Robotham's, who in an observation on the contemporary difference between the islands suggests that "Barbadian prosperity [is] based on . . . [a] *pragmatic* racial contract".[43]

While other analyses of the diverging paths taken by post-independence Jamaica and Barbados do not mirror Robotham's errors, it is difficult to escape the conclusion that Barbados functions as a counterpoint for commentators largely interested in providing alternatives to the wrenching social and economic problems of Jamaica.⁴⁴ Nor does this view emanate solely from Jamaica, as Ralph Gonsalves, prime minister of St Vincent, has shown in an incredible attempt to sketch what he terms "the idea of Barbados".⁴⁵ This comes at the price of an attenuated knowledge of the scholarship on post-independence Barbadian society, resulting in uncritical readings of its contemporary sociopolitical scene as one of harmony and social cohesion.

There is much to consider here about regional and global perceptions of Barbados, and the lived realities of that island nation. The "success" of Barbados, and its touting as the best-run majority-black independent society in the world, would suggest, in a global order under the hegemony of liberal democracy, that it has one of the most settled and extensive black middle classes to be found in the community of nations. This contains a kernel of historical truth, albeit with other limitations. As Winston James has noted, "from the eighteenth century, Barbadians have been among the most literate and educated black populations in the world", and particularly since the nineteenth century, Barbadian lower-middle-class professionals – particularly teachers, civil servants and policemen – have travelled the Caribbean, and the Commonwealth, in search of labour opportunities.⁴⁶ However, this migrant class did not historically have a strong local counterpart – or, put differently, the stultifying social conditions of white supremacy and paternalism meant that Barbados developed a self-confident, assertive black middle class later than countries like its neighbour Trinidad and Tobago.⁴⁷ This legacy of racial apartheid was only frontally challenged (notwithstanding the signally important 1937 rebellion) in the social and public sphere by black cultural organizations and black power in the 1970s, by the scholarship of a number of progressive social scientists and historians in the 1980s, and in a critique of white economic power from the late 1980s to the early 1990s.⁴⁸

In 1990, the political scientist Hilbourne Watson accused the middle classes of a "pathological indifference to, and cynicism about, racism" and a pragmatism that scarcely hid a "disconcerting anti-intellectualism".⁴⁹ The record of the decades preceding this statement is one of a middle class making definitive socio-economic advances, but arguably even more filled with anxieties about downward mobility than their middle-class peers in other parts of the Caribbean, and captive through employment to the whims of either the two leading, white minority–controlled conglomerates or alternating parties in government, both with a statecraft mired in client politics.

A 2001 report on social stratification and the status of the black middle class noted that the size of that class in Barbados was proportionately bigger than its counterparts in Jamaica and Trinidad and Tobago, though the "stratification system is not significantly different". It also concluded that this middle class had stagnated in the 1990s, following the impressive gains of the previous generation.[50] Over a decade later, in the midst of the second most difficult economic situation the country has faced since independence, and with debates swirling about the viability of the free health care and tertiary education system that Barbadians have enjoyed since independence, the question of whether the relatively straightforward ascendancy to middle-class status will become dramatically curtailed is a pressing concern.[51] And this is the context of Rihanna's rise to global celebrity.

RIHANNA'S FUN

> Many blacks, in short, simply want to be beautiful and successful.
> —Lewis Gordon, *Her Majesty's Other Children*[52]

> Cheers to the fricken' weekend
> I drink to that, yeah yeah . . .
> There's a party at the bar, everybody putcha glasses up and I'll drink to that
> —Rihanna, "Cheers (Drink to That)"

Bishop Husbands's admonishment that Rihanna is "always doing foolishness" strikes one as less of a condemnation than, surely inadvertently for him, a bit of a tease. In the arena of popular culture, to be strange is the point; controversy sells; and, as popularized by Michael Jackson, "bad" is good. Even the word *foolishness* in Caribbean creoles is hardly necessarily an insult, being more suggestive of the silly than the savage. Husbands follows the well-worn path of other Barbadian state managers who often speak grimly about "deviant behaviour" among the youth and press for the eradication of "subcultures". Yet, for the cultural critic, the subculture is often the meeting point of cultural creativity and counter-hegemonic resistance.[53] Husbands's comment feels more like a tease than a condemnation because its haughty tone belies the fact that Rihanna is hardly a child, but is instead a global cultural icon whose power makes the warblings of religious ministers seem anachronistic and more than a little dull.

And what a global cultural icon Rihanna has become. As of April 2014, she had sold more digital tracks than any other artist in the United States, the world's largest national consumer market. She has also been unofficially crowned the queen of Facebook and of YouTube; at the time of writing, she had more views of her page and videos, respectively, on those media than any other artist.[54] Facebook, the world's most heavily utilized social networking website, with over one billion users, and YouTube, the dominant video-sharing website, are two of the most powerful sites of the currently evolving online-entertainment revolution, and Rihanna's current capture of both is a stunning success. Further, Rihanna has thirteen *Billboard* Hot 100 number-one hits, making her the youngest artist to reach that number. At the American Music Awards in 2013, she received their first Icon Award, and she was honoured with the Council of Fashion Designers of America's Fashion Icon Award in June 2014. With over 30 million albums and 120 million singles sold, she is on course to become one of the top-selling artists of all time.

It is fascinating to consider the case of Garfield Sobers, arguably Barbados's best-known living citizen before Rihanna. Both grew up in poor neighbourhoods in the greater Bridgetown area: Sobers in the Bayland, Rihanna in Westbury Road. At the height of their success, both were lauded as the greatest of their time – Sobers as the finest all-round cricketer the world had ever seen, and Rihanna as the most successful pop singer to emerge in the first decade of the twenty-first century. Yet a look at the contrasts between the two more clearly situates the generational shift they represent. The knowledge and awe of Sobers extends throughout the Commonwealth, the result of his mastery and transformation of that British colonial game, cricket. Rihanna's appeal is to a global audience, made possible by a widespread fascination with black popular culture – and with one of its most mesmerizing creations, the rhythm and blues/hip-hop/urban pop music genre.

The claim here is not that Rihanna represents the move from a British cultural influence in the anglophone Caribbean to an American hegemony, a shift considered by many to have decisively taken place with the decline in British power in the aftermath of World War II. This historical trajectory misses too much about the circulation of Caribbean cultures through North America and back to the region in the early twentieth century and about the investment of Caribbean publics in consumer products from America throughout the last century.[55] It is worth remembering that 2012 commemorated the one hundredth anniversary of the recording of the first calypso record, not in Trinidad but in New York, and the borrowings and cross-fertilizations between the United States and Jamaica that have created reggae and hip-hop, to name just two massively popular contemporary art forms, are too well known to rehearse again here. However, the creation of Rihanna as a distinctively pop icon, rather than one tied to any specific black diasporic musical tradition, along with her dizzying, quite outrageous success, creates wonder and concern in many – not least of all in her country, Barbados.

Heather Russell has done a fine job of theorizing and documenting the multiple anxieties and discourses surrounding Rihanna in the Barbadian public sphere.[56] These range from the (tired and tiring) "role model" argument, to the ageist arrogance (pervasive in the Caribbean, though far less critiqued) that portrays her to be a little girl in need of prayer, support and stern rebuke, and, finally, the blissfully colonizing arguments that Barbados must own, control and manage the profile of this product of their soil, who may provide revenue for the state and its people. The weight of being Barbados's first superstar in the media-saturated American market, as Russell suggests, has placed a particularly heavy scrutiny on Rihanna at home, particularly in that all-pervasive linchpin of respectability, the arena of sexuality. Thus, Russell rightly notes that much of the anger over Rihanna and her claim to be a legitimate national representative relates to her sexuality, as "to be acknowledged as possessing an autonomous sexuality [is] to be necessarily stripped of all legitimate claims to national recognition".[57]

I want to press these critiques by Russell further, partly through my observations of the last couple of years since her essay was completed. I would suggest that in that time, Rihanna has felt less of an interest or need to respond to Barbadian society's ambivalence about her, and that the reinventions of her public image as explored by Russell suggest a randomness based on both a marketing project and a yearning for a new aesthetic style, as well as on the tumble and silliness of celebrity leisure practices, and a sense of fun. There is an almost frantic quality to the burgeoning stories of risqué behaviour emanating from the Rihanna camp, and much of dubious merit.[58] We are told of a new tattoo, a topless pose. There is a duet with Chris Brown, followed by angry tweets between them. Rihanna posts to her Twitter account a picture of herself hooked up to an IV on a hospital bed; nude pictures circulate on the Internet. Jay-Z reportedly tells her to enter rehab or he will drop her from his label.[59] It is through such ruses that Rihanna secures her position as the "most controversial person of the year", as she was dubbed by her hometown paper, and – more concretely, and more importantly for her career – outstanding visibility and commercial success.[60]

In a discerning essay on hip-hop, Lewis Gordon suggests that one of the difficulties of presenting that genre as a singular example of authentic black culture is its status as an "adolescent culture", a form of "cultural play" which, while enjoyable in itself, has its limits. Gordon is not suggesting that hip-hop culture remains innocent of progressive politics. Rather, he suggests that the effervescence of the genre and its appeals to pleasure make sense when we understand it as a youth culture, as "part of being young is behaving in ways that stretch the limits of culture marked by the weight of responsibility".[61] Gordon's argument has undeniable merit; however, it is worth appreciating that in even the less politicized urban pop music of which Rihanna is the unofficial queen, her performances and image have resulted in a salvo of intense discussions about gender, sexuality and commodification on websites like the Crunk Feminist Collective and the Feminist Wire.[62]

What some of the writers of these highly provocative exchanges seem to miss is the extent to which artists like Rihanna are removed from the creation of most of their hits. It is difficult to discuss Rihanna's song "Man Down" as a personal response to a past abusive relationship when we know it was written in a writing camp in twelve minutes.[63] The point is not to diminish her achievements by pointing to the intensely commodified nature of today's popular-music industry, for as John Seabrook points out, Rihanna "embodies a song in the way an actor inhabits a role – and no one expects the actor to write the script".[64] I would suggest, though, that this may be a better way of comprehending the Rihanna of the last few years, with the new tattoos, intimations of marijuana use, outlandish outfits and partying. It is partly the allure of acting out a particularly carefully crafted marketing brand, but, just as crucially, it is also youthful fun writ large on the global stage provided by celebrity.

The reactions to this from respectable black middle-class society in Barbados and elsewhere are so predictable that it all seems almost like a choreographed series of steps of risqué performance followed by haughty moral retort. Even here, though, there is a twist. The Barbadian state has sufficiently pinned its marketing hopes for its major industry, tourism, on its most recognizable citizen, and with this financial imperative comes the need for a cautious tone from the political directorate, and an occasional defence from officialdom.[65] This means that the minister of family, culture, sports and youth can appeal to Barbadians to stop criticizing Rihanna, suggesting that she is an appropriate role model for the youth, while two months later he can condemn the abundance of sexuality and the promotion of homosexuality on television.[66]

What can we make of these middle-class anxieties that continue to reverberate into the second decade of the twenty-first century? Fanon and James, two of the Caribbean's greatest thinkers, could speak so clearly about them because their revolutionary commitment was unmistakable and the world they imagined had an unequivocal option: neo-colonialism or a sovereign socialist postcolonial society. The contemporary question is in part the debris of middle-class formation in emerging liberal democracies – middle-classness as the normative genre of the human wedded to coloniality; but since coloniality now exists largely devoid of revolutionary critique in the Caribbean public sphere, middle-classness exists as a state of being we cannot *not* want.

It is clear that for the black middle class, Rihanna can only serve as an endlessly problematic symbol, as they are attracted to the fame and the money she has wrested from white capitalism but are scandalized at her agency to behave in ways they consider to be not respectable. She has enough money to buy legitimacy and a form of erotic freedom which they yearn for but cannot possess. Middle-class respectability becomes what Lindon Barrett once described as a "crush of racial, gendered, domestic, and commercial prohibitions and imperatives".[67] It is likely why Rihanna can still produce a thrill, sardonic and otherwise, among non-elite communities in Barbados.

NOTES

1. Mike King, "Rihanna 'Not Fit' ", *Daily Nation* (Barbados), 21 November 2011, http://www.nationnews.com/nationnews/news/289/rihanna-fit.
2. C.L.R. James, *Party Politics in the West Indies* (San Juan, Trinidad and Tobago: Vedic Enterprises, 1962), 133.
3. Frantz Fanon, *The Wretched of the Earth*, trans. Constance Farrington (London: Penguin, 1990), 37.
4. Ibid., 141, 122.
5. Ibid., 119.
6. Ibid., 131.
7. James, *Party Politics*, 131.
8. Ibid., 139.
9. See here W.E.B. Du Bois's landmark essay "The Study of the Negro Problems", *Annals of the American Academy of Political and Social Science* 11 (January 1898): 1–23. Thanks to Lewis Gordon for alerting me to the existence of this essay. See Gordon, "Du Bois's Humanistic Philosophy of Human Sciences", *Annals of the American Academy of Political and Social Science* 568 (March 2000): 265–80.
10. Greg Thomas, "Sexual Imitation and the Lumpen-Bourgeoisie: Race and Class as Erotic Conflict in E. Franklin Frazier", in *The Sexual Demon of Colonial Power: Pan-African Embodiment and Erotic Schemes of Empire* (Bloomington: Indiana University Press, 2006), 58.
11. Ibid., 74.
12. Oliver Cox, introduction to *The Black Anglo-Saxons*, by Nathan Hare (New York: Marzani and Munsell, 1965), 13. This work by Hare is a devastating indictment of the black elites, influenced enough by Frazier for Cox to refer to them in his critical introduction as part of the same school of thought. The critique of this work from the left in the figure of Oliver Cox takes Frazier and Hare as its targets and reaches the conclusion that their work is beset with methodological problems, resulting in flawed readings of this class, particularly in their descriptions of black institutions, as well as in their reading of the black upper class as fundamentally rootless, partly as a result of an overplaying of their ideological investments.
13. Patrick Bryan, "The Black Middle Class in Nineteenth Century Jamaica", in *Caribbean Freedom: Economy and Society from Emancipation to the Present*, ed. Hilary McD. Beckles and Verene Shepherd (Kingston: Ian Randle, 1993); Bridget Brereton, "The Development of an Identity: The Black Middle Class of Trinidad in the Later Nineteenth Century", in Beckles and Shepherd, *Caribbean Freedom*.

14. Belinda Edmondson, *Caribbean Middlebrow: Leisure Culture and the Middle Class* (Ithaca: Cornell University Press, 2009).
15. Lloyd Braithwaite, *Social Stratification in Trinidad* (Kingston: Institute of Social and Economic Research, University of the West Indies, 1975). Originally published in *Social and Economic Studies* 2, nos. 2–3 (1953).
16. Ibid., 107.
17. Edward Kamau Brathwaite, *The Development of Creole Society in Jamaica, 1770–1820* (Oxford: Oxford University Press, 1971), 311.
18. Walter Rodney, "Contemporary Political Trends in the English-Speaking Caribbean", *Black Scholar* 7, no. 1 (September 1975): 15–21.
19. Rodney, "Contemporary Political Trends", 15. In this essay, Rodney shows an tremendous debt to Frantz Fanon, specifically to the analysis of the colonial transitioning to independent Third World state as developed by Fanon in *The Wretched of the Earth*.
20. Ibid., 15.
21. Ibid., 18.
22. Don Robotham, "Blackening the Jamaican Nation: The Travails of a Black Bourgeoisie in a Globalized World", *Identities* 7, no. 1 (March 2000): 1–37; Rupert Lewis, "Reconsidering the Role of the Middle Class in Caribbean Politics", in *New Caribbean Thought: A Reader*, ed. Brian Meeks and Folke Lindahl (Kingston: University of the West Indies Press, 2001).
23. Robotham, "Blackening the Jamaican Nation", 3.
24. Ibid., 8.
25. Lewis, "Reconsidering", 140.
26. Ibid. See Lewis's comments on entrepreneurial activity, 133, 135, 139.
27. For an important argument on entrepreneurship, neoliberalism, middle-classness and the Barbadian state, see Carla Freeman, "The 'Reputation' of Neoliberalism", *American Ethnologist* 34, no. 2 (2007): 252–67, and her forthcoming book *Entrepreneurial Selves: Neoliberal Respectability and the Making of a Caribbean Middle Class* (Durham, NC: Duke University Press, 2014)
28. Peter J. Wilson, "Reputation and Respectability: A Suggestion for Caribbean Ethnology", *Man* 4, no. 1 (1969): 70–84; Peter J. Wilson, *Crab Antics: The Social Anthropology of English-Speaking Negro Societies of the Caribbean* (New Haven: Yale University Press, 1973). See also Rhoda E. Reddock, ed., *Interrogating Caribbean Masculinities: Theoretical and Empirical Analyses* (Kingston: University of the West Indies Press, 2004).
29. See the discussion in Daniel Miller, *Modernity: An Ethnographic Approach, Dualism and Mass Consumption in Trinidad* (Oxford: Berg, 1994).
30. Jean Besson, "Reputation and Respectability Reconsidered: A New Perspective

on Afro-Caribbean Peasant Women", in *Women and Change in the Caribbean: A Pan-Caribbean Perspective*, ed. Janet Momsen (Bloomington: Indiana University Press, 1993), 19. See also Wilson, *Crab Antics*, 234.

31. Shalini Puri, "Beyond Resistance: Notes Towards a New Caribbean Cultural Studies", *Small Axe* 7, no. 2 (2003): 23–38; David A.B. Murray, *Flaming Souls: Homosexuality, Homophobia and Social Change in Barbados* (Toronto: University of Toronto Press, 2012).
32. Puri, "Beyond Resistance", 24.
33. See here George L. Mosse's introduction, "Nationalism and Respectability", to his work *Nationalism and Sexuality: Respectability and Abnormal Sexuality in Modern Europe* (New York: Howard Fertig, 1985).
34. Wilson, *Crab Antics*, 233.
35. Diane J. Austin, "Culture and Ideology in the English-Speaking Caribbean: A View from Jamaica", *American Ethnologist* 10, no. 2 (May 1983): 236.
36. See here Brian Meeks, "The Political Moment in Jamaica: The Dimensions of Hegemonic Dissolution", in *Radical Caribbean: From Black Power to Abu Bakr* (Kingston: University of the West Indies Press, 1993), 124–43; Percy Hintzen, "Afro-Creole Nationalism as Elite Domination: The English-Speaking West Indies", in *Foreign Policy and the Black (Inter)National Interest*, ed. Charles P. Henry (New York: State University of New York Press, 2000), 185–215; Aaron Kamugisha, "The Coloniality of Citizenship in the Contemporary Anglophone Caribbean", *Race and Class* 49, no. 2 (2007): 20–40.
37. Neil Lazarus, *Nationalism and Cultural Practice in the Postcolonial World* (Cambridge: Cambridge University Press, 1999), 19; emphasis in original.
38. I chart some of these stereotypes in my essay "The Survivors of the Crossing and the Impossibility of Late Colonial Revolt", introduction to *The Survivors of the Crossing*, by Austin Clarke (Leeds: Peepal Tree Press, 2012).
39. Tony Best, "Barbados Shines", 8 November 2010, *Daily Nation* (Barbados), http://www.nationnews.com/nationnews/news/41742/barbados-shines.
40. In 2012, Barbados was ranked number one in the Caribbean in the *Global Information Technology Report*. See "Barbados Is the Best in the Caribbean According to Latest Report", MNI Alive, 26 April 2012, http://www.mnialive.com/articles/barbados-is-the-best-in-the-caribbean-according-to-latest-report. On car ownership, Barbados is cited as having the sixth-densest road network in the world and as being twenty-third in the world with respect to number of cars per kilometre of road. "Car Ownership among Highest", *Saturday Sun* (Barbados), 31 March 2012, 16.
41. Courtney Blackman, "The Barbados Model", *Caribbean Affairs* 8, no. 1 (1998): 61–68.

42. Don Robotham, *Vision and Volunteerism: Reviving Volunteerism in Jamaica*, Grace Kennedy Foundation Lecture, 1998 (Kingston: Grace Kennedy Foundation, 1998), 29.
43. Robotham, "Blackening the Jamaican Nation", 7 (emphasis added). Readers of Charles Mills's acclaimed work *The Racial Contract* will have much to ponder about Robotham's use of this term, or on how indeed a racial contract can be pragmatic. See Charles W. Mills, *The Racial Contract* (Ithaca: Cornell University Press, 1997).
44. Peter Blair Henry and Conrad Miller, "Institutions versus Policies: A Tale of Two Islands", *American Economic Review* 99, no. 2 (2009): 261–67; Brian Meeks, *Envisioning Caribbean Futures: Jamaican Perspectives* (Kingston: University of the West Indies Press, 2007), 95–97. For two alternative discussions of the Barbados/Jamaica connection, see Winston James, *Holding Aloft the Banner of Ethiopia: Caribbean Radicalism in Early Twentieth-Century America* (London: Verso, 1998), 114–19; and, for a particularly witty and revealing rumination, Hilary McD. Beckles, "Historicising Conversations with Michael Manley", *Caribbean Quarterly* 48, no. 1 (2002): 31–44.
45. Ralph Gonsalves, "The Idea of Barbados", *Barbados Today*, 3 April 2014, http://www.barbadostoday.bb/2014/04/03/the-idea-of-barbados/. Gonsalves's article strains towards a Hegelian-type philosophy of Caribbean history and is lavishly filled with similarly ahistorical and deeply problematic formulations. What is most telling is that, while supposedly praising Barbados, the article has little interest in the neocolonial conditions under which contemporary Barbadians labour. Such has been the case of much writing on Barbados – it is caricatured by polemicists who care so little about it.
46. James, *Holding Aloft the Banner*, 118.
47. The irony being, as Winston James points out, that Barbadian migrants did much to create this black, educated and frequently radical middle class in Trinidad.
48. For important overviews of this entire period, see Hilary McD. Beckles, "Independence and the Social Crisis of Nationalism in Barbados", in Beckles and Shepherd, *Caribbean Freedom*, 528–39; Linden Lewis, "The Contestation of Race in Barbadian Society and the Camouflage of Conservatism", in Meeks and Lindahl, *New Caribbean Thought*, 144–55. See also Christine Barrow, "Ownership and Control of Resources in Barbados: 1834 to the Present", *Social and Economic Studies* 32, no. 3 (1983): 83–120; Anthony Layne, "Racial Injustice and National Development in Post-Colonial Barbados", *Bulletin of Eastern Caribbean Affairs* 15, no. 6 (January/February 1990): 46–61; Hilbourne Watson, "Beyond Ideology: The Question of the Black Middle Class in Barbados", *Bulletin of Eastern Caribbean Affairs* 15, no. 6 (January–February 1990): 16–31. For the classic text that docu-

ments the struggle against white economic hegemony in Barbados, see Hilary McD. Beckles, *Corporate Power in Barbados: The Mutual Affair* (Bridgetown, Barbados: Lighthouse Communications, 1989).

49. Watson, "Beyond Ideology", 18.
50. Ian Boxill, Dillon Alleyne and Andrew Downes, *Social Stratification in Barbados: An Analysis of the State of the Black Middle Class*, vols. 1–2. Report prepared for the Nation Publishing Company, Barbados, July 2001.
51. The most challenging economic crisis Barbados has experienced in its post-independence history is the balance of payments crisis of the early 1990s. For one account of this, see Neville C. Duncan, "Barbados and the IMF: A Case Study", in *Structural Adjustment, Public Policy and Administration in the Caribbean*, ed. John La Guerre (St Augustine: School for Continuing Studies, University of the West Indies, 1994), 54–87.
52. Lewis Gordon, "Race, Biraciality, and Mixed Race – In Theory", in *Her Majesty's Other Children: Sketches of Racism from a Neocolonial Age* (Lanham, MD: Rowman and Littlefield, 1997), 59.
53. I allude here to Dick Hebdige, *Subculture: The Meaning of Style* (London: Routledge, 1991).
54. "Rihanna's Queen of YouTube", *Daily Nation* (Barbados), 11 January 2012, http://www.nationnews.com/nationnews/news/45275/rihanna-8217-queen-youtube.
55. Here, we may consider Caribbean migrations to the United States in the first decades of the twentieth century, along with the transformations in the Caribbean public's tastes, styles and access to capital as a result of the building of the Panama Canal. See James, *Holding Aloft the Banner*. See also Harvey Neptune, *Caliban and the Yankees: Trinidad and the United States Occupation* (Chapel Hill: University of North Carolina Press, 2007).
56. Heather Russell, "Whose Rihanna? Diasporic Citizenship and the Economies of Crossing Over", in *Archipelagos of Sound: Transnational Caribbeanities, Women and Music*, ed. Ifeona Fulani (Kingston: University of the West Indies Press, 2012), 301–22.
57. Ibid., 310.
58. I refer to the "Rihanna camp" as it is obvious that most of these portrayals are being crafted by a media team rather than by the idiosyncratic warblings of its rich and talented singer.
59. "Jay-Z to Rihanna: 'Go to Rehab' ", *Daily Nation* (Barbados), 14 June 2012, http://www.nationnews.com/nationnews/news/45990/jay-rihanna-8216-rehab-8217.
60. The *Nation*, Barbados's leading newspaper, called Rihanna "the most controversial person of the year" for 2011. See Ricky Jordan, "Rihanna Does It All in 2011", *Sunday Sun*, 1 January 2012, 23A.

61. Lewis R. Gordon, "The Problem of Maturity in Hip Hop", *Review of Education, Pedagogy, and Cultural Studies* 27 (2005): 368.
62. "Sound Off: Black Women Writers Respond to Rihanna's 'Pour It Up' ", *Feminist Wire* (blog), 11 October 2013, http://thefeministwire.com/2013/10/sound-off-black-women-writers-respond-to-rihannas-pour-it-up/; Muna Mire, "Talkback: In Defense of Rihanna", *Feminist Wire*, 16 October 2013, http://thefeministwire.com/2013/10/rihanna/; "Man Down: On Rihanna, Rape and Violence", *Crunk Feminist Collective* (blog), 2 June 2011, http://crunkfeministcollective.wordpress.com/2011/06/02/man-down-on-rihanna-rape-and-violence/.
63. Zoe Chace, "How Much Does It Cost to Make a Hit Song?", NPR online, 30 June 2011, http://www.npr.org/blogs/money/2011/07/05/137530847/how-much-does-it-cost-to-make-a-hit-song.
64. John Seabrook, "The Song Machine: The Hitmakers behind Rihanna", *New Yorker* online, 26 March 2012, http://www.newyorker.com/reporting/2012/03/26/120326fa_fact_seabrook?currentPage=all.
65. For a rare, thoughtful counter to this, see Robert Chase, "BTA Off-Key on Rihanna", *Sunday Sun* (Barbados), 5 February 2012, 21A.
66. Mike King, "Stop Bashing Rihanna", *Daily Nation* (Barbados), 5 March 2011, http://www.nationnews.com/nationnews/news/21935/stop-bashing-rihanna; "Too Much Sex on Television", *Daily Nation*, 18 May 2011, http://www.nationnews.com/nationnews/news/33554/sex-television. For a later tribute to Rihanna from the same minister on the floor of the House of Assembly, see "Lashley Praises Rihanna", *Daily Nation*, 29 January 2014, 19A.
67. Lindon Barrett, "Black Men in the Mix: Badboys, Heroes, Sequins, and Dennis Rodman", *Callaloo* 20, no. 1 (1997): 125.

8

RIHANNA

Diaspora Citizen, Bajan Daughter, Global Superstar

HEATHER D. RUSSELL

Writing brilliantly and eerily prophetically almost forty years ago, the Barbadian author Austin Clarke, in his novel *The Prime Minister* (1977), depicts the complex imbrications, heavy encumbrances and fraught exigencies that come when government, tourism, culture, globalization, art and national identity simultaneously converge and inevitably collide.[1] The novel begins with John Moore (the fictionalized Austin Clarke), the poet turned politician who returns to Barbados after twenty years to assume the position of director of national culture of the newly independent nation-state.[2]

As the plane carrying John Moore "home" descends, the novel's central character "looked at his country going past his view like the frames in a magic lantern, shown at too fast a speed for concentration and identification".[3] Here, Barbados is presented as bewitchingly alluring and yet elusive, dynamically shifting, resisting any attempts to fix it. Barbados, like its anglophone Caribbean neighbours, is a nascent postcolonial nation-in-process-of-becoming. Throughout the novel, poignant scenes capture the dialectical tug of nation-building and exilic freedom. "You never know how free you are," John Moore ruminates, "how much freedom you have living in an alien society, until you come back to your own free and independent country."[4] His conclusions here resoundingly echo the sentiments about returning home expressed in Dennis Scott's poem "Exile": "To travel / is to return / to strangers".[5]

In the end, absolute church power, easily corruptible state interests, ruthless collusion between elites, the suppression of free cultural expression and a manipulable general public lead a disillusioned John Moore to abandon the nation-building project, which is seemingly doomed to fail, to return to his exilic existence. He concludes by the novel's end, as the plane ascends and he once again surveys Barbados, "Paradise . . . a country such as this does look like paradise. . . . Perhaps . . . it is the idea of flight and departure that comes as a natural consequence of arrival, that makes the tourists regard only this aspect of a country" (190). In other words, to see Barbados as paradisiacal, one must necessarily be in flight.

As he gazes upon Barbados's "naked purity for the last time", John Moore, former director of national culture, poignantly observes that "the land is beautiful, the only truly beautiful thing about this country" (191). Of course, we know that the narrator is being painfully ironic. Clarke's novel provides, however, in strikingly resonant ways an interesting, early framing of some of the critical currents surrounding Barbados's most famous cultural ambassador, Robyn "Rihanna" Fenty.

DIASPORA CITIZENSHIP

In the pages that follow, I examine Rihanna as "diaspora citizen" as a way to tease out the politics of her multiple and multiply inflected locations. According to Alexander Weheliye, "The phrase 'diasporic citizenship' excavates and magnifies [the] tension between the national and transnational, rather than subsuming one under the other."[6] In other words, to be a diaspora citizen is to simultaneously negotiate the entailments of civic responsibility, public discourse, nostalgia, nationhood, belonging *and* migration, transnational cultural affiliations and shifting/fluid subject positionalities across material and symbolic boundaries. If, as Weheliye argues, diasporic citizenship "occupies the interstices of the nation-state and other forms of politicized community" outside of national borders, its practice demands a deft negotiation of culture, politics, and *de jure* and *de facto* rules of engagement across multiple spaces. Eschewing both the tendency in traditional social science to foreground the nation-state as the principal unit of organization and the tendency in cultural and postcolonial studies to privilege transnationalism and cultural hybridity, Weheliye affirms, and I fully concur, that "the national and the transnational should be understood as quasidialectical partners in the movement of globalization."[7]

Simultaneously identified as Barbadian "daughter" and global "superstar", Rihanna must navigate inevitably conflicting, contesting and reinforcing sites of national and transnational belongings. In other words, she is a Barbadian citizen shining in a US-global sphere within which most citizens can hardly find Barbados on the map. She is a hugely commercially successful artist operating in a popular-cultural market dictated by US-global musical tastes. At the same time, Rihanna is Barbados's honorary ambassador of youth and culture and has signed a multi-year deal to promote Barbados for the Barbados Tourism Authority. Moreover, local discussions surrounding Barbadian national pride, Victorian notions of female propriety and Christian ideas about decency which Rihanna's emergence and ascendancy have provoked, continue to capture the Barbadian public's imaginations and dominate the opinions expressed in their newspaper columns and call-in programmes.

Rihanna is, on the one hand, a pop star, attiring and expressing herself within the popular-cultural marketplace in ways that reify her commercial appeal and (not to strip her of agency here) that perhaps conform to her own necessarily dynamic ideological choices about self-presentation. But as the first Barbadian superstar of such magnitude, she implicitly carries the burden, the sheer weight, of representing the entire nation (willingly or not); for it is especially true in the case of black people that in the absence of multiple, diverse public images, "the one" is always already construed as both representative and representation.

If for a diasporic citizen, as Weheliye has argued, "the problematic of belonging" concerns where "subjects locate their political and cultural affiliations" and how these allegiances are "circumscribed by various political, economic and cultural constraints", in the face of such competing, coeval, national and transnational interests, how can Rihanna productively locate her political and cultural affiliations?[8] If she simultaneously belongs to Barbados and to her global consumers, and is thus answerable to (at least) both constituencies, then what challenges does she continue to face in terms of negotiating her status as diaspora citizen? Finally, then, through a reading of popular responses to Rihanna, her (re)presentations and respective entailments (including the aforementioned nationally bestowed honour of serving as Barbados's ambassador of youth and culture and her promotional agreement with the Barbados Tourism Authority), my chapter carries forward these questions of Rihanna's diaspora citizenship in an attempt to tease out how ideas around nation, diaspora, gender, identity, sexuality and global economy converge in illuminating ways, necessary for reading Caribbean cultural production in the age of postmodernity.

ROOTINGS AND ROUTINGS

When pop superstar Rihanna burst on the scene in 2005 with her hybrid reggae/hip-hop/R&B style, signalled by her highly successful single "Pon de Replay", audiences hurriedly googled to find information about her origins: "Barbados? Barbados!" Conventionally known for its progressive civility, its culture of cricket excellence, its internationally renowned writers Paule Marshall, George Lamming, Kamau Brathwaite and Austin Clarke – that Barbados would be the site of national origin for one of the most internationally recognized and commercially successful pop stars of the twenty-first century caught many non-Caribbeans, and admittedly some Caribbean non-Bajans, by surprise. More curious, though, and decidedly more revelatory, have been the ensuing conversations surrounding Rihanna on topics ranging from sex, commerce and citizenship to domestic violence, sadomasochism and globalization.

In the case of Rihanna, such dynamics dramatically resound within several discursive domains, including a radically divergent public dialogue in Barbados that on the one hand critiques her for the overly sexualized representations and morally questionable behaviour perceived by many, but on the other demands formal national recognition of her for having placed the nation "on the map". The wide-ranging debate around Rihanna culminates with the more recently articulated belief that Rihanna as Bajan citizen bears responsibility to help Barbados with its developmental strategy. As one Barbadian news commentator recently put it in her article "What Can Rihanna Do for Her Country?", "To whom much is given, much is expected."[9]

In addition, Rihanna's self-conscious choice to feature the Barbadian flag, especially the trident, in her transnational cultural production, as well as her resistance to standardize her "accent" to conform to US expectations, are noteworthy articulations of Barbadian national belonging that signify globally. At the same time, however, economic rewards accrue from aesthetically "crossing over" into the US-global mainstream market, thus creating a disjuncture between her global rhythmic and national soundings. It is true that Rihanna returns, musically, to her Caribbean roots from time to time, the most recent notable instances being the highly controversial reggae/dancehall single "Man Down" (2011) and her performance at the 2013 Grammy Awards in tribute to Bob Marley. Still, "Man Down" enjoyed only moderate success in comparison to her more rhythmically and lyrically conventional pop hits like "Only Girl (in the World)", "We Found Love" and, most recently, "Diamonds". There is no question then that the "Bimshire" artist has unequivocally crossed over into the mainstream of popular culture through her musical production, if not in her public performances of national/cultural subjectivity.[10] However, while Rihanna may be crossing, she is unequivocally not passing, a point to which I shall return.

The invocation of Rihanna as "the face of Barbados" produces a veritable phantasmagoria of colonial history, nationalism, globalization and sexual politics. With her light complexion and green-amber eyes, Rihanna is not phenotypically characteristic of the majority of Afro-Barbadians, who constitute the principal racial group in the nation. Thus, her acceptance in the global popular-cultural marketplace as a sex symbol who embodies crossover appeal raises a complex of issues. The Barbadian public's imagination of itself is inevitably fraught with what Alice Walker calls "contrary instincts".[11] The nation-state invariably feels simultaneously proud and protective of its native daughter. And yet, from an economic standpoint, the selfsame nation-state must concede the expediency of *marketing* its daughter as "Bajan" commodity on the global exchange with full awareness that Rihanna's commercial viability rests upon enduring colonial legacies which idealize and reward brown skin.

In fact, the thorny issue of skin colour and race in Barbados entered the US public sphere a few years ago, when Rihanna revealed in a 2007 interview with *Allure* magazine that during her childhood, she was "bullied at school – for being 'white'". "So I was cultured in a very 'black way'", she said. "But when I go to school, I'm getting called 'white'. They would look at me and curse me out."[12] Here, Rihanna reveals the cultural conflation of light skin with the term *white*, which in the Bajan context does not necessarily refer to race – a conflation that undoubtedly seems odd and thus salacious to *Allure*'s primary readers, consuming from the highly racially charged space of the United States. In the United States, "one drop" of black blood historically determined black racial identity. "Brown privilege" notwithstanding, clearly defined divisions between whites and blacks, irrespective of the latter's colour diversity, remain firmly entrenched. What Rihanna points to here, at least inferentially, are the ways in which colour signifies differently across national borders. In other words, the terms *white* and *black* have attendant cultural meanings that are not simply transferable transnationally. At the same time, when she admits that she was raised in "a very 'black way' ", in her purposeful usage, *black* comes to stand in not for race per se, but for a kind of cultural nationalism which construes Barbados as a black nation.

Within Barbados, the response to the *Allure* article, especially in the *Barbados Free Press*, took a particularly interesting national twist: Rihanna's revelations were appropriated for political fodder. The *Allure* article, which appeared in the January 2008 issue of the magazine, on which Rihanna graced the cover, was actually released in December 2007, one month before elections were to be held in Barbados. The Barbados Labour Party's (BLP) leadership of the country, under the helm of Prime Minister Owen Arthur, was being contested by the David Thompson–led Democratic Labour Party (DLP). In a *Barbados Free Press* article from that month, under the headline "The Ugly Secret of Barbados Revealed Worldwide: Rihanna 'I Was Bullied at School for Being White' ", the writer declares, "This might be the best thing that ever happened to those of us on this island who have shades of skin that are 'not dark enough' – because it will focus world attention on that dirty little Bajan secret that we all live with: *a virulent new strain of racism is alive and well in Barbados and it is being nurtured by our own government to serve a partisan agenda.*"[13]

Pointing to the "Barbados political elite" as purveyors of a politico-cultural environment of reverse discrimination against brown and white Bajans, the *Free Press* article argued that the BLP both tacitly and overtly deployed a discourse of black/dark skin legitimacy to affirm its loyalty to, and thus suitability to continue to address, the needs of the black Bajan majority. Highlighting the absence of "lighter-skinned persons of African heritage or mixed race persons" on the BLP's website and the claims from a supposed BLP insider's post on the *Free Press* website that light-complexioned opposition leader

"David Thompson is a white man who believes that any success gained by a black man is by way of corruption", the article argued that the "racial slurs of the Barbados government" revealed a political system rife with its own racist agenda to delegitimize and silence brown Barbadians. Ironically, the physical differences between the two party leaders was arguably a matter of semantics, for both former prime minister Owen Arthur and (since-deceased) prime minister David Thompson were, for all intents and purposes, phenotypically brown men. Crossing the border back into her nation-state, the cultural and political meanings of Rihanna's public revelations in an American magazine of having been bullied in Barbados "for being white" became fascinatingly co-opted, caught within the critical maelstrom of national electoral fervour, in which race, colour, history and politics existed – as they always do, particularly in the postcolonial world – in highly conflictual interrelation to each other.

"PRETTY LI'L GIRL RIHANNA"

On 22 February 2008, one month after assuming his post as prime minister, David Thompson named Rihanna an honorary youth and cultural ambassador of Barbados.[14] I shall return to the transnational implications of Rihanna's cultural production and its global/economic dimensions, but for the moment, I want to explore the historical, ideological and political trajectory framing Rihanna's journey towards the bestowal of this national honour. As Weheliye relevantly reminds us, "being a diasporic citizen entails culturally and politically aligning oneself with communities beyond the borders of the nation-state in which one dwells, in addition to negotiating legal and cultural positionalities in relation to this very nation-state."[15]

The dialectical relationship between transnational and nationally inflected "cultural positionalities" (along with unmistakable gender implications) resounds in the following poem, which appeared in the Barbadian daily newspaper the *Nation* in honour of both Rihanna's first Grammy Award and her designation as youth and cultural ambassador of Barbados:

> *Rihanna*
> Pretty little Bajan island girl
> You have put Barbados on the map of the world
> Like a glimmer of sunshine

> You came with a song
> And had the world at your feet before too long
> Your sweetness and innocence go a long way
> To reach the hearts of those you endear
> Keep up the good work, pretty little island girl
> Keep on putting Barbados on top of the world.
> Keep up the good work and may you continue
> to be blessed.[16]

To many in Barbados, the honour bestowed by Prime Minister Thompson upon "the pretty li'l Bajan girl" was long overdue. As exemplified by several editorials published in 2007,[17] demands that the "gem of Barbados" be given national recognition had permeated the Barbados press: "Rihanna is the 'biggest thing' (person) to come out of Barbados ever. Yet to date, not a word of acknowledgement at the national level. How can this be?"[18] While the BLP had in fact launched a tourism campaign in 2006 that featured Rihanna, many in the public believed it was an insufficient attempt at capitalizing on the ascendancy of the Bajan superstar. The advertisement featured Rihanna in an early incarnation, singing. She does not speak, and thus does not clearly, concretely and definitively situate herself squarely as *belonging* to Barbados and her history. The absence of such public proclamations of belonging showed, in the opinion of many, that the government's efforts were bereft of vision and belied an ambiguous commitment to making Rihanna and her nation coterminous in the public's imagination.

On the eve of the 2007 MTV Video Music Awards, for example, one writer castigated the BLP government's inaction in publicly recognizing Rihanna's achievements:

> Here, it is important to question whether the Ministry of Tourism continues to have strong links with this star, and if they do, what programmes are they hoping to put in place where her international recognition *can be used* to help develop and further penetrate markets to promote Barbados? Likewise, what developmental programmes has the Ministry of Culture established? . . . So far both agencies' silence on these matters has been deafening.[19]

At that time, much of the dominant pro-Rihanna public discourse that permeated print media and radio call-in programmes was undecidedly yoked to an articulation of national pride on the one hand and to an unmistakable and concomitant recognition of Rihanna as utilitarian commodity in the global marketplace on the other. For example, a newspaper column penned by the People's Empowerment Party declared, "Now, if the Ministry of Tourism and the Barbados Tourism had any vision, they would have already established a Rihanna tourism development project dedicated to *utilizing her* phenomenal international market penetration *to promote* Barbados as a tourism destination."[20] Implying that the Arthur government (BLP) lacked the "vision, intelligence [and] self-respect *to claim* international musical sensation for Barbados", the People's Empowerment Party column claimed it would "step into the breach".[21]

There was, in the end, no need for alarm, as the Democratic Labour Party victory on 15 January 2008 inaugurated the stemming of this "breach", and Robyn Rihanna Fenty was finally given her "just deserts" as part of the DLP's Youth Manifesto: "Where there has been exclusion there will be inclusion. . . . Our Youth Manifesto as presented is a contract between the DLP and the young people of Barbados. It is against this background that the Prime Minister signalled the intention to honour our Grammy Award-winning superstar."[22]

In addition to bestowing the aforementioned national honour, the Thompson government also announced its plan to give Rihanna "a piece of the rock", a portion of land in the prestigious Apes Hill development, a move that itself has provoked a fascinating discussion of class, geography, access and political sparring within Barbados.

In response to the land-donation resolution introduced into the House of Assembly in June 2010 by DLP minister of housing and lands Michael Lashley, a member of parliament from the recently replaced Arthur government, Gline Clarke, questioned the choice of Apes Hill as opposed to Westbury, where Rihanna is from, or some other locale. Clarke reportedly queried "why Government was paying millions of dollars for land for someone who was making millions of dollars in the entertainment industry".[23] Minister Lashley responded by asserting that the government was "rewarding" the young Barbadian for her efforts, particularly because "it is not easy to penetrate the American music industry"; he chided Clarke for his "audacity" and suggested that the query revealed a "snobbish attitude" on his part, and by implication on the part of other BLP representatives, who thought that perhaps "the exclusive community was too good" for Rihanna.[24] Here, we have a national debate about the feasibility and efficacy of donating materially a particular tract of scarce and prime Barbadian land to a global superstar who is also a Barbadian daughter from a working-class community, as a symbolic gesture for having achieved unprecedented transnational success, at the centre of an ideological debate about the government's role in rewarding national achievement and accusations of class bias, all of which is taking place in a stagnated and insecure economic climate within which the working classes, from whom Rihanna emerges, invariably suffer most. Such are the complexities of diasporic citizenship.

In the end, it is clear that the DLP's rectification of what was, by their judgement, a monumental and glaring oversight – the prior administration's failure to bestow national public recognition on their daughter, Rihanna – was more than just political ploy, and yet their move to capitalize on the singer's historic Grammy win alongside their newly acquired national mandate certainly added sweet succour to their political ascendancy.

It is important at this juncture to note that the artist herself has never equivocated on the subject of national belonging. Upon winning the Grammy in 2008, Rihanna's concluding remark in her acceptance speech, "Barbados, I love you, we got one", enunciated with unmistakable Bajan inflection, was, of course, emblematic. While it has been the case that some artists from the Caribbean who have won such international awards have retained their "mother tongues", and I am thinking here of Jamaican artists like Shaggy, Ziggy Marley, Sean Paul, Damian Marley and the like, these artists have generally won in the Best Reggae Album category. Their acceptance speeches are usually not telecast on the primetime airing of the award shows. When televised, however, their purposive West Indian inflections are also integral to the artists' promulgation of cultural "authenticity".[25] Oftentimes, though, Caribbean-born artists (from Harry Belafonte to Heather Headley and now Nicki Minaj) who win international awards don the American "twang" and linguistically pass for US-born Americans.[26] As Barbados *Nation* news commentator Mavis Beckles writes of the Rihanna Grammy moment, "Ya did not try to speak or act like other people who have gone there before; ya didn't act as though you were pretending; your Bajan accent came across the airwaves as clear as day. . . . Thank you for holding the Barbados flag high for the whole world to see it, without any prompting or help from any o' we bout here."²⁷

Rihanna's Bajan-speak remains consistent and was evident even as recently as her August 2012 interview with Oprah Winfrey for *Oprah's Next Chapter*, which was actually filmed in Barbados and which scored the second-highest ratings in the history of the Oprah Winfrey Network.²⁸

Most notable in terms of Rihanna's symbolic/semiotic articulation of Barbadian national belonging is the fact that she has featured the Barbados flag, and the trident which is emblazoned on its blue and gold bands, on several of her album covers and in many of her music videos. It is precisely this issue of "marketing" Barbados through her cultural products, however, that created a firestorm beginning in the Barbados media in June 2007.

In an interview with *Entertainment Weekly*, the then nineteen-year-old musician responded to a question concerning her post-fame home excursions. Rihanna's response stirred the proverbial cou-cou pot:²⁹

> *Rihanna:* A lot of them hate me, but a lot of them love me. I don't really let the ones that hate me stop me from doing what I wanna do. They always have something to say about what I'm wearing or what I'm not wearing, like in the "Umbrella" video. If I wear a swimsuit to the beach, it's a problem, they put it on the front of the newspaper and call in programs. It really annoys me when people that I try to represent and I try to put them on the map as much as I can – you know, I didn't have to put tridents in my videos.
> *Interviewer:* Put what in your videos?
> *Rihanna:* Trident, which is the symbol of the flag. I didn't have to talk about them. I didn't have to even mention that I'm from Barbados. But I do and people kind of take it for granted. They hate me. They talk s—— about me all the time. But I'm like, "Whatever. I'm still doing this 'cause I love to do it and you're not going to stop me."³⁰

For the next few months, myriad and frequently ideologically incommensurate Bajan responses to the interview dominated the media. She was saint. She was sinner. She was the proverbial second coming, holding a distant second only to Barack Obama, to whom, in two articles, she was compared. She was the Whore of Babylon, scantily clad, "gyrating" inappropriately, and a terrible role model for young Barbadian girls to emulate.

This dichotomous configuration of Rihanna's identity imbricated within the conventional madonna/whore paradigm has, of course, historical roots, in particular for black women. As Donna Aza Weir-Soley cogently points out, "From the time of the black woman's first appearance on the New World stage, her moral character was beleaguered by vituperative stereotypes steeped in pseudoscientific myth, virulent rumour and salacious fallacy. As a consequence, black women were conflicted regarding the issue of sexuality. How could they not be?"[31] Such distortions of black women's sexuality invariably drove their sexuality underground if they desired bourgeois respectability. Having been historically barred from and hence naturally desirous of assuming such status, black women entered the twentieth century both inadvertently and sometimes quite consciously reifying conventional Victorian ideals regarding the dichotomy between sexuality (and its expression) and Christianity.

These values still persist and perpetuate simplistic, over-determined and rigid ideas about black female sexual expressivity. Although it can be argued that within the music entertainment industry there has historically been greater fluidity in terms of black women's sexual expression (and I am thinking here, for instance, of the early twentieth-century blues singers, all the way through contemporary R&B icons like Beyoncé and Janet Jackson), Rihanna bears the additional burden of singularly representing the entire nation of Barbados on the international stage.[32] It is no coincidence, for example, that in the aforementioned celebratory poem, "Rihanna", she is necessarily constructed as a "sweet", "innocent" "girl", aesthetically and ostensibly stripped of sexual allure, sexuality and womanhood.

In one pro-Rihanna article in the *Nation*, "When Is Rihanna Going to Get Her Just Deserts?", as if anticipating the public's (and by implication the government's) moralistically steeped reticence at honouring Rihanna because of the perception of her sexual suggestiveness, the writer ends by asking, "What is going to happen if we produce a successful movie star who has to perform a bedroom scene similar to those in [soap operas]?"[33] Here, the argument is that Rihanna's questionable moral decency is at least manageable since the Barbados public does not have to witness one of their native daughters simulating sex (the nude photos of Rihanna had not yet been leaked to the press). In her analysis of "the Rihanna debate", Alyson Holder, in the *Barbados Advocate*, writes that "one of the strongest arguments I have heard so far [against honouring Rihanna] is that Barbados is a predominantly Christian society and therefore such 'behaviour' should not be condoned."[34]

As a consequence, many responses to the *Entertainment Weekly* interview castigated Rihanna for her arrogant articulation regarding having "put Barbados on the map", with a concomitant denouncement of her moral character. One of the most fascinating convergences of nationalism and Victorian and Christian idealism, however, was offered in a piece published in the Barbados *Nation* called "Pray for Rihanna". In this editorial, Phillip Knight enjoins not only the Bajan public but all Caribbean Community (CARICOM) citizens to have a prayer for Rihanna *every six months* in all churches:

> This *young child* . . . needs our prayers and 100 per cent Bajan support . . . *her tiny body* is going through some mental and physical battering [referencing her work schedule]. . . . Do not envy her . . . She is correct to return to Barbados every month or two. . . . We have to keep her in our prayers so her health, wisdom, understanding and compassion are endless, thanks to the blessings and mercy of God Almighty . . . we must share her with the world. We must protect her from this same world. Yes, we must pray to God to protect her now and for all time.³⁵

Here, the paternalistic infantilization of Rihanna is revelatory. She is a young, tiny-bodied child subjected to the potential evils of an immorally encroaching globalized world. Safety and protection from such secular exploitation are to be found in the coterminously operative domains of the church and the nation-state, which must, according to Knight, necessarily operate in lockstep.

Responses to Knight's editorial were as ideologically problematic and as discursively revelatory as the article itself. Beginning with a sardonic assessment of "this little country" which "possesses human resources out of all proportion to its size", one commenter, Olutuye Walrond, writes, "Where else would we find the extraordinary ideas of a Phillip Knight?" Picking up on the idea of the proposed biannual CARICOM prayer for their Bajan daughter, Walrond offers her own spiritual recommendations:

> So let's all pray for Rihanna . . . this poor "child" [who] has so much limited control over her own life, that she has to work like the proverbial "Kendal mule" . . . Let us pray that one day she will regain this control [and cease] *the kinds of erotic gyrations* she indulges in on stage. And while we are praying *let us ask God to turn her into a true role model* for young girls, who may not want to walk around with three-quarters of their bodies exposed.³⁶

No longer the eternal innocent, unequivocally *not* a "child", and certainly not a victim of the tyrannical entertainment industry, here Rihanna is the corrupter incarnate, the despoiler of young girls bereft of decent role models, who, properly covered, comport themselves with moral rectitude and Christian decency.

In a similar vein, another response to Knight's editorial, "Who's Envying Rihanna?", written by Etta Best and published in the *Nation*, commences with the author's admission that she was "astounded by this man's foolishness about the people of Barbados envying Rihanna". Continuing, she rhetorically queries, "What is there to be jealous of . . . What is so important about a young woman holding a mike in her hand on a stage and gyrating? Is that the kind of role model you want our future generation to emulate? . . . What do you want Barbadians to do, Mr Knight – idolize Rihanna like an ancient deity?" Best's concluding statement, the only declarative juxtaposed against a litany of interrogatives, recalls the moral admonitions of the aforementioned response from Walrond: "Accepting God as our mediator and being baptized is what we Barbadians should be very proud of, not Rihanna's accomplishments."[37]

Thus, in the months leading up to the bestowal of the 2008 Barbados national honour, Rihanna was caught up in a maelstrom of controversy regarding her suitability as national representative. Deified on the one hand, demonized on the other, in neither case was she liberated from the strictures of the society's ingrained Victorian codes governing female sexuality and the deeply entrenched discourse of Christian decency. To be sanctioned in the public domain was to be necessarily stripped of all markers of womanliness – to be forever the "pretty li'l Bajan girl". To be acknowledged as possessing an autonomous sexuality was to be necessarily stripped of all legitimate claims to national recognition.

Arguably, Rihanna, whether in her profession or in private, has never relinquished her rights to fully express her sexual desires, nor has she tempered her unrepentant sexual display; and at the same time, she has in fact received tremendous official and non-official national acknowledgement in Barbados. The tension between moral and national imaginings is a dichotomy that is not of her making; neither has she capitulated to it. What this dynamic speaks to, however, are the ways in which discourses of national identity and belonging invariably remain yoked to the operations of heterosexist patriarchy. It becomes important, then, to recognize the debates surrounding Rihanna as a part of a longer-standing historical and contemporary journey which underscores the unfinished business of rooting out sexism, and by extension heterosexism, from Caribbean societies.

BAD GIRL DONE BEST

In the midst of these aforementioned dichotomous/dialectical national permutations, Rihanna's sound, her physical appearance and her demeanour began to reflect a hardening, darkening, anarchic quality.[38] By the close of 2007, Rihanna could no longer be legitimately claimed as the pretty li'l Bajan girl, as signalled overtly by her self-reflexive designation as a "good girl gone bad", the title of her third studio album. As I have argued in an earlier version of this essay, in the aftermath of the domestic abuse she suffered in 2009 during her tumultuous and extremely public relationship with singer Chris Brown, as an attempt to resist the designation of "victim", Rihanna appeared to invoke and emulate her iconic, iconoclastic, outlaw, powerful, androgynous and defiant Caribbean forebear Grace Jones, whose nonconformist deconstruction of traditional sex and gender roles, invocation of phallic power, and hard, edgy sexuality explode fully the dichotomy between victim and perpetrator into which Rihanna had been read in 2009.[39]

Since that time, Rihanna's popular-cultural (re)presentations have undergone numerous incarnations, including her post-assault emphases in song lyrics and especially in music videos on the themes of sadomasochism, rape and domestic violence. These figured prominently during 2011 with the release of her hugely controversial music videos for "S&M", which was banned in eleven countries for its sexual content; "Man Down", filmed in Jamaica, which depicts a rape survivor's revenge killing of her perpetrator; and "We Found Love", which portrays an unhealthy, drug-filled, intensely sexual, co-dependent love relationship. All of the above were denounced by various Barbadian and international entities.[40]

It is outside of the purview of this essay to make an argument about the degree to which artists should be able to exercise full poetic licence, and whether or not pop stars bear any responsibility to be role models for their fans. Such a discussion gets into the thorny issues of whose vantage point and whose ideological/moral compass dictate such determinations. What I am interested in, however, are the ways in which the national and transnational overtly and semiotically converge in particularly revelatory ways, primarily in Rihanna's video for "S&M".

Accusations of plagiarism notwithstanding, the video for "S&M" is a fascinating and powerful exploration of sex, media, sovereignty, transnationalism, power and representation.[41] If, as Josh Kun has argued, an "audiotopia" is a "transformative social and sonic space [in which] transported by the technologies of transnational capital, music becomes an experiential network of connection and intersection that enables global simultaneity by juxtaposing the same with the different, bridging the near with the far, and confusing the local with the global",[42] then the music video for "S&M" is a veritable "ocutopia" of national and transnational images and imaginings.

While there has been some concern expressed about the degree to which we can grant Rihanna full attribution for the creative and aesthetic choices made in her song lyrics and videos, there is copious evidence to suggest that she is a hugely instrumental part of a collaborative process, particularly in terms of the creative content of her videos.[43] As she self-reflexively asserted in a *GQ* interview in 2012, "Sometimes a person looks at me and sees dollars. They see numbers and they see a product. I look at me and see art. If I didn't like what I was doing, then I would say *I was committing slavery.*"[44] This is a powerful and clearly intentional analogy for someone emerging from the first of the heinous British slave societies – Barbados.

The most notable recent instance of Rihanna's clear creative control is her co-direction of the video for the 2013 single "Pour It Up", which features Rihanna along with actual strippers in an all-female, highly stylized striptease in which she is both sex worker and consumer. The highly controversial video, described by one cultural critic as "pro-queer and deeply feminist", portrays themes that are consistent with both her earlier work, like "S&M", and her extremely public stance (evident on Twitter and YouTube and in the blogosphere), which has remained consistent, about her belief in a woman's right to full sexual and erotic expressivity.[45]

The "S&M" video begins with Rihanna, dressed in a haute couture gown made of fabric with newspaper headlines, being dragged into a press conference room by reporters who pinion her to the wall using a large plastic sheath held in position by black electrical tape in the shape of bold *X*'s, which are placed by members of the press corps. From beneath the plastic wrap (clearly associative with safe, lesbian oral sex), Rihanna smiles coyly to the bevy of reporters, many of whom have either bright pink or black leather bondage gags in their mouths, while she sensually sings the opening lines, which start with "Feels so good being bad". Furiously, and yet clearly taking pleasure in it, the newspaper reporters scribble frenetically on notepads, nodding their heads like automatons at Rihanna's utterances; most legible is the word *slut*, which appears several times, while flashes of derogatory headlines about Rihanna stream across the screen in orgiastic assault. "Cox News", perched to televise Rihanna's "news conference" – an obvious play on the ultra-conservative, US-based Fox News and a homonym for the derisive term *cocks* – is the only identifiable TV station. The scene shifts to Rihanna, adorned in light brown leather, corseted, cigarette in one hand, riding crop in the other, leading around on his hands and knees by leash famed celebrity gossip and entertainment mogul Perez Hilton – the source of everything tabloid.

During this sadomasochistic, ritualized enactment of power reversal and exchange, as Donna Aza Weir-Soley and Esther Jones cogently point out in earlier chapters, at the end of the battle of words, Rihanna clearly comes out on top. As she sardonically sings, "Sticks and stones may break my bones, but chains and whips excite me", Rihanna is, of course, playing on the well-known children's rhyme which retorts, "Sticks and stones may break my bones, but words will never hurt me." She thereby subjugates her media detractors, whose weak (signalled by the soft, pink terrycloth restraints in which she is barely and pleasurably entangled) attempts to subordinate, shame and punish her (all features of S/M) with their words have failed to be permanent or enduring; Rihanna is dominatrix extraordinaire.

Still, as Elizabeth Freeman has argued, S/M role playing can also function as a kind of historiographic re-enactment of insidious and long-standing power relations that utilize the queer body, always situated in a temporal space of experiential deferral (pain/pleasure), as a means of addressing history.[46] In other words, the queer subjugated and/or dominating body corporeally plays with and in history, militating against its violent and traumatic hold. At the heart of the "ocutopia" that "S&M" creates is the history of black women's thwarted and thorny relationship to sexual desire – a tangled and tornadic web of commodification, distortion, public display, resistance and sexual expression. Towards the video's conclusion, an iconic image of Rihanna appears; she is adorned with a 1920s coiffure held in place beneath a profusion of exotic flowers, while she sensuously peels and eats a banana. To a viewer not fitted with what Vèvè Clark has called "diaspora literacy", the image is facilely transparent, but there is clearly much more going on. To my view, in addition to playing out and with the enduring, globally exported, stereotypical image of the Caribbean woman bearing fruit on her head (like, for example, the iconic Carmen Miranda), Rihanna seems also to be homaging the incredibly controversial, talented and successful "Black Venus", Josephine Baker. Baker, like Rihanna, was a diaspora citizen, operating simultaneously, nationally and transnationally between Paris and the United States, pushing the borders and boundaries of black women's public performance.[47] Clearly, there is more to the S/M play in this video than simply a commentary on "Scandals and Media", Rihanna's tweeted explanation for the title's acronym.

In fact, I would also argue that in the "S&M" video, Rihanna's queer body is engaged in a ritualized exchange of power/play between herself and her nation in ways that only an "insider" might unveil. It is here that the local and global productively converge. As mentioned, in the opening scenes, Rihanna is wearing a gown made of newsprint. At the top of the gown is the unmistakable word *Barbados*. Just below, though slightly less perceptible, is the word *nation*. For a non-Barbadian, non-Caribbean viewer, the term *nation* is an ironized reference to postcolonial cultural belonging and displacement. However, in this S/M performance of pain/pleasure between Rihanna and the media, at the top of her list, featured most prominently, is clearly the *Nation* newspaper, which for obvious reasons is the source of both her greatest humiliations and her greatest triumphs, her shaming and her adulation. Barbados will always, in a primal sense, be home. As the video opens, the female reporter who rips black electrical tape with her mouth to secure the plastic wrap bears eerily striking physical similarity to the highly prominent opposition leader for the BLP, Mia Mottley.

According to Weheliye, "'Diasporic citizenship' *refuses to sublate* the fraught and violent traffic between national and global assemblages; instead it *raucously* brings to the fore the tensions that require complex ways of mediating between [and, I would add, reading] contradictory forces as they are scripted and sounded through the bodies and psyches of Afro-diasporic subjects."[48] Herself a target of media speculation and aspersions cast regarding her alleged lesbian sexual identity in a region infamous for its heterosexism, Mottley has managed to enjoy a long, successful career at the centre of Barbadian politics, despite attempts to discredit her suitability to lead her nation. At the same time, as leader of the BLP, she represents the party critiqued for not giving Rihanna her "just deserts".

In a raucously fraught, violently and productively suggestive moment of S/M diaspora citizenship performed, Rihanna and the media reps reappear in a basement whose walls are covered with surveillance cameras. Every member of the press, including the female reporter, is tied up, while a futuristic-looking Rihanna, clad in pink latex, engages in various acts of bondage/discipline/sadism/masochism (BDSM), in particular, whipping a white male reporter who is tied to the bed – he is perhaps the worst offender. Sauntering over to the Mottley lookalike, who is bound and pinioned against the wall as the singer was earlier, a clear moment of shared experiential identification, Rihanna places a strip of the same black electrical tape used previously to affix her, over the reporter's mouth; gently, she kisses her and then smiles coyly at the camera. If, as Freeman argues, S/M role playing is a "means of addressing history" and its legacies, "as an idiom of pleasure" which "offers up a temporal means of reconfiguring the possible" in the ocutopia of this particular scene, Rihanna and (by inference) her fellow Bajan and black diaspora sisters are simultaneously entrapped and empowered actors queerly and deftly navigating across national/transnational spaces of possibility, transformation and power, which historically and contemporarily seek to script and conscript their sexual mobility.[49]

NATIONALIST SOUNDINGS

Debates in Barbados, however, about Rihanna's suitability to continue serving as ambassador for youth and culture and as the face of the Barbados Tourism Authority (BTA), which surfaced in the aftermath of the contentious "S&M" video, reignited in light of the "cunt-roversy" fomented by photographs of the star wearing a necklace bearing the word *cunt* and her response to international press queries that Bajans "use the *c*-word" the way "African-Americans use the *n*-word to their brothers".⁵⁰ In a quintessential moment emblematic of her diasporic citizenship, translating cross-culturally, Rihanna revealed to her Euro-American audiences that she had not been cognizant of the pejorative meanings associated with the term *cunt* until she left Barbados; "at home", the appellative, according to her, carries associations more closely aligned to African Americans' vernacular practice of signifying on the word *nigger*, emptying it of its derisive associations and radically transforming it into *nigguh*. Thus, the circulation of the word *cunt* becomes problematic only when it enters into a diasporically illiterate global marketplace into which Rihanna, and by extension Barbados, is inevitably interpellated.⁵¹

In the Barbados press, however, both mainstream and otherwise, Rihanna (as usual) had her defenders and detractors regarding the validity of her claims about, as one *Barbados Free Press* editorial cleverly put it, her "cuntry". Invoking "the cunt controversy" as yet another instance affirming her unsuitability to serve as BTA representative, the *Free Press* article exposes how insidiously classism signifies across global circuits of meaning. Rather than steeping their objections in the language of morality (as is common), the authors support their assertions using the language of pragmatism. According to them, the kind of "upscale" tourists that Barbados seeks to attract are not Rihanna's demographic, since, as they put it, the country cannot be "competitive in mass-market tourism" and thus is reliant on promoting high-end, boutique, exclusive hotels. Rihanna, as spokesperson for the BTA, they argue, "doesn't resonate with the folks who have money . . . or class".⁵² In other words, Barbados is a "classy place" for "classy tourists". As with the Apes Hill land donation controversy, this question of "class" once again rears its ugly head. Here, the Westbury girl and her "mass-market" consumers are coded as "classless", ill-fitting cogs in an ill-conceived government tourism project.

But perhaps the most overtly troubling publicly expressed opinions are those that call for the government of Barbados to "revoke" Rihanna's title as ambassador of youth and culture by forging linkages between her artistic expression and serious criminal behaviour. In a letter to the editor published in the *Barbados Advocate* under the heading "Youth Need a New Ambassador", the writer suggests that "Ri-Ri" has been "*promoting sexual tourism* with her . . . sexually explicit images".⁵³ In a follow-up editorial published in the *Jamaica Observer* on 26 August 2012, "Caricom's Challenge of Declining Moral Values",

Rickey Singh creates a tangled skein of associations between Rihanna's (mis)behaviour, "criminality and declining moral values" across the region, and the pervasiveness of a "'wuk-up' culture" spreading from the usual (albeit worsening) locales of Trinidad and Jamaica and invading the "quiet pastoral Caribbean society of Barbados", wherein "declining moral values and a penchant for lewdness and conflicts" have pervaded the youth.[54]

Then, in a turn even more problematic than the idea that Rihanna is single-handedly promoting sex tourism, Singh cites the suggestion made by the president of Barbados's National Organisation of Women that "lewd acts" captured by the media during Kadooment Day, the children's portion of the annual Crop Over festival, constitute "child abuse". Singh is very cautious to avoid attributing direct causality to Rihanna, but his implications are clear. These published opinions suggest the extremes to which national and regional discourses around Rihanna sometimes devolve so as to yoke her aesthetic corpus to the illegalities of sex tourism and child abuse that are truly gripping our Caribbean nation-states. RiRi, it seems, is an easy scapegoat.

Members of the Barbados government, however, have remained steadfast in their support of Rihanna, rejecting such calls for revocation and reaffirming their commitment to embracing their "daughter of the soil".[55] Minister of education Ronald Jones and minister of family, culture, sports and youth Stephen Lashley have been unequivocal in their public support, with Jones defending her poetic licence and Lashley pointing to her unprecedented success as a potential motivator for young Barbadians. Such public declarations, however, should not be read simply as magnanimous gestures of nationalistic support, without recognition of the operations and allure of transnational capital which she wields. Thus, the three-year partnership between Rihanna and the Barbados Tourism Authority was solidified with a deal for Rihanna to end her hugely successful Loud tour in Barbados in August 2011.

In the aftermath of the deal, minister of tourism Richard Sealy affirmed, "In the hearts of every Barbadian, Rihanna is known as the girl down the road", a local image that became globally consumed during the previously discussed Oprah Winfrey interview, which featured Rihanna driving Oprah around her country in an SUV, stopping on the roadside at intervals to enquire after family and friends, and being called simply "Robyn" by her fellow Bajans.[56] Still, as Hilary Beckles reminds us in this volume, Rihanna is indeed a Westbury girl, and the loud protestations regarding "morality" – a point echoed by Aaron Kamugisha – are deeply and profoundly inflected by "middle-classness".

BAJAN DAUGHTER, GLOBAL SUPERSTAR

From all reports, the Loud concert was "Ri-markable", as the Bajan daughter who continues to Ri-write global pop history put on a show-stopping performance in her homeland. Towards the end of the concert, in an emotional, articulated moment of national belonging and claiming for the singer and her audience, Rihanna revealed, "I travel everywhere in the world, and nothing feels like this place. It started about two streets away from here, in Westbury Road, where I grew up." As one commentator wrote, describing the emotionally charged space of the Westbury woman's homecoming, "As she sang her first Grammy Award-winning hit ['Umbrella', to close the historic evening], it rained confetti on the audience, some of whose eyes were wet."[57]

John Moore, it seems, got it wrong. Barbados is truly beautiful. At least, in all of the ways that beauty is inextricable from that which is palpably affective. I am reminded of the poet Langston Hughes's treatise on art, race, respectability and aesthetic freedom, "The Negro Artist and the Racial Mountain" (1926). Writing about the right of young black artists to freely and fully express themselves, Hughes declared to the conservative black middle-class intelligentsia, "We younger Negro artists who create now intend to express our individual dark-skinned selves without fear or shame. . . . We know we are beautiful. And ugly too."[58]

In the end, despite the poignancy of Rihanna's performance, public discourse surrounding the concert inevitably intervened, because such cannot be delinked from the incumbencies of commerce, class and national pride. Here was an international star performing at a historic national site, to a global audience, as part of a state tourism strategy. Barbados was on stage with her. Thus, complaints from the "higher-end consumers" (those located in the VIP and VVIP sections) about poorly planned and executed logistics fomented suggestions that the BTA improve their end of product delivery, "for the sake of the country and its reputation".[59] More significantly, the concert commenced without the singing of "In Plenty and in Time of Need", the Barbados national anthem – "our Bajan way to start every show".[60] In addition, there were complaints that the BTA failed to welcome the twenty-five thousand audience members to Barbados's "cricketing mecca", Kensington Oval, where the concert was performed. Still, as one commentator aptly put it, troping on the amazing performance of their "good girl gone bad", which served to mitigate the BTA's insufficiencies, "In life you have to take the bad with the good."[61] Indeed.

Current questions in the Caribbean about revenues (actual and potential) derived from Rihanna's global brand have already been wonderfully dealt with in this volume. I was struck, however, by an article in the *Caribbean Journal* reporting on a speech given at a Caribbean regional meeting of culture and sport ministers, in which Adrian Augier, the co-chair of CARICOM'S Regional Task Force on Cultural Industries, reminded the audience that Rihanna "is a billion-dollar business" from whom Barbados "earns relatively little in taxes and other revenues".[62] My critical pause is not related to Augier's argument; it makes perfect sense to me that all of the Caribbean region could stand to improve its infrastructural and strategic plans around cultural branding and intellectual property, and *should* work to incentivize global artists with local roots to assist with development.

It was the verb use that struck me: Rihanna *is* as opposed to *has* a billion-dollar business. Rihanna, after all, is a person. But perhaps I too am guilty of being a bit protective here, for like many other women of the black diaspora, I am deeply sensitive to the multiple locations we inhabit simultaneously that sometimes put us at risk. To this end, Michaeline Crichlow's admonition to engage in "trans/nationalizing and (re)homing" the debates that surround the movement of people, commodities, capital, identities and ideologies across territories is a useful one for thinking outside of binary oppositions that can still entrap, despite modernity's liberations: citizen/visitor, home/foreign, strange/familiar, good/bad, and even the one I am guilty of imposing in my critique above, artist/product.[63] As Crichlow puts it, such acts, which position the national and transnational as dialectically engaged, "recompose current debates about globalization and localization by revealing practices and processes that go beyond the postulations of false-dichotomous locations . . . replac[ing them] instead with 'une poétique de la Relation' – a cross-cultural poetics evocative of co-relational and intertwined histories".[64] In other words, we are always already bound up in each other.

Perhaps, in the end, Rihanna, as with other artists who dare to transgress entrenched, hallowed borders and boundaries, who are unafraid to test the limitations and explore the possibilities of (re)presentation, trans/nationalisms and (re)homing, is more a projection of our own best and most productive anxieties, fears, dreams, desires and unrestrained imaginings, engendering as a result not just a sense of who we are, or think we are, but who we might just become once we are willing to play.

NOTES

1. An earlier version of this article, "Whose Rihanna? Diasporic Citizenship and the Economies of Crossing Over", was published in *Archipelagos of Sound: Transnational Caribbeanities, Women and Music*, ed. Ifeona Fulani (Kingston: University of the West Indies Press), 299–320.
2. Austin Clarke returned to Barbados to serve as cultural officer and adviser to Prime Minister Tom Adams from 1975 to 1978.
3. Austin Clarke, *The Prime Minister* (Markham, ON: PaperJacks, 1977), 10.
4. Ibid., 44.
5. Dennis Scott, *Uncle Time* (Pittsburgh: University of Pittsburgh Press, 1973), 5.
6. Alexander Weheliye, *Phonographies: Grooves in Sonic Afro-Modernity* (Durham, NC: Duke University Press, 2005), 149.
7. Ibid.
8. Weheliye, Ibid, 147.
9. Carol Martindale, "What Can Rihanna for her Country?", *Daily Nation* (Barbados), 22 May 2012, http://www.nationnews.com/nationnews/news/5778/rihanna-country.
10. *Bimshire* is a familiar appellation for Barbados.
11. Alice Walker, *In Search of Our Mothers' Gardens* (New York: Harvest Books, 1984), 235.
12. "Rihanna Says She Was Bullied at School – for Being 'White'", *Showbiz Spy*, 18 December 2007, http://www.showbizspy.com/article/56792.
13. "The Ugly Secret of Barbados Revealed Worldwide", *Barbados Free Press*, 19 December 2007, http://barbadosfreepress.wordpress.com/2007/12/19/the-ugly-secret-of-barbados-revealed-worldwide-rihanna-i-was-bullied-at-school-for-being-white/(emphasis in original).
14. The title of this section comes from an article by Mavis Beckles, "Good Tidings and Great Joy", *Daily Nation* (Barbados), 22 December 2007.

15. Weheliye, *Phonographies*, 148.
16. Sylvia Barrow-Green, "Keep On Winning, Rihanna", *Daily Nation* (Barbados), 21 February 2008.
17. See, for example, Alaistair Haynes, "When Is Rihanna Going to Get Her Just Deserts?", *Daily Nation* (Barbados), 20 November 2007.
18. Jerome Davis, "Let Us Recognize Rihanna's Success", *Daily Nation* (Barbados), 6 November 2007.
19. "What Rihanna Means to Us", *Daily Nation* (Barbados), 17 November 2007 (emphasis added).
20. People's Empowerment Party, "She is Our Rihanna", *Weekend Nation* (Barbados), 17 August 2007 (emphasis added).
21. Ibid. (emphasis added).
22. "All Hail Rihanna", *Weekend Nation* (Barbados), 22 February 2008.
23. "Controversy over Gift of Land to Rihanna", *Daily Nation* (Barbados), 16 June 2010, http://www.nationnews.com/nationnews/news/23314/controversy-gift-land-rihanna.
24. Ibid.
25. These Caribbean artists primarily reside in their countries of origin, also contributing to their language retention.
26. *Twanging* is Caribbean vernacular used to refer to someone from the Caribbean who puts on a fake American accent to hide his or her national origins.
27. Mavis Beckles, "Well Done Rihanna", *Daily Nation* (Barbados), 15 February 2008.
28. "'Oprah's Next Chapter' Rihanna Interview Ranks #1 in Key Women Demos in Time Period", OWN press release, *The Futon Critic*, 21 August 2012, http://www.thefutoncritic.com/ratings/2012/08/21/.
29. Cou-cou is a part of the Barbadian national dish; it is made of slowly turned cornmeal that is cooked in a pot.
30. Margeaux Watson, "Caribbean Queen: Rihanna", *Entertainment Weekly* online, 21 June 2007, http://www.ew.com/ew/article/0,,20043298,00.html.
31. Donna Aza Weir-Soley, *Eroticism, Spirituality and Resistance in Black Women's Writings* (Gainesville: University Press of Florida, 2009), 12.
32. Although Alison Hinds and Rupert "Rupee" Clarke have both enjoyed major national, regional and international acclaim, they have primarily done so in the area of soca/calypso music and have not enjoyed the kind of broad crossover that is a hallmark of Rihanna's career.
33. Haynes, "Just Deserts".
34. "Our World of Entertainment: The Rihanna Debate", *Barbados Advocate*, 24 February 2008.

35. Phillip Knight, "Pray for Rihanna", *Daily Nation* (Barbados), 5 November 2007 (emphasis added).
36. Olutoye Walrond, "Some Praying for Poor Rihanna", *Daily Nation* (Barbados), 29 November 2007 (emphasis added).
37. Etta Best, "Who's Envying Rihanna?", *Weekend Nation* (Barbados), 16 November 2007.
38. The phrase "bad girl done best" was given to me by my co-editor, Hilary McD. Beckles.
39. Russell, "Whose Rihanna?", 316.
40. "US Pressure Groups Call for Rihanna's Video for 'Man Down' to Be Banned", *NME* online, 2 June 2011, http://www.nme.com/news/rihanna/57031; "Rihanna Causes Controversy with 'S&M' Video", *Mirror Online*, 2 February 2011, http://www.mirror.co.uk/3am/celebrity-news/rihanna-causes-controversy-with-sm-video-108051.
41. Photographers David LaChapelle and Phillipp Paulus have both sued Rihanna and her creative director for plagiarism. Rihanna settled with LaChapelle in 2011 after a court agreed that the images in the music video very closely resembled those from LaChapelle's photographic fantasy series on BDSM for Italian *Vogue* in 2002. "Rihanna Settles with Dave LaChapelle", *Huffington Post*, 21 October 2011, http://www.huffingtonpost.com/2011/10/20/rihanna-settles-with-davi_n_1023067.html; Mara Siegler, "Rihanna Faces New Plagiarism Charge", *New York Post*, 17 February 2014, http://pagesix.com/2014/02/17/rihanna-faces-plagiarism-charge-from-another-photographer/. The charges levelled by LaChapelle are also discussed in Eriq Gardner, "Rihanna's 'S&M' Video Elicits Photographer's Copyright Infringement Lawsuit, Again", *Billboardbiz*, 29 June 2011, http://www.billboard.com/biz/articles/news/1177276/rihannas-sm-video-elicits-photographers-copyright-infringement-lawsuit.
42. In Nadia Celis's essay on Shakira, "The Rhetoric of Hips", she quotes Kun to talk about what she has elsewhere called Shakira's "corporeal consciousness". In Fulani, *Archipelagos of Sound*, 193–215.
43. See John Seabrook, "The Song Machine: The Hitmakers behind Rihanna", *New Yorker* online, 26 March 2012, http://www.newyorker.com/reporting/2012/03/26/120326fa_fact_seabrook?currentPage=all.
44. See Jay Bulger, "Rihanna: Obsession of the Year", *GQ* online, December 2012, http://www.gq.com/moty/2012/rihanna-cover-story-gq-men-of-the-year-2012?currentPage=1 (emphasis added).
45. See Muna Mire, "Talkback: In Defense of Rihanna", *Feminist Wire* (blog), 16 October 2013, http://thefeministwire.com/2013/10/rihanna/.
46. Special thanks to my colleague Steven Blevins for pointing me to Elizabeth

Freeman's work. See Elizabeth Freeman, "Turn the Beat Around: Sadomasochism, Temporality, History", *Journal of Feminist Cultural Studies* 19, no. 1 (2008): 34–35.
47. It is rumoured that Rihanna is shortlisted to play Josephine Baker in an upcoming biopic. Annabel Venning, "Wilder than Her Pet Cheetah, the Sex-Mad Black Venus Who Outwitted the Nazis: Remarkable Story of Josephine Baker as Rihanna Is Set to Play Legendary Seductress in Biopic", *Mail Online*, 22 August 2013, http://www.dailymail.co.uk/tvshowbiz/article-2400416/Rihanna-set-play-Josephine-Baker-biopic-legendary-seductress.html.
48. Weheliye, *Phonographies*, 150 (emphasis added).
49. Freeman, "Turn the Beat Around", 34–35.
50. "Rihanna Defends Use of C-Word, Claims It's Common in Barbados", *AceShowbiz*, 4 October 2011, http://www.aceshowbiz.com/news/view/00044186.html.
51. Vèvè A. Clark, "Developing Diaspora Literacy: Allusion in Maryse Condé's *Heremakhonon*", in *Out of the Kumbla: Caribbean Women and Literature*, ed. Carole Boyce Davies and Elaine Savory Fido (Trenton: Africa World Press, 1990), 303–19.
52. "Rihanna Explains to *Vogue* Readers How Bajans Normally Call Each Other C_nt", *Barbados Free Press*, 4 October 2011, https://barbadosfreepress.wordpress.com/2011/10/04/rihanna-explains-to-vogue-readers-how-bajans-normally-call-each-other-c_nt/.
53. Pamela Cumberbatch, "Youth Need a New Ambassador", *Barbados Advocate*, 17 August 2012, http://www.barbadosadvocate.com/newsitem.asp?more=letters&NewsID=26413.
54. Rickey Singh, "Caricom's Challenge of Declining Moral Values", *Jamaica Observer*, 26 August 2012, http://www.jamaicaobserver.com/columns/Caricom-s-challenge-of-declining-moral-values_12340078.
55. Mike King, "Stop Bashing Rihanna", *Saturday Sun* (Barbados), 5 March 2011, http://www.nationnews.com/nationnews/news/21935/stop-bashing-rihanna.
56. "Rihanna Seals Barbados Deal", *Daily Nation* (Barbados), 15 June 2011, http://www.nationnews.com/nationnews/news/41127/rihanna-seals-barbados-deal.
57. Ricky Jordan, "Ri-Markable", *Daily Nation* (Barbados), 7 August 2011, http://www.nationnews.com/articles/view/ri-markable/.
58. Henry Louis Gates Jr and Nellie McKay, eds. *The Norton Anthology of African American Literature* (New York: Norton, 1997), 1267.
59. Carol Martindale, "LOUD Concerns about Rihanna Show", *Daily Nation* (Barbados), 10 August 2011, http://www.nationnews.com/nationnews/news/39167/loud-concerns-about-rihanna.
60. Ibid.
61. Ibid.

62. "Caribbean Could Derive Significant Revenue from Artists Like Rihanna", *Caribbean Journal*, 8 February 2012, http://www.caribjournal.com/2012/02/08/caribbean-could-derive-significant-revenue-from-artists-like-rihanna/.
63. Michaeline Crichlow, *Globalization and the Post-Creole Imagination* (Durham, NC: Duke University Press, 2009), 207.
64. Ibid.

CONTRIBUTORS

HILARY McD. BECKLES is Professor of Economic History, Pro-Vice Chancellor and Principal, University of the West Indies, Cave Hill, Barbados.

HEATHER D. RUSSELL is Associate Professor of English, Florida International University, Miami, Florida.

MIKE ALLEYNE is Professor, Department of Recording Industry, Middle Tennessee State University, Murfreesboro, Tennessee.

CURWEN BEST is Professor of Popular Culture and Literary Study Chair, Department of Language, Linguistics, and Literature, University of the West Indies, Cave Hill, Barbados.

ESTHER L. JONES is Assistant Professor of English, E. Franklin Frazier Professor of African American Literature, Theory and Culture, Clark University, Worcester, Massachusetts.

AARON KAMUGISHA is Senior Lecturer in Cultural Studies, University of the West Indies, Cave Hill, Barbados.

DON MARSHALL is Senior Lecturer and Deputy Dean, Globalization and Global Governance, University of the West Indies, Cave Hill, Barbados.

DONNA AZA WEIR-SOLEY is Associate Professor of English, Florida International University, Miami, Florida.

ACKNOWLEDGEMENTS

The editors wish to thank those who helped make the present collection of essays a reality. We wish to acknowledge the Caribbean Studies Association, where this collection began, first as a panel on Rihanna for the annual conference held in Barbados in 2010. In this vein, special thanks to Ifeona Fulani, at New York University, who first published Heather Russell's essay in her wonderful collection *Archipelagos of Sound: Transnational Caribbeanities, Women and Music*, which fomented the initial scholarly interest in this project. We are indebted to Linda Speth and her team at the University of the West Indies Press for their professionalism and support. Very special thanks to the gifted artist Jonna Twigg, whose stunning and insightful cover was specifically designed for this book. Finally, we could not have achieved such a fine collection without the incisive brilliance and unreserved support for this somewhat unique project from all of our contributors.

CPSIA information can be obtained at www.ICGtesting.com
Printed in the USA
LVOW11s0816070315

429583LV00001B/1/P